Progressing AI Driverless Cars

Practical Advances in Artificial Intelligence and Machine Learning

Dr. Lance B. Eliot, MBA, PhD

 First Edition.

ISBN: 978-1-73-630319-1

DEDICATION

To my incredible daughter, Lauren, and my incredible son, Michael.

Forest fortuna adiuvat (from the Latin; good fortune favors the brave).

DEDICATION

To my incredible daughter, Lauren, and my incredible son, Michael.

Forest fortuna adiuvat (from the Latin; good fortune favors the brave).

CONTENTS

ACKNOWLEDGMENTS

I have been the beneficiary of advice and counsel by many friends, colleagues, family, investors, and many others. I want to thank everyone that has aided me throughout my career. I write from the heart and the head, having experienced first-hand what it means to have others around you that support you during the good times and the tough times.

To Warren Bennis, one of my doctoral advisors and ultimately a colleague, I offer my deepest thanks and appreciation, especially for his calm and insightful wisdom and support.

To Mark Stevens and his generous efforts toward funding and supporting the USC Stevens Center for Innovation.

To Lloyd Greif and the USC Lloyd Greif Center for Entrepreneurial Studies for their ongoing encouragement of founders and entrepreneurs.

To Peter Drucker, William Wang, Aaron Levie, Peter Kim, Jon Kraft, Cindy Crawford, Jenny Ming, Steve Milligan, Chis Underwood, Frank Gehry, Buzz Aldrin, Steve Forbes, Bill Thompson, Dave Dillon, Alan Fuerstman, Larry Ellison, Jim Sinegal, John Sperling, Mark Stevenson, Anand Nallathambi, Thomas Barrack, Jr., and many other innovators and leaders that I have met and gained mightily from doing so.

Thanks to Ed Trainor, Kevin Anderson, James Hickey, Wendell Jones, Ken Harris, DuWayne Peterson, Mike Brown, Jim Thornton, Abhi Beniwal, Al Biland, John Nomura, Eliot Weinman, John Desmond, and many others for their unwavering support during my career.

And most of all thanks as always to Lauren and Michael, for their ongoing support and for having seen me writing and heard much of this material during the many months involved in writing it. To their patience and willingness to listen.

INTRODUCTION

This is a book that provides the newest innovations and the latest Artificial Intelligence (AI) advances about the emerging nature of AI-based autonomous self-driving driverless cars. Via recent advances in Artificial Intelligence (AI) and Machine Learning (ML), we are nearing the day when vehicles can control themselves and will not require and nor rely upon human intervention to perform their driving tasks (or, that allow for human intervention, but only *require* human intervention in very limited ways).

Similar to my other related books, which I describe in a moment and list the chapters in the Appendix A of this book, I am particularly focused on those advances that pertain to self-driving cars. The phrase "autonomous vehicles" is often used to refer to any kind of vehicle, whether it is ground-based or in the air or sea, and whether it is a cargo hauling trailer truck or a conventional passenger car. Though the aspects described in this book are certainly applicable to all kinds of autonomous vehicles, I am focused more so here on cars.

For this book, I am going to borrow my introduction from those companion books, since it does a good job of laying out the landscape of self-driving cars and my overall viewpoints on the topic.

INTRODUCTION TO SELF-DRIVING CARS

This is a book about self-driving cars. Someday in the future, we'll all have self-driving cars and this book will perhaps seem antiquated, but right now, we are at the forefront of the self-driving car wave. Daily news bombards us with flashes of new announcements by one car maker or another and leaves the impression that within the next few weeks or maybe months that the self-driving car will be here. A casual non-technical reader would assume from these news flashes that in we must be on the cusp of a true self-driving car.

We are still quite a distance from having a true self-driving car. A true self-driving car is akin to a moonshot. In the same manner that getting us to the moon was an incredible feat, likewise, is achieving a true self-driving car. Anybody that suggests or even brashly states that the true self-driving car is nearly here should be viewed with great skepticism. Indeed, you'll see that I often tend to use the word "hogwash" or "crock" when I assess much of the decidedly ***fake news*** about self-driving cars.

Indeed, I've been writing a popular blog post about self-driving cars and hitting hard on those that try to wave their hands and pretend that we are on the imminent verge of true self-driving cars. For many years, I've been known as the AI Insider. Besides writing about AI, I also develop AI software. I do what I describe. It also gives me insights into what others that are doing AI are really doing versus what it is said they are doing.

Many faithful readers had asked me to pull together my insightful short essays and put them into another book, which you are now holding.

For those of you that have been reading my essays over the years, this collection not only puts them together into one handy package, I also updated the essays and added new material. For those of you that are new to the topic of self-driving cars and AI, I hope you find these essays approachable and informative. I also tend to have a writing style with a bit of a voice, and so you'll see that I am times have a wry sense of humor and poke at conformity.

As a former professor and founder of an AI research lab, I for many years wrote in the formal language of academic writing. I published in referred journals and served as an editor for several AI journals. This writing here is not of the nature, and I have adopted a different and more informal style for these essays. That being said, I also do mention from time-to-time more rigorous material on AI and encourage you all to dig into those deeper and more formal materials if so interested.

For those of you that are reading this book and have a penchant for writing code, you might consider taking a look at the open-source code available for self-driving cars. This is a handy place to start learning how to develop AI for self-driving cars. There are also many new educational courses spring forth. There is a growing body of those wanting to learn about and develop self-driving cars, and a growing body of colleges, labs, and other avenues by which you can learn about self-driving cars.

This book will provide a foundation of aspects that I think will get you ready for those kinds of more advanced training opportunities. If you've already taken those classes, you'll likely find these essays especially interesting as they offer a perspective that I am betting few other instructors or faculty offered to you. These are challenging essays that ask you to think beyond the conventional about self-driving cars.

THE MOTHER OF ALL AI PROJECTS

In June 2017, Apple CEO Tim Cook came out and finally admitted that Apple has been working on a self-driving car. As you'll see in my essays, Apple was enmeshed in secrecy about their self-driving car efforts. We have only been able to read the tea leaves and guess at what Apple has been up to. The notion of an iCar has been floating for quite a while, and self-driving engineers and researchers have been signing tight-lipped Non-Disclosure Agreements (NDA's) to work on projects at Apple that were as shrouded in mystery as any military invasion plans might be.

Tim Cook said something that many others in the Artificial Intelligence (AI) field have been saying, namely, the creation of a self-driving car has got to be the mother of all AI projects. In other words, it is in fact a tremendous moonshot for AI. If a self-driving car can be crafted and the AI works as we hope, it means that we have made incredible strides with AI and that therefore it opens many other worlds of potential breakthrough accomplishments that AI can solve.

Is this hyperbole? Am I just trying to make AI seem like a miracle worker and so provide self-aggrandizing statements for those of us writing the AI software for self-driving cars? No, it is not hyperbole. Developing a true self-driving car is really, really, really hard to do. Let me take a moment to explain why. As a side note, I realize that the Apple CEO is known for at times uttering hyperbole, and he had previously said for example that the year 2012 was "the mother of all years," and he had said that the release of iOS 10 was "the mother of all releases" – all of which does suggest he likes to use the handy "mother of" expression. But, I assure you, in terms of true self-driving cars, he has hit the nail on the head. For sure.

When you think about a moonshot and how we got to the moon, there are some identifiable characteristics and those same aspects can be applied to creating a true self-driving car. You'll notice that I keep putting the word "true" in front of the self-driving car expression. I do so because as per my essay about the various levels of self-driving cars, there are some self-driving cars that are only somewhat of a self-driving car. The somewhat versions are ones that require a human driver to be ready to intervene. In my view, that's not a true self-driving car. A true self-driving car is one that requires no human driver intervention at all. It is a car that can entirely undertake via automation the driving task without any human driver needed. This is the essence of what is known as a Level 5 self-driving car. We are currently at the Level 2 and Level 3 mark, and not yet at Level 5.

Getting to the moon involved aspects such as having big stretch goals, incremental progress, experimentation, innovation, and so on. Let's review how this applied to the moonshot of the bygone era, and how it applies to the self-driving car moonshot of today.

Big Stretch Goal

Trying to take a human and deliver the human to the moon, and bring them back, safely, was an extremely large stretch goal at the time. No one knew whether it could be done. The technology wasn't available yet. The cost was huge. The determination would need to be fierce. Etc. To reach a Level 5 self-driving car is going to be the same. It is a big stretch goal. We can readily get to the Level 3, and we are able to see the Level 4 just up ahead, but a Level 5 is still an unknown as to if it is doable. It should eventually be doable and in the same way that we thought we'd eventually get to the moon, but when it will occur is a different story.

Incremental Progress

Getting to the moon did not happen overnight in one fell swoop. It took years and years of incremental progress to get there. Likewise, for self-driving cars. Google has famously been striving to get to the Level 5, and pretty much been willing to forgo dealing with the intervening levels, but most of the other self-driving car makers are doing the incremental route. Let's get a good Level 2 and a somewhat Level 3 going. Then, let's improve the Level 3 and get a somewhat Level 4 going. Then, let's improve the Level 4 and finally arrive at a Level 5. This seems to be the prevalent way that we are going to achieve the true self-driving car.

Experimentation

You likely know that there were various experiments involved in perfecting the approach and technology to get to the moon. As per making incremental progress, we first tried to see if we could get a rocket to go into space and safety return, then put a monkey in there, then with a human, then we went all the way to the moon but didn't land, and finally we arrived at the mission that actually landed on the moon.

Self-driving cars are the same way. We are doing simulations of self-driving cars. We do testing of self-driving cars on private land under controlled situations.

We do testing of self-driving cars on public roadways, often having to meet regulatory requirements including for example having an engineer or equivalent in the car to take over the controls if needed. And so on. Experiments big and small are needed to figure out what works and what doesn't.

Innovation

There are already some advances in AI that are allowing us to progress toward self-driving cars. We are going to need even more advances. Innovation in all aspects of technology are going to be required to achieve a true self-driving car. By no means do we already have everything in-hand that we need to get there. Expect new inventions and new approaches, new algorithms, etc.

Setbacks

Most of the pundits are avoiding talking about potential setbacks in the progress toward self-driving cars. Getting to the moon involved many setbacks, some of which you never have heard of and were buried at the time so as to not dampen enthusiasm and funding for getting to the moon. A recurring theme in many of my included essays is that there are going to be setbacks as we try to arrive at a true self-driving car. Take a deep breath and be ready. I just hope the setbacks don't completely stop progress. I am sure that it will cause progress to alter in a manner that we've not yet seen in the self-driving car field. I liken the self-driving car of today to the excitement everyone had for Uber when it first got going. Today, we have a different view of Uber and with each passing day there are more regulations to the ride sharing business and more concerns raised. The darling child only stays a darling until finally that child acts up. It will happen the same with self-driving cars.

SELF-DRIVING CARS CHALLENGES

But what exactly makes things so hard to have a true self-driving car, you might be asking. You have seen cruise control for years and years. You've lately seen cars that can do parallel parking. You've seen YouTube videos of Tesla drivers that put their hands out the window as their car zooms along the highway, and seen to therefore be in a self-driving car. Aren't we just needing to put a few more sensors onto a car and then we'll have in-hand a true self-driving car? Nope.

Consider for a moment the nature of the driving task. We don't just let anyone at any age drive a car. Worldwide, most countries won't license a driver until the age of 18, though many do allow a learner's permit at the age of 15 or 16. Some suggest that a younger age would be physically too small to reach the controls of the car. Though this might be the case, we could easily adjust the controls to allow for younger aged and thus smaller stature. It's not their physical size that matters. It's their cognitive development that matters.

To drive a car, you need to be able to reason about the car, what the car can and cannot do. You need to know how to operate the car. You need to know about how other cars on the road drive. You need to know what is allowed in driving such as speed limits and driving within marked lanes. You need to be able to react to situations and be able to avoid getting into accidents. You need to ascertain when to hit your brakes, when to steer clear of a pedestrian, and how to keep from ramming that motorcyclist that just cut you off.

Many of us had taken courses on driving. We studied about driving and took driver training. We had to take a test and pass it to be able to drive. The point being that though most adults take the driving task for granted, and we often "mindlessly" drive our cars, there is a significant amount of cognitive effort that goes into driving a car. After a while, it becomes second nature. You don't especially think about how you drive, you just do it. But, if you watch a novice driver, say a teenager learning to drive, you suddenly realize that there is a lot more complexity to it than we seem to realize.

Furthermore, driving is a very serious task. I recall when my daughter and son first learned to drive. They are both very conscientious people. They wanted to make sure that whatever they did, they did well, and that they did not harm anyone. Every day, when you get into a car, it is probably around 4,000 pounds of hefty metal and plastics (about two tons), and it is a lethal weapon. Think about it. You drive down the street in an object that weighs two tons and with the engine it can accelerate and ram into anything you want to hit. The damage a car can inflict is very scary. Both my children were surprised that they were being given the right to maneuver this monster of a beast that could cause tremendous harm entirely by merely letting go of the steering wheel for a moment or taking your eyes off the road.

In fact, in the United States alone there are about 40,000 deaths per year by auto accidents, which is more than 100 per day. Given that there are about 263 million cars in the United States, I am actually more amazed that the number of fatalities is not a lot higher.

During my morning commute, I look at all the thousands of cars on the freeway around me, and I think that if all of them decided to go zombie and drive in a crazy maniac way, there would be many people dead. Somehow, incredibly, each day, most people drive relatively safely. To me, that's a miracle right there. Getting millions and millions of people to be safe and sane when behind the wheel of a two-ton mobile object, it's a feat that we as a society should admire with pride.

So, hopefully you are in agreement that the driving task requires a great deal of cognition. You don't' need to be especially smart to drive a car, and we've done quite a bit to make car driving viable for even the average dolt. There isn't an IQ test that you need to take to drive a car. If you can read and write, and pass a test, you pretty much can legally drive a car. There are of course some that drive a car and are not legally permitted to do so, plus there are private areas such as farms where drivers are young, but for public roadways in the United States, you can be generally of average intelligence (or less) and be able to legally drive.

This though makes it seem like the cognitive effort must not be much. If the cognitive effort was truly hard, wouldn't we only have Einstein's that could drive a car? We have made sure to keep the driving task as simple as we can, by making the controls easy and relatively standardized, and by having roads that are relatively standardized, and so on. It is as though Disneyland has put their Autopia into the real-world, by us all as a society agreeing that roads will be a certain way, and we'll all abide by the various rules of driving.

A modest cognitive task by a human is still something that stymies AI. You certainly know that AI has been able to beat chess players and be good at other kinds of games. This type of narrow cognition is not what car driving is about. Car driving is much wider. It requires knowledge about the world, which a chess playing AI system does not need to know. The cognitive aspects of driving are on the one hand seemingly simple, but at the same time require layer upon layer of knowledge about cars, people, roads, rules, and a myriad of other "common sense" aspects. We don't have any AI systems today that have that same kind of breadth and depth of awareness and knowledge.

As revealed in my essays, the self-driving car of today is using trickery to do particular tasks. It is all very narrow in operation. Plus, it currently assumes that a human driver is ready to intervene. It is like a child that we have taught to stack blocks, but we are needed to be right there in case the child stacks them too high and they begin to fall over.

AI of today is brittle, it is narrow, and it does not approach the cognitive abilities of humans. This is why the true self-driving car is somewhere out in the future.

Another aspect to the driving task is that it is not solely a mind exercise. You do need to use your senses to drive. You use your eyes as vision sensors to see the road ahead. You vision capability is like a streaming video, which your brain needs to continually analyze as you drive. Where is the road? Is there a pedestrian in the way? Is there another car ahead of you? Your senses are relying a flood of info to your brain. Self-driving cars are trying to do the same, by using cameras, radar, ultrasound, and lasers. This is an attempt at mimicking how humans have senses and sensory apparatus.

Thus, the driving task is mental and physical. You use your senses, you use your arms and legs to manipulate the controls of the car, and you use your brain to assess the sensory info and direct your limbs to act upon the controls of the car. This all happens instantly. If you've ever perhaps gotten something in your eye and only had one eye available to drive with, you suddenly realize how dependent upon vision you are. If you have a broken foot with a cast, you suddenly realize how hard it is to control the brake pedal and the accelerator. If you've taken medication and your brain is maybe sluggish, you suddenly realize how much mental strain is required to drive a car.

An AI system that plays chess only needs to be focused on playing chess. The physical aspects aren't important because usually a human moves the chess pieces or the chessboard is shown on an electronic display. Using AI for a more life-and-death task such as analyzing MRI images of patients, this again does not require physical capabilities and instead is done by examining images of bits.

Driving a car is a true life-and-death task. It is a use of AI that can easily and at any moment produce death. For those colleagues of mine that are developing this AI, as am I, we need to keep in mind the somber aspects of this. We are producing software that will have in its virtual hands the lives of the occupants of the car, and the lives of those in other nearby cars, and the lives of nearby pedestrians, etc. Chess is not usually a life-or-death matter.

Driving is all around us. Cars are everywhere. Most of today's AI applications involve only a small number of people. Or, they are behind the scenes and we as humans have other recourse if the AI messes up. AI that is driving a car at 80 miles per hour on a highway had better not mess up. The consequences are grave.

Multiply this by the number of cars, if we could put magically self-driving into every car in the USA, we'd have AI running in the 263 million cars. That's a lot of AI spread around. This is AI on a massive scale that we are not doing today and that offers both promise and potential peril.

There are some that want AI for self-driving cars because they envision a world without any car accidents. They envision a world in which there is no car congestion and all cars cooperate with each other. These are wonderful utopian visions.

They are also very misleading. The adoption of self-driving cars is going to be incremental and not overnight. We cannot economically just junk all existing cars. Nor are we going to be able to affordably retrofit existing cars. It is more likely that self-driving cars will be built into new cars and that over many years of gradual replacement of existing cars that we'll see the mix of self-driving cars become substantial in the real-world.

In these essays, I have tried to offer technological insights without being overly technical in my description, and also blended the business, societal, and economic aspects too. Technologists need to consider the non-technological impacts of what they do. Non-technologists should be aware of what is being developed.

We all need to work together to collectively be prepared for the enormous disruption and transformative aspects of true self-driving cars.

WHAT THIS BOOK PROVIDES

What does this book provide to you? It introduces many of the key elements about self-driving cars and does so with an AI based perspective. I weave together technical and non-technical aspects, readily going from being concerned about the cognitive capabilities of the driving task and how the technology is embodying this into self-driving cars, and in the next breath I discuss the societal and economic aspects.

They are all intertwined because that's the way reality is. You cannot separate out the technology per se, and instead must consider it within the milieu of what is being invented and innovated, and do so with a mindset towards the contemporary mores and culture that shape what we are doing and what we hope to do.

WHY THIS BOOK

I wrote this book to try and bring to the public view many aspects about self-driving cars that nobody seems to be discussing.

For business leaders that are either involved in making self-driving cars or that are going to leverage self-driving cars, I hope that this book will enlighten you as to the risks involved and ways in which you should be strategizing about how to deal with those risks.

For entrepreneurs, startups and other businesses that want to enter into the self-driving car market that is emerging, I hope this book sparks your interest in doing so, and provides some sense of what might be prudent to pursue.

For researchers that study self-driving cars, I hope this book spurs your interest in the risks and safety issues of self-driving cars, and also nudges you toward conducting research on those aspects.

For students in computer science or related disciplines, I hope this book will provide you with interesting and new ideas and material, for which you might conduct research or provide some career direction insights for you.

For AI companies and high-tech companies pursuing self-driving cars, this book will hopefully broaden your view beyond just the mere coding and development needed to make self-driving cars.

For all readers, I hope that you will find the material in this book to be stimulating. Some of it will be repetitive of things you already know. But I am pretty sure that you'll also find various eureka moments whereby you'll discover a new technique or approach that you had not earlier thought of. I am also betting that there will be material that forces you to rethink some of your current practices.

I am not saying you will suddenly have an epiphany and change what you are doing. I do think though that you will reconsider or perhaps revisit what you are doing.

For anyone choosing to use this book for teaching purposes, please take a look at my suggestions for doing so, as described in the Appendix. I have found the material handy in courses that I have taught, and likewise other faculty have told me that they have found the material handy, in some cases as extended readings and in other instances as a core part of their course (depending on the nature of the class).

In my writing for this book, I have tried carefully to blend both the practitioner and the academic styles of writing.

It is not as abstract as is typical academic journal writing, but at the same time offers depth by going into the nuances and trade-offs of various practices.

The word "deep" is in vogue today, meaning getting deeply into a subject or topic, and so is the word "unpack" which means to tease out the underlying aspects of a subject or topic. I have sought to offer material that addresses an issue or topic by going relatively deeply into it and make sure that it is well unpacked.

In any book about AI, it is difficult to use our everyday words without having some of them be misinterpreted. Specifically, it is easy to anthropomorphize AI. When I say that an AI system "knows" something, I do not want you to construe that the AI system has sentience and "knows" in the same way that humans do. They aren't that way, as yet. I have tried to use quotes around such words from time-to-time to emphasize that the words I am using should not be misinterpreted to ascribe true human intelligence to the AI systems that we know of today. If I used quotes around all such words, the book would be very difficult to read, and so I am doing so judiciously. Please keep that in mind as you read the material, thanks.

Some of the material is time-based in terms of covering underway activities, and though some of it might decay, nonetheless I believe you'll find the material useful and informative.

COMPANION BOOKS BY DR. ELIOT

1. **"Introduction to Driverless Self-Driving Cars"** by Dr. Lance Eliot
2. **"Innovation and Thought Leadership on Self-Driving Driverless Cars"**
3. **"Advances in AI and Autonomous Vehicles: Cybernetic Self-Driving Cars"**
4. **"Self-Driving Cars: The Mother of All AI Projects"** by Dr. Lance Eliot
5. **"New Advances in AI Autonomous Driverless Self-Driving Cars"**
6. **"AV Driverless Self-Driving Cars & AI"** by Dr. Lance Eliot and Michael B. Eliot
7. **"Transformative Artificial Intelligence Driverless Self-Driving Cars"**
8. **"Disruptive Artificial Intelligence and Driverless Self-Driving Cars"**
9. "**State-of-the-Art AI Driverless Self-Driving Cars**" by Dr. Lance Eliot
10. "**Top Trends in AI Self-Driving Cars**" by Dr. Lance Eliot
11. **"AI Innovations and Self-Driving Cars"** by Dr. Lance Eliot
12. **"Crucial Advances for AI Driverless Cars"** by Dr. Lance Eliot
13. **"Sociotechnical Insights and AI Driverless Cars**" by Dr. Lance Eliot.
14. **"Pioneering Advances for AI Driverless Cars"** by Dr. Lance Eliot
15. **"Leading Edge Trends for AI Driverless Cars"** by Dr. Lance Eliot
16. **"The Cutting Edge of AI Autonomous Cars"** by Dr. Lance Eliot
17. **"The Next Wave of AI Self-Driving Cars"** by Dr. Lance Eliot
18. **"Revolutionary Innovations of AI Driverless Cars"** by Dr. Lance Eliot
19. **"AI Self-Driving Cars Breakthroughs"** by Dr. Lance Eliot
20. **"Trailblazing Trends for AI Self-Driving Cars"** by Dr. Lance Eliot
21. **"Ingenious Strides for AI Driverless Cars"** by Dr. Lance Eliot
22. **"AI Self-Driving Cars Inventiveness"** by Dr. Lance Eliot
23. **"Visionary Secrets of AI Driverless Cars"** by Dr. Lance Eliot
24. **"Spearheading AI Self-Driving Cars"** by Dr. Lance Eliot
25. **"Spurring AI Self-Driving Cars"** by Dr. Lance Eliot
26. **"Avant-Garde AI Driverless Cars"** by Dr. Lance Eliot
27. **"AI Self-Driving Cars Evolvement"** by Dr. Lance Eliot
28. **"AI Driverless Cars Chrysalis"** by Dr. Lance Eliot
29. **"Boosting AI Autonomous Cars"** by Dr. Lance Eliot
30. **"AI Self-Driving Cars Trendsetting"** by Dr. Lance Eliot
31. **"AI Autonomous Cars Forefront"** by Dr. Lance Eliot
32. **"AI Autonomous Cars Emergence"** by Dr. Lance Eliot
33. **"AI Autonomous Cars Progress"** by Dr. Lance Eliot
34. **"AI Self-Driving Cars Prognosis"** by Dr. Lance Eliot
35. **"AI Self-Driving Cars Momentum"** by Dr. Lance Eliot
36. **"AI Self-Driving Cars Headway"** by Dr. Lance Eliot
37. **"AI Self-Driving Cars Vicissitude"** by Dr. Lance Eliot
38. **"AI Self-Driving Cars Autonomy"** by Dr. Lance Eliot
39. **"AI Driverless Cars Transmutation"** by Dr. Lance Eliot
40. **"AI Driverless Cars Potentiality"** by Dr. Lance Eliot
41. **"AI Driverless Cars Realities"** by Dr. Lance Eliot
42. **"AI Self-Driving Cars Materiality"** by Dr. Lance Eliot
43. **"AI Self-Driving Cars Accordance"** by Dr. Lance Eliot
44. **"AI Self-Driving Cars Equanimity"** by Dr. Lance Eliot
45. **"AI Self-Driving Cars Divulgement"** by Dr. Lance Eliot
46. **"AI Self-Driving Cars Consonance"** by Dr. Lance Eliot
47. **"Revelatory AI Self-Driving Cars"** by Dr. Lance Eliot
48. **"Edifying AI Self-Driving Cars"** by Dr. Lance Eliot
49. **"Apprising AI Driverless Cars"** by Dr. Lance Eliot
50. **"Improving AI Self-Driving Cars"** by Dr. Lance Eliot
51. **"Progressing AI Driverless Cars"** by Dr. Lance Eliot

These books are available on Amazon and at other major global booksellers.

CHAPTER 1

ELIOT FRAMEWORK FOR AI SELF-DRIVING CARS

This chapter is a core foundational aspect for understanding AI self-driving cars and I have used this same chapter in several of my other books to introduce the reader to essential elements of this field. Once you've read this chapter, you'll be prepared to read the rest of the material since the foundational essence of the components of autonomous AI driverless self-driving cars will have been established for you.

When I give presentations about self-driving cars and teach classes on the topic, I have found it helpful to provide a framework around which the various key elements of self-driving cars can be understood and organized (see diagram at the end of this chapter). The framework needs to be simple enough to convey the overarching elements, but at the same time not so simple that it belies the true complexity of self-driving cars. As such, I am going to describe the framework here and try to offer in a thousand words (or more!) what the framework diagram itself intends to portray.

The core elements on the diagram are numbered for ease of reference. The numbering does not suggest any kind of prioritization of the elements. Each element is crucial. Each element has a purpose, and otherwise would not be included in the framework. For some self-driving cars, a particular element might be more important or somehow distinguished in comparison to other self-driving cars.

You could even use the framework to rate a particular self-driving car, doing so by gauging how well it performs in each of the elements of the framework. I will describe each of the elements, one at a time. After doing so, I'll discuss aspects that illustrate how the elements interact and perform during the overall effort of a self-driving car.

At the AI Self-Driving Car Institute, we use the framework to keep track of what we are working on, and how we are developing software that fills in what is needed to achieve Level 5 self-driving cars.

D-01: Sensor Capture

Let's start with the one element that often gets the most attention in the press about self-driving cars, namely, the sensory devices for a self-driving car.

On the framework, the box labeled as D-01 indicates "Sensor Capture" and refers to the processes of the self-driving car that involve collecting data from the myriad of sensors that are used for a self-driving car. The types of devices typically involved are listed, such as the use of mono cameras, stereo cameras, LIDAR devices, radar systems, ultrasonic devices, GPS, IMU, and so on.

These devices are tasked with obtaining data about the status of the self-driving car and the world around it. Some of the devices are continually providing updates, while others of the devices await an indication by the self-driving car that the device is supposed to collect data. The data might be first transformed in some fashion by the device itself, or it might instead be fed directly into the sensor capture as raw data. At that point, it might be up to the sensor capture processes to do transformations on the data. This all varies depending upon the nature of the devices being used and how the devices were designed and developed.

D-02: Sensor Fusion

Imagine that your eyeballs receive visual images, your nose receives odors, your ears receive sounds, and in essence each of your distinct sensory devices is getting some form of input. The input befits the nature of the device. Likewise, for a self-driving car, the cameras provide visual images, the radar returns radar reflections, and so on. Each device provides the data as befits what the device does.

At some point, using the analogy to humans, you need to merge together what your eyes see, what your nose smells, what your ears hear, and piece it all together into a larger sense of what the world is all about and what is happening around you. Sensor fusion is the action of taking the singular aspects from each of the devices and putting them together into a larger puzzle.

Sensor fusion is a tough task. There are some devices that might not be working at the time of the sensor capture. Or, there might some devices that are unable to report well what they have detected. Again, using a human analogy, suppose you are in a dark room and so your eyes cannot see much. At that point, you might need to rely more so on your ears and what you hear. The same is true for a self-driving car. If the cameras are obscured due to snow and sleet, it might be that the radar can provide a greater indication of what the external conditions consist of.

In the case of a self-driving car, there can be a plethora of such sensory devices. Each is reporting what it can. Each might have its difficulties. Each might have its limitations, such as how far ahead it can detect an object. All of these limitations need to be considered during the sensor fusion task.

D-03: Virtual World Model

For humans, we presumably keep in our minds a model of the world around us when we are driving a car. In your mind, you know that the car is going at say 60 miles per hour and that you are on a freeway.

You have a model in your mind that your car is surrounded by other cars, and that there are lanes to the freeway. Your model is not only based on what you can see, hear, etc., but also what you know about the nature of the world. You know that at any moment that car ahead of you can smash on its brakes, or the car behind you can ram into your car, or that the truck in the next lane might swerve into your lane.

The AI of the self-driving car needs to have a virtual world model, which it then keeps updated with whatever it is receiving from the sensor fusion, which received its input from the sensor capture.

D-04: System Action Plan

By having a virtual world model, the AI of the self-driving car is able to keep track of where the car is and what is happening around the car. In addition, the AI needs to determine what to do next. Should the self-driving car hit its brakes? Should the self-driving car stay in its lane or swerve into the lane to the left? Should the self-driving car accelerate or slow down?

A system action plan needs to be prepared by the AI of the self-driving car. The action plan specifies what actions should be taken. The actions need to pertain to the status of the virtual world model. Plus, the actions need to be realizable.

This realizability means that the AI cannot just assert that the self-driving car should suddenly sprout wings and fly. Instead, the AI must be bound by whatever the self-driving car can actually do, such as coming to a halt in a distance of X feet at a speed of Y miles per hour, rather than perhaps asserting that the self-driving car come to a halt in 0 feet as though it could instantaneously come to a stop while it is in motion.

D-05: Controls Activation

The system action plan is implemented by activating the controls of the car to act according to what the plan stipulates.

This might mean that the accelerator control is commanded to increase the speed of the car. Or, the steering control is commanded to turn the steering wheel 30 degrees to the left or right.

One question arises as to whether or not the controls respond as they are commanded to do. In other words, suppose the AI has commanded the accelerator to increase, but for some reason it does not do so. Or, maybe it tries to do so, but the speed of the car does not increase.

The controls activation feeds back into the virtual world model, and simultaneously the virtual world model is getting updated from the sensors, the sensor capture, and the sensor fusion. This allows the AI to ascertain what has taken place as a result of the controls being commanded to take some kind of action.

By the way, please keep in mind that though the diagram seems to have a linear progression to it, the reality is that these are all aspects of the self-driving car that are happening in parallel and simultaneously. The sensors are capturing data, meanwhile the sensor fusion is taking place, meanwhile the virtual model is being updated, meanwhile the system action plan is being formulated and reformulated, meanwhile the controls are being activated.

This is the same as a human being that is driving a car. They are eyeballing the road, meanwhile they are fusing in their mind the sights, sounds, etc., meanwhile their mind is updating their model of the world around them, meanwhile they are formulating an action plan of what to do, and meanwhile they are pushing their foot onto the pedals and steering the car. In the normal course of driving a car, you are doing all of these at once. I mention this so that when you look at the diagram, you will think of the boxes as processes that are all happening at the same time, and not as though only one happens and then the next.

They are shown diagrammatically in a simplistic manner to help comprehend what is taking place. You though should also realize that they are working in parallel and simultaneous with each other. This is a tough aspect in that the inter-element communications involve latency and other aspects that must be taken into account. There can be delays in one element updating and then sharing its latest status with other elements.

D-06: Automobile & CAN

Contemporary cars use various automotive electronics and a Controller Area Network (CAN) to serve as the components that underlie the driving aspects of a car.

There are Electronic Control Units (ECU's) which control subsystems of the car, such as the engine, the brakes, the doors, the windows, and so on.

The elements D-01, D-02, D-03, D-04, D-05 are layered on top of the D-06, and must be aware of the nature of what the D-06 is able to do and not do.

D-07: In-Car Commands

Humans are going to be occupants in self-driving cars. In a Level 5 self-driving car, there must be some form of communication that takes place between the humans and the self-driving car. For example, I go into a self-driving car and tell it that I want to be driven over to Disneyland, and along the way I want to stop at In-and-Out Burger. The self-driving car now parses what I've said and tries to then establish a means to carry out my wishes.

In-car commands can happen at any time during a driving journey. Though my example was about an in-car command when I first got into my self-driving car, it could be that while the self-driving car is carrying out the journey that I change my mind. Perhaps after getting stuck in traffic, I tell the self-driving car to forget about getting the burgers and just head straight over to the theme park. The self-driving car needs to be alert to in-car commands throughout the journey.

D-08: V2X Communications

We will ultimately have self-driving cars communicating with each other, doing so via V2V (Vehicle-to-Vehicle) communications. We will also have self-driving cars that communicate with the roadways and other aspects of the transportation infrastructure, doing so via V2I (Vehicle-to-Infrastructure).

The variety of ways in which a self-driving car will be communicating with other cars and infrastructure is being called V2X, whereby the letter X means whatever else we identify as something that a car should or would want to communicate with.

The V2X communications will be taking place simultaneous with everything else on the diagram, and those other elements will need to incorporate whatever it gleans from those V2X communications.

D-09: Deep Learning

The use of Deep Learning permeates all other aspects of the self-driving car. The AI of the self-driving car will be using deep learning to do a better job at the systems action plan, and at the control's activation, and at the sensor fusion, and so on.

Currently, the use of artificial neural networks is the most prevalent form of deep learning. Based on large swaths of data, the neural networks attempt to "learn" from the data and therefore direct the efforts of the self-driving car accordingly.

D-10: Tactical AI

Tactical AI is the element of dealing with the moment-to-moment driving of the self-driving car. Is the self-driving car staying in its lane of the freeway? Is the car responding appropriately to the controls commands? Are the sensory devices working?

For human drivers, the tactical equivalent can be seen when you watch a novice driver such as a teenager that is first driving. They are focused on the mechanics of the driving task, keeping their eye on the road while also trying to properly control the car.

D-11: Strategic AI

The Strategic AI aspects of a self-driving car are dealing with the larger picture of what the self-driving car is trying to do. If I had asked that the self-driving car take me to Disneyland, there is an overall journey map that needs to be kept and maintained.

There is an interaction between the Strategic AI and the Tactical AI. The Strategic AI is wanting to keep on the mission of the driving, while the Tactical AI is focused on the particulars underway in the driving effort.

If the Tactical AI seems to wander away from the overarching mission, the Strategic AI wants to see why and get things back on track. If the Tactical AI realizes that there is something amiss on the self-driving car, it needs to alert the Strategic AI accordingly and have an adjustment to the overarching mission that is underway.

D-12: Self-Aware AI

Very few of the self-driving cars being developed are including a Self-Aware AI element, which we at the Cybernetic Self-Driving Car Institute believe is crucial to Level 5 self-driving cars.

The Self-Aware AI element is intended to watch over itself, in the sense that the AI is making sure that the AI is working as intended. Suppose you had a human driving a car, and they were starting to drive erratically. Hopefully, their own self-awareness would make them realize they themselves are driving poorly, such as perhaps starting to fall asleep after having been driving for hours on end. If you had a passenger in the car, they might be able to alert the driver if the driver is starting to do something amiss.

This is exactly what the Self-Aware AI element tries to do, it becomes the overseer of the AI, and tries to detect when the AI has become faulty or confused, and then find ways to overcome the issue.

D-13: Economic

The economic aspects of a self-driving car are not per se a technology aspect of a self-driving car, but the economics do indeed impact the nature of a self-driving car. For example, the cost of outfitting a self-driving car with every kind of possible sensory device is prohibitive, and so choices need to be made about which devices are used. And, for those sensory devices chosen, whether they would have a full set of features or a more limited set of features.

We are going to have self-driving cars that are at the low-end of a consumer cost point, and others at the high-end of a consumer cost point. You cannot expect that the self-driving car at the low-end is going to be as robust as the one at the high-end.

I realize that many of the self-driving car pundits are acting as though all self-driving cars will be the same, but they won't be. Just like anything else, we are going to have self-driving cars that have a range of capabilities. Some will be better than others. Some will be safer than others. This is the way of the real-world, and so we need to be thinking about the economics aspects when considering the nature of self-driving cars.

D-14: Societal

This component encompasses the societal aspects of AI which also impacts the technology of self-driving cars. For example, the famous Trolley Problem involves what choices should a self-driving car make when faced with life-and-death matters. If the self-driving car is about to either hit a child standing in the roadway, or instead ram into a tree at the side of the road and possibly kill the humans in the self-driving car, which choice should be made?

We need to keep in mind the societal aspects will underlie the AI of the self-driving car. Whether we are aware of it explicitly or not, the AI will have embedded into it various societal assumptions.

D-15: Innovation

I included the notion of innovation into the framework because we can anticipate that whatever a self-driving car consists of, it will continue to be innovated over time. The self-driving cars coming out in the next several years will undoubtedly be different and less innovative than the versions that come out in ten years hence, etc.

Framework Overall

For those of you that want to learn about self-driving cars, you can potentially pick a particular element and become specialized in that aspect. Some engineers are focusing on the sensory devices. Some engineers focus on the controls activation. And so on. There are specialties in each of the elements.

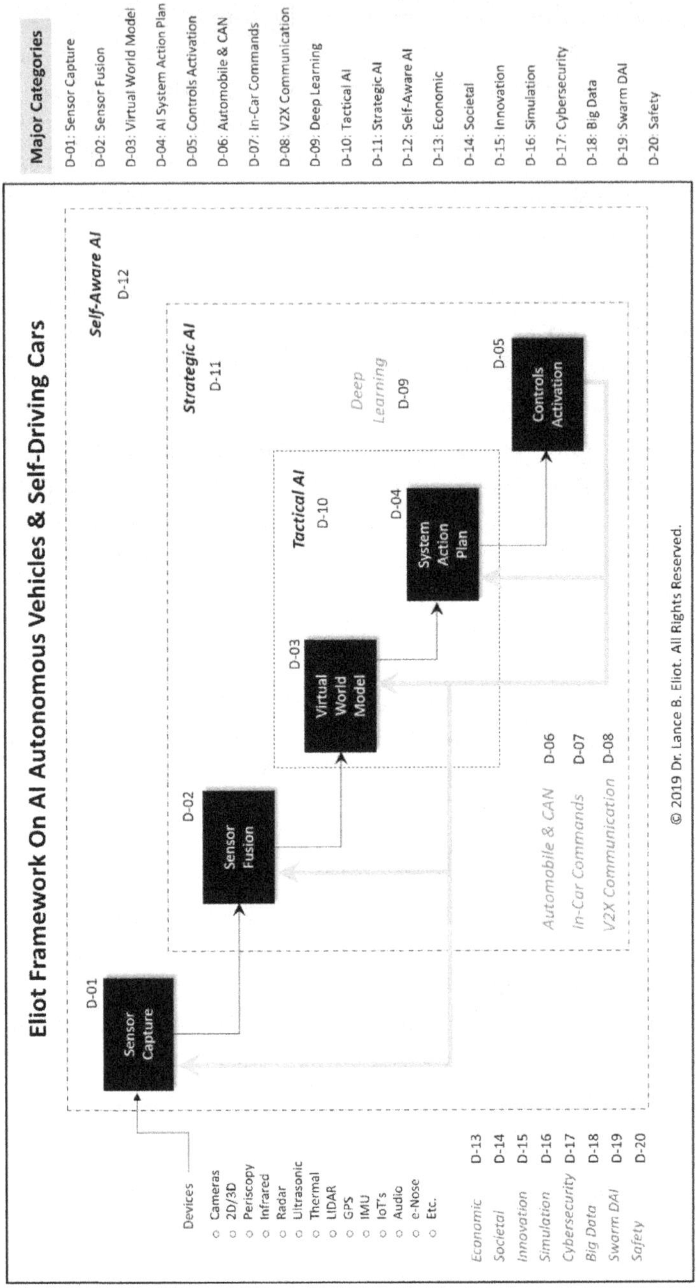
Major Categories
D-01: Sensor Capture
D-02: Sensor Fusion
D-03: Virtual World Model
D-04: AI System Action Plan
D-05: Controls Activation
D-06: Automobile & CAN
D-07: In-Car Commands
D-08: V2X Communication
D-09: Deep Learning
D-10: Tactical AI
D-11: Strategic AI
D-12: Self-Aware AI
D-13: Economic
D-14: Societal
D-15: Innovation
D-16: Simulation
D-17: Cybersecurity
D-18: Big Data
D-19: Swarm DAI
D-20: Safety
Eliot Framework On AI Autonomous Vehicles & Self-Driving Cars
Self-Aware AI
D-12
Strategic AI
D-11
Tactical AI
D-10
Deep Learning
D-09
D-01
Sensor Capture
D-02
Sensor Fusion
D-03
Virtual World Model
D-04
System Action Plan
D-05
Controls Activation
Automobile & CAN D-06
In-Car Commands D-07
V2X Communication D-08
Devices
Cameras
2D/3D
Periscopy
Infrared
Radar
Ultrasonic
Thermal
LIDAR
GPS
IMU
IoT's
Audio
e-Nose
Etc.
Economic D-13
Societal D-14
Innovation D-15
Simulation D-16
Cybersecurity D-17
Big Data D-18
Swarm DAI D-19
Safety D-20
© 2019 Dr. Lance B. Eliot. All Rights Reserved.

CHAPTER 2

HOLIDAY TRAVEL AND SELF-DRIVING CARS

Here they come!

It's time for a deserved road trip, a refreshing getaway, a chance to finally stretch your legs and see someplace other than your own domicile and escape those brooding four walls that you've been staring at for over a year now.

I'm talking about the upcoming Memorial Day weekend and the plain fact that a tremendous amount of travel is afoot, that's for darned sure.

People have been cooped up and are abundantly eager to hit the road. According to the AAA, an estimated 34 million Americans will travel by car at least 50 miles from their homes this three-day weekend. Some people consider the Memorial Day weekend to be the start of summer and they want to go see friends and friendly, ostensibly for collegial interaction and also downright outlandish partying.

A caution though is warranted.

First, the cars that people will be driving are bound to no longer be getaway viable.

The odds are that many of these vehicles have been sitting idle for a year or so. There wasn't a need to make that daily commute to the office. Your car perhaps sat in your driveway or out on the street. Sure, you used your car, but barely. Driving over to the grocery store was maybe in the cards, though even that was a skittish act due to concerns about going into the store and being near other people.

Trying to suddenly opt to take your out-of-shape and somewhat unused car onto the wide-open roads is a recipe for calamity and potential disaster. When was the last time you had the oil changed? When was the last time that you had a tune-up done? Are those tires properly inflated or have they lost a lot of air and are now suspect for any sustainable driving distances? Etc.

Sadly, we might see a lot of those travelers getting stuck on the roadways, sitting in their broken-down vehicles, and wondering what happened. Besides the ruination of what was supposed to be an enjoyable escape, there is a concern too about impacting traffic and the adverse results thereof. Cars that are sitting at the side of a freeway or highway are an unmitigated hazard to all.

People that are in that car are essentially sitting ducks if another car rams into the halted vehicle. Anyone that decides to get out of the car to take a look at the vehicle to ascertain what has gone wrong can readily be hit by passing cars. Fast-moving cars will likely pass the vehicle within inches, possibly sideswiping it or striking it entirely.

This might seem a bit downtrodden and you might also be skeptical that other drivers would make the mistake of veering into a car that is parked in an emergency lane or at the edge of a thoroughfare. Sorry to be further demoralizing but you ought to assume that there will be quite a mixture of bad drivers on the roads this Memorial Day weekend.

That leads us to the second key point, namely that the drivers for this weekend are likely to be out-of-touch or (at least) rusty while at the wheel.

Here's the skinny.

Drivers that haven't been driving for much of the last year are unaccustomed to being at the wheel of a moving car. Their reflexes are dulled. That natural driving instinct that was previously built up by daily commuting has gradually and inexorably decayed. Reaction times are slower than they used to be. The ability to nimbly spot dour situations and take proactive preventive driving measures is out the window.

In short, there will be tons of drivers that are not going to be very sharp at the wheel and can readily fall into or get ensnared in a myriad of ugly car accidents, entailing serious property damage, human injury, and potentially life-or-death consequences.

If the situation was more normal, most of those drivers would be already up-to-speed. They would have been doing their usual driving chores each day, each week, and be at the standard level of their driving prowess. Now, they have dropped below such a threshold. They don't know it. They wouldn't like to admit it.

Nonetheless, it is the bare and decidedly harsh truth.

That covers the drivers that *care* about their driving.

We also need to account for the drivers that are careless and outright insidious about their driving, especially on a three-day partying-going weekend. You can certainly expect a lot of drinking and driving. Once again, some of those intoxicated drivers will think they are fine to get on the road and misjudge their level of drunkenness, while others will be completely out of their gourd and simply don't care.

It is a twofer for the three-day driving spree.

There are the drivers that are quite rusty and slovenly in being able to adroitly drive, mixed with drivers that are over the limit and should not be at the wheel. The rest of the pack consists of everyday drivers that are merely intent on getting to their desired destination, safely so. Those conscientious drivers need to be especially wary of the overabundance of the bad drivers.

We can also take a look at the mindful driver's too.

Dare I say it, a lot of them will be going over the speed limit.

Come on, you've got to admit that it is easy to do and when taking a long driving trip it is bound to happen. In addition, since the rest of the traffic will likely be speeding along on the highways and byways, you figure that if everyone else is doing so, you might as well too (the herd mentality rears up).

Trying to proceed at just the speed limit can be a daunting task these days. Other drivers will come right up upon your bumper. They will flash their headlights. They might honk their horn. If they decide to go around you, the chances are that they will do so with a flourish and then extend a designated finger in your direction. Road rage can erupt.

All told, this usually causes the most legally minded drivers to give in to peer pressure and push the pedal to the metal. You can justify speeding by rationalizing that if you don't proceed at the prevailing speed of traffic, you are actually a hazard to traffic. Going at a presumed snail's pace in comparison to those zipping by your vehicles is seemingly going to provoke a car collision of one kind or another.

Heightened speeds tend to reduce available reaction time and increase the chances of a car crash. There is also the aspect that at higher speeds the car colliding impacts are usually much more fierce. Yes, speed kills. Besides the death-defying aspects, any speeding will subject you, the driver, to the chances of getting a speeding ticket, incurring points on your driving record, and all-around putting a damper on your weekend retreat.

There will be a lot of traffic too, which again is different than what was seen this last year.

Fewer cars had been on the roadways. For those people that did much driving, they had the roads to themselves. You can bet that the three-day weekend will not be the grand open roads that might dreamily be swimming in your escapism noggin. Instead, the traffic will be unrelenting and occur while on major pathways and perhaps on the side streets too.

We can toss some interesting statistics into this discussion.

A survey undertaken via Erie Insurance earlier this year had asked drivers about their overall driving habits. Around 72% of the respondents indicated that they sometimes or often speed. That's not a good sign. It does though seem to ring true. One might argue that the percentage ought to be even higher and maybe the other 28%

aren't willing to openly admit to the full degree of their driving transgressions.

Approximately 62% indicated that sometimes or often they will drive while they are tired. That's yet another scary sign. And about one-third admitted that they use their cell phone while driving, doing so for texting, or to access social media, and for other purposes.

Let's unpack some of those additionally admitted qualms by contemporary drivers.

For this three-day weekend, we can readily assume that there will be drivers that opt to drive while they are tired or worn out. It stands to reason.

You go to see your buddies and end up having a wonderful couple of days, relishing the time with them that was forsaken this past year. At some point, you have to drive home. There is that comforting and warm feeling from having been with your year-long Zoom-seen acquaintances for a while, yet you also used up a huge amount of personal energy in being up close and personal with them. During the drive home, you are so tired that you can barely keep your eyes open and are only partially able to concentrate on the driving chore.

Add those kinds of weary drivers into the weekend unnerving mixture.

During the three-day weekend, we can readily also assume that there will be distracted drivers on our highways and byways.

Go with this typical scenario. You are getting on the road and heading to see those pals that are avidly awaiting your arrival. They text you and ask how much longer will you be? You text them back, even though you are supposed to have both hands on the steering wheel. Another text comes in that asks if you can pick up some extra chips and other goodies. You use your smartphone to search for a grocery store near the destination. You then use the mapping app to showcase how to get there.

That is par for the course and amped on steroids during the Memorial Day traveling.

People are going to be using their smartphones while driving, regrettably and inappropriately so. We need to add into the weekend ruinous mixture the fact that drivers will be allowing themselves to become distracted by their cellphones.

By combining all of the preceding elements and impacts related to drivers for this Memorial Day traveling, you've got 34 million that are unknowingly entering into the Twilight Zone, as it were, meaning that they are unwittingly going to be in amidst heightened danger and probably have no suspicion or realization about it.

Some might assert that they perhaps they ought to not be made aware and ergo be able to revel in their blissful ignorance, on the other hand, if drivers are cognizant that this particular occasion of driving might be especially perilous, maybe those drivers will seek stridently to remain safe and likewise aid others in being safe too.

Let's certainly hope so.

Shifting gears, the future of cars consists of self-driving cars. AI-based true self-driving cars are driven by an AI driving system. There isn't a human driver at the wheel.

This brings up an intriguing question: *What will the traditional Memorial Day traveling be like once we reach an era of prevalent AI-based true self-driving cars?*

Maybe the driving aspects will be better for us all, or then again, there might be some gotchas.

Before jumping into the details, I'd like to clarify what is meant when referring to true self-driving cars.

Self-Driving Cars And Memorial Day Traveling

For Level 4 and Level 5 true self-driving vehicles, there won't be a human driver involved in the driving task.

All occupants will be passengers.

The AI is doing the driving.

One aspect to immediately discuss entails the fact that the AI involved in today's AI driving systems is not sentient. In other words, the AI is altogether a collective of computer-based programming and algorithms, and most assuredly not able to reason in the same manner that humans can.

Why this added emphasis about the AI not being sentient?

Because I want to underscore that when discussing the role of the AI driving system, I am not ascribing human qualities to the AI. Please be aware that there is an ongoing and dangerous tendency these days to anthropomorphize AI. In essence, people are assigning human-like sentience to today's AI, despite the undeniable and inarguable fact that no such AI exists as yet.

With that clarification, you can envision that the AI driving system won't natively somehow "know" about the facets of driving. Driving and all that it entails will need to be programmed as part of the hardware and software of the self-driving car.

Let's dive into the myriad of aspects that come to play on this topic.

First, and perhaps overly obvious, when going on a driving journey during the Memorial Day weekend you won't need to be worried about finding a driver. The driver is essentially built into the vehicle, somewhat. All told, the AI driving system will be doing the entirety of the driving and there is no need for a human to be at the wheel.

This also lets you off the hook of potentially doing all that laborious driving when you'd prefer to be taking things easy on an extended weekend.

You can merely jump into the car and away you go. Give the desired destination to the AI driving system and it will dutifully drive you there. You can meanwhile daydream, look out the window and leisurely enjoy the passing scenery, and otherwise feel confident that there is a driver and that it is going to be driving relatively safely. The driver won't be drinking and driving, it won't be distracted by using a cellphone, it won't get tired or weary, and it won't even be caught catnapping whilst watching cat videos.

On top of that, if you wanted to just hang around at home and not go on a trip, which didn't use to be an option because you were perchance considered the driver of the household, that's a possibility now too. Others that you know and previously relied upon your driving prowess won't need you to do their driving for them. The AI driving system will do so.

Another facet entails what the traveling activity can consist of.

The normal expectation is that everyone inside a conventional car has to be respectful of the driver sitting in the driver's seat and try not to bump them, distract them, or interfere with the driving chore. This meant that the driver was unable to (shall we say) party throughout the long drive and it also forced the passengers to be cautious and somewhat muted too.

With the AI driving system doing the driving, you and the other passengers will all be able to have a joyous time and possibly party during the trip (within reason, of course). Whoop it up! None of that will adversely impact the AI driving system. You can party and party and party, all the way to your destination, and likewise all the way back home.

The interior of self-driving cars will ultimately be differently structured than conventional cars.

Existing conventional cars must allocate space for a driver's seat and accommodate the requisite driving controls such as a steering wheel and pedals. This is in a fixed position inside the vehicle. That is a constraint on how else you might design the rest of the interior. For self-driving cars, the interior becomes an open space that no longer has those types of stipulated requirements and restrictions.

Some automakers and self-driving tech firms are aiming to use swiveling seats and have a popup table that will be between the several seats. Passengers will be able to swivel in whatever direction they might wish to face. For some of the trip, you might be looking outside the windows and at other points during the trip be facing each other. This allows for improved face-to-face engagement in dialogues, maybe play a round of cards or chess, etc.

The expectation is that the seats of self-driving cars are probably going to be reclinable. Since many of the Memorial Day weekend driving trips are lengthy, you can lay back and catch a nap. Imagine how refreshed you will be when you reach your destination. Similarly, on the trek back home, you can get lots of sleep and be ready to immerse yourself into your usual daily schedule again.

One aspect that might arise would be people choosing to take trips over the Memorial Day weekend that are longer than they feel comfortable doing currently. You might be basing the distance of travel on how far you can endure doing the driving. With the AI driving system, it will work 24x7, thus you can do a sleepover in the vehicle and let the self-driving car continue on the journey.

It could be that instead of reporting on the notion of Americans traveling 50 miles or more during the Memorial Day weekend, the number of miles will increase substantially. You could scramble into a self-driving car on a late Friday afternoon and by the next morning be 500 miles from where you started the trip.

Hopefully, the roads will be safer for driving because there won't be drunk drivers. The AI driving system will be continually attentive and driving in a considered safe manner, including not speeding (the AI driving system could certainly go faster than the speed limit, but the assumption is that the programming will limit doing so). You will feel more confident that the Memorial Day weekend trek will occur without difficulty and you can focus entirely on whatever you'll be doing at the destination of your traveling.

Conclusion

Wish we could let things conclude with that rather rosy portrayal encompassing the advent of self-driving cars and what might therefore occur during the rush of Memorial Day weekend traveling. The thing is, there are various downsides and potential gotchas.

We ought to be thinking about those too. I know it seems like a bummer but facing reality will help to shape proper expectations.

We don't yet know how widespread self-driving cars will be. Pundits anticipate that they will gradually become quite prevalent. The traveling cost is supposed to be low, presumably lower than the cost of existing ridesharing that entails a human driver. Many tout that we might be heading toward a mobility-for-all nirvana.

That's a nice aspiration.

It could take a long time to reach that ambitious goal. Meanwhile, some worry that self-driving cars might be extraordinarily costly and only affordable by the wealthy, sorely falling short of the mobility-for-all mantra.

Your interest in using a self-driving car over Memorial Day weekend might be dashed by the lack of availability or the exorbitant cost.

Another concern is that there will be an ongoing mixture of human-driven cars and self-driving cars on our highways and byways.

No matter how safely a self-driving car might attempt to drive, all it takes is for a drunk driver to ram into a self-driving car and there wasn't much that the AI driving system could have done to avert the crash. You can forget about the outstretched claims that self-driving cars will incur zero fatalities, which is just not realistic.

Yet another qualm is that people might misbehave while traveling inside a self-driving car. I earlier emphasized that you could party to your heart's content since the AI driving system is doing the driving.

Yes, that's the case, but will those passengers become crazed revelers, and will the advent of self-driving cars spur people toward doing more drinking (a seemingly inadvertent and unexpected consequence)? You can argue that at least they aren't driving, though this is not the only way that intoxicated people can get themselves into trouble.

Well, I'll stop for now on this sobering look at some of the potential drawbacks associated with self-driving cars. Don't want to ruin your day, especially when there is a ton of really positive outcomes related to driverless cars.

The especially good news is that we can all shape how the future will unfold and provide insightful guidance as the emergence of self-driving cars takes place. Those aforementioned gotchas will hopefully spark attention to topics that will need some focus and tender loving care. We can mindfully avert falling into foul traps during the adoption of autonomous vehicles and self-driving cars.

The big picture is that self-driving cars are assuredly going to boost our traveling and enable a much easier, safer, and enjoyable effort while trying to relish and honor the three-day Memorial Day weekend.

I think that is cause for great celebration and reflection.

.

CHAPTER 3

FORBIDDEN KNOWLEDGE AND SELF-DRIVING CARS

I have a vexing question for you.

Are there things that we must not know?

This is an age-old question.

Some assert that there is the potential for knowledge that ought to not be known. In other words, there are ideas, concepts, mental formulations, and other at times tangible and yet somewhat intangible facets of knowledge that if we should become aware of that knowledge it could be our downfall. The discovery or invention of some new innovation or way of thinking could be unduly dangerous. It would be best to not go there, as it were, and avoid ever landing into such knowledge.

A common means to refer to such knowledge is to coin it as forbidden knowledge.

The typical basis for wanting to forbid the discovery or emergence of so-called forbidden knowledge is that the adverse consequences are overwhelming. By overwhelming, the emphasis is that even if the knowledge was possibly helpful and had merits, the end result is so devastating and undercutting that the bad side outweighs the good that could be derived from the knowledge.

It is conceivable that there might be knowledge that is so bad that it has no good possibilities at all. Thus, rather than trying to balance or weigh the good versus the bad, the knowledge has no counterbalancing effects. It is just plain bad. This would seem to be harder to try and declare as worthy of consideration in such an extreme case.

We are usually though faced with the matter of knowledge that has both the good and the bad as to how it might be utilized or employed. This then leads to a dogged debate about whether the bad is so bad that it outweighs the good. On top of this, there is the unrealized bad and the unrealized good, which could be differentiated from the realized bad and the realized good (in essence, the knowledge might be said to be either good or bad, though this is purely conceptual and not put into real-world conditions to attest or become realized as such).

The most familiar reference to forbidden knowledge is likely evoked via the Garden of Eden and the essence of forbidden fruit.

A contemporary down-to-earth example often discussed about forbidden knowledge consists of the atomic bomb. Some suggest that the knowledge devised or invented to ultimately produce a nuclear bomb provides a quite visible and overt exemplar of the problems associated with knowledge. Had the knowledge about being able to attain an atomic bomb never been achieved, there presumably would not be any such device. In debates about the topic, it is feasible to take a resolute position favoring the attainment of an atomic bomb and there are equally counterbalancing contentions sternly disfavoring this attainment.

One perplexing problem about forbidden knowledge encompasses knowing beforehand the kind of knowledge that might end up in the forbidden category. This is a bit of a Catch-22 or circular type of puzzle. You might discover knowledge and then ascertain it ought to be forbidden, but the cat is kind of out of the bag due to the knowledge having been already uncovered or rendered. Oopsie, you should have in advance decided to not go there and therefore have avoided falling into the forbidden knowledge zone.

On a related twist, suppose that we could beforehand declare what type of knowledge is to be averted because it is predetermined as forbidden. Some people might accidentally discover the knowledge, doing so by happenstance, and now they've again potentially opened Pandora's box. Meanwhile, there might be others that regardless of being instructed to not derive any such stated forbidden knowledge, do so anyway.

This then takes us to a frequently used retort about forbidden knowledge, namely, if you don't seek the forbidden knowledge there is a chance that someone else will, and you'll be left in the dust because they got there first. In that preemptive viewpoint, the claim is that it is better to go ahead and forage for the forbidden knowledge and not get caught behind the eight ball when someone else beats you to the punch.

Round and round we can go.

The main thing that most would agree to is that knowledge is power.

The alluded to power could be devastating and destroy others, possibly even leading to the self-destruction of the wielder of the knowledge. Yet there is also the potential for knowledge to be advantageous and save humanity from other ills.

Maybe we ought to say that knowledge is powerful. Despite that perhaps obvious proclamation, we might also add that knowledge can decay and gradually become outdated or less potent. Furthermore, since we are immersing ourselves herein into the cauldron of the love-it or hate-it knowledge conundrum, knowledge can be known and yet undervalued, perhaps only becoming valuable at a later time and in a different light.

There is a case to be made that humankind has a seemingly irresistible allure toward more and more knowledge. Some philosophers suggest you are unlikely to be able to bottle up or stop this quest for knowledge. If that's the manner of how humanity will be, this implies that you must find ways to control or contain knowledge and give up on the belief that we can altogether avoid landing into forbidden knowledge.

There is a relatively new venue prompting a lot of anxious hand wringing pertaining to forbidden knowledge, namely the advent of Artificial Intelligence (AI).

Here's the rub.

Suppose that we are able to craft AI systems that make use of knowledge about how humans can think. There are two major potential gotchas.

First, the AI systems themselves might end up doing good things and they also might end up doing bad things. If the bad outweighs the good, maybe we are shooting our own foot by allowing AI to be put into use.

Secondly, perhaps this could be averted entirely by deciding that there is forbidden knowledge about how humans think, and we ought to not discover or reveal those mental mechanisms. It is the classic stepwise logic that step A axiomatically leads to step B. We won't need to worry about AI systems (step B), if we never allow the achievement of step A (figuring out how humans think and then imparting that into computers), since the attainment of AI would presumably not arise.

In any case, there is inarguably a growing concern about AI.

Plenty of efforts are underway to promulgate a semblance of AI Ethics, meaning that those developers and indeed all stakeholders that are conceiving of, building, and putting into use an AI system needs to consider the ethical aspects of their efforts. AI systems have been unveiled and placed into use that is replete with all sorts of notable concerns, including incorporating unsavory biases and other problems.

All told, one bold and somewhat stark argument is that the pursuit of AI is being underpinned or stoked by the discovery and then exploitation of forbidden knowledge.

Be aware that many would scoff at this allegation.

There are those deeply immersed in the field of AI that would laugh that there is anything in the entirety of AI to date that constitutes potential forbidden knowledge. The technology and technological elements are relatively ho-hum, they would argue. You would be hard-pressed to pinpoint what AI-related knowledge that is already known comes anywhere near the ballpark of forbidden knowledge.

For those that concur with that posture, there is the reply that it might be future knowledge that we have not yet attained that is the upcoming forbidden kind, and for which we are heading pell-mell down that path. Thus, they would concede that we haven't arrived at forbidden knowledge at this juncture, but this is an insidious distractor due to the aspect that it masks or belies our qualms entailing the possibility that it lays in wait at the next turn.

One area where AI is being actively used is to create Autonomous Vehicles (AVs).

We are gradually seeing the emergence of self-driving cars and can expect self-driving trucks, self-driving motorcycles, self-driving drones, self-driving planes, self-driving ships, self-driving submersibles, etc.

Today's conventional cars are eventually going to give way to the advent of AI-based true self-driving cars. Self-driving cars are driven via an AI driving system. There isn't a need for a human driver at the wheel, and nor is there a provision for a human to drive the vehicle.

Here's an intriguing question that has arisen: *Might the crafting of AI-based true self-driving cars take us into the realm of discovering forbidden knowledge, and if so, what should be done about this?*

Before jumping into the details, I'd like to clarify what is meant when referring to true self-driving cars.

Self-Driving Cars And Forbidden Knowledge

For Level 4 and Level 5 true self-driving vehicles, there won't be a human driver involved in the driving task.

All occupants will be passengers.

The AI is doing the driving.

One aspect to immediately discuss entails the fact that the AI involved in today's AI driving systems is not sentient. In other words, the AI is altogether a collective of computer-based programming and algorithms, and most assuredly not able to reason in the same manner that humans can.

Why this added emphasis about the AI not being sentient?

Because I want to underscore that when discussing the role of the AI driving system, I am not ascribing human qualities to the AI. Please be aware that there is an ongoing and dangerous tendency these days to anthropomorphize AI. In essence, people are assigning human-like sentience to today's AI, despite the undeniable and inarguable fact that no such AI exists as yet.

With that clarification, you can envision that the AI driving system won't natively somehow "know" about the facets of driving. Driving and all that it entails will need to be programmed as part of the hardware and software of the self-driving car.

Let's dive into the myriad of aspects that come to play on this topic.

The crux here is whether or not there is forbidden knowledge lurking within the existing and ongoing efforts to achieve AI-based true self-driving cars. We'll begin by considering the status of the existent efforts and then shift into speculation about the future of such efforts.

Per the earlier discussion about whether there is forbidden knowledge that has already perchance been revealed or discovered via the efforts toward today's AI systems all told, the odds seem stacked against such a notion at this time, and likewise the same could be said about the pursuit of self-driving cars. Essentially, there doesn't seem to be any forbidden knowledge per se that has been discovered or revealed during the self-driving cars development journey so far, at least with respect to the conventional wisdom about what forbidden knowledge might entail.

One could try to argue that it is premature to reach such a conclusion and that we might, later on, realize that forbidden knowledge was indeed uncovered or invented, and we just didn't realize it. That is a rabbit hole that we'll not go down for now, though you are welcome to keep that presumption at hand if so desired.

That covers the present, and ergo we can turn our attention to the future.

Generally, the efforts underway today have been primarily aimed at achieving Level 4, and the hope is that someday we will go beyond Level 4 and attain Level 5. To get to a robust Level 4, most would likely say that we can continue the existing approaches.

Not everyone would agree with that assumption. Some believe that we will get stymied within Level 4. Furthermore, the inability to produce a robust Level 4 will ostensibly preclude us from being able to attain Level 5. There is a contingent that suggests we need to start over and set aside the existing AI approaches, which otherwise are taking us down a dead-end or blind alley. An entirely new way of devising AI for autonomous vehicles is needed, they would vehemently argue.

There is also a contingent that asserts the Level 4 itself is a type of dead-end. In brief, those proponents would say that we will achieve a robust Level 4, though this will do little good towards attaining Level 5. Once again, their view is similar to the preceding remark that we will need to come up with some radically new understandings about AI and the nature of cognitive acumen in order to get self-driving cars into the Level 5 realm.

Aha, it is within that scope of having to dramatically revisit and revamp what AI is and how we can advance significantly in the pursuit of AI that the forbidden knowledge question can reside. In theory, perhaps the only means of attaining Level 5 will be to strike upon some knowledge that we do not yet know and that for which bodes for falling within the realm of forbidden knowledge.

To some, this seems farfetched.

They would emphatically ask; just what kind of knowledge are you even talking about?

Here's their logic. Humans are able to drive cars. Humans do not seem to need or possess forbidden knowledge as it relates to the act of driving a car. Therefore, it seems ridiculous on the face of things to claim or contend that the only means to get AI-based true self-driving cars, for which they would be driven on an equal basis as human drivers can drive, would require the discovery or invention of whatever might be construed as forbidden knowledge.

Seems like pretty ironclad logic.

The retort is that humans have common-sense reasoning. With common-sense reasoning, we seem to know all sorts of things about the world around us. When we drive a car, we intrinsically make use of our common-sense reasoning. We take for granted that we do have a common-sense reasoning capacity, and similarly, we take for granted that it integrally comes to the fore when driving a car.

Attempts to create AI that can exhibit the equivalent of human common-sense reasoning have made ostensibly modest or some would say minimal progress (to clarify, those pursuing this line of inquiry are to be lauded, it's just that no earthshattering breakthroughs seem to have been reached and none seem on the immediate horizon).

Yes, there are some quite fascinating and exciting efforts underway, but when you measure those against the everyday common-sense reasoning of humans, there is no comparison. They are night and day. If this were a contest, the humans win hands down, no doubt about it, and the AI experimental efforts encompassing common-sense reasoning are mere playthings in contrast.

You might have gleaned where this line of thought is headed.

The belief by some is that until we crack open the enigma of common-sense reasoning, there is little chance of achieving a Level 5, and perhaps also this will hold back the Level 4 too. It could be that a secret ingredient of sorts for autonomous vehicles is the need to figure out and include common-sense reasoning into AI-based driving and piloting systems.

If you buy into that logic, the added assertion is that maybe within the confines of how common-sense reasoning takes place is a semblance of forbidden knowledge. On the surface, you would certainly assume that if we knew entirely how common-sense reasoning works, there would not appear to be any cause for alarm or concern. The act of employing common-sense reasoning does not seem to necessarily embody forbidden knowledge.

The twist is that perhaps the underlying cognitive means that gives rise to the advent of common-sense reasoning is where there is forbidden knowledge. Some deep-rooted elements in the nature of human thought and how we form common sense and undertake common-sense reasoning are possibly a type of knowledge that will be shown as crucial and a forbidden knowledge formulation.

Conclusion

Wow, that's quite a bit of pondering, contemplation, and (some would say) wild thinking.

Maybe so, but it is a consideration that some would wish that we gave at least some credence toward and devoted attention to. There is the angst that we might find ourselves by happenstance stumbling into forbidden knowledge on these voracious self-driving cars quests.

For however you might emphasize that having AI-based true self-driving cars will be a potential blessing, proffering mobility-for-all and leading to reducing the number of car crash-related fatalities, there is a sneaking suspicion that it will not be all-good. The catch or trap could be that there is some kind of forbidden knowledge that will get brought to the eye and we will inevitably kick ourselves that we didn't see it coming.

The next time you are munching on a delicious apple, give some thought to whether self-driving cars might be forbidden fruit.

We are on the path to taking a big bite, and we'll have to see where that takes us.

CHAPTER 4
ACCELERATION AND SELF-DRIVING CARS

I feel the need, the need for speed.

We all know that famous line.

I feel the need, the need for acceleration.

That's a line that doesn't quite roll off the tongue.

It is also a somewhat different way to frame or discuss the need or rapt desire for speed. If you are driving a car, there is the notion of a moment-in-time aspect entailing the speed of the vehicle. We are legally supposed to not go over the stated speed limit. Our speed might be relatively slow when in a school zone and might be relatively high or fast when driving on an open freeway.

Some drivers relish driving fast and at times exceeding the speed limit. Perhaps they are late for work and are in a hurry to get to the office. Maybe the driver is someone that just relishes going fast. The posted speed limit might not necessarily be on their minds, other than as a general guide as to what their speed is supposed to be.

Acceleration is the attainment of speed based on increasing velocity over time. We all viscerally know this somewhat mathematical notion by the seat of our pants and experience it routinely while driving or perhaps outrightly when enjoying a breathtaking ride on a roller coaster.

Think about driving a car. Upon coming up to a red light, you bring your car to a stop and are no longer moving. Once the light turns green, you give your vehicle a bit of gas or push down on the accelerator pedal and the car rolls forward. Some drivers like to do those jackrabbit starts, pushing the pedal to the metal and skyrocketing down the street. Other drivers prefer a steady and gradual pace of acceleration.

Are you the type of driver that likes to do a quick snap from a standing position and gun your engine as you zoom along, or are you the type that prefers a calmer incremental semblance of acceleration?

In some ways, our driving laws tend to allow for a bit of latitude in your acceleration, whilst being tight or stern when it comes to speeding. There usually isn't a stipulated rule that says you cannot do those rocketing accelerations. If you want to go from zero to 45 miles per hour on a street that has a speed limit of 45 miles per hour, you can choose generally how fast you want to get to that top speed. No rule normally exists that says you can only proceed at a pace of some X number of feet per second.

That being said, there is no question that you can get busted if your acceleration causes traffic-related problems. A driver that zips forward might disturb other traffic. Pedestrians that are crossing the street might be endangered. In short, though acceleration itself is not specially regulated, your acceleration can create unsafe roadway conditions and you can be appropriately cited accordingly.

On top of that possibility of a traffic violation, we ought to also consider the dangers of rapid acceleration. A driver that is screeching forward would seem more likely to get themselves into driving trouble. Your control of the car is lessened and you have less reaction time for any sudden appearance of an obstruction or coping with a dire issue such as a tire blowing out.

The rule of thumb usually is steady as things go.

Take your time. That doesn't mean that you crawl at a snail's pace. A really slow acceleration can be bad too. Not because you cannot control the vehicle, but because it might be confounding to other nearby drivers.

Someone that does acceleration like a turtle is bound to get an adverse reaction from other drivers nearby. Why is that person not going faster and getting more quickly up-to-speed? Other cars will tend to try and go around the slowpoke, which can produce a cavalcade of potential near collisions as vehicles jockey back and forth.

Confusion can also arise in that some other drivers might assume that there is a need to accelerate slowly, maybe due to a dog that has come onto the street or some other related factor. Those other drivers will start looking around and needlessly be distracted by the belief that a phantom reason exists for this driving behavior.

Someone that does acceleration as though being shot out of a canon will also usually get an adverse reaction from other drivers. Is that driver showing off? Indeed, this can induce other drivers to accelerate rapidly too. All of a sudden, a street race has been instigated. This worsens the situation since you now have a multitude of cars accelerating, whereas at least up until then it was just one vehicle doing so.

Road rage can readily erupt as a result of acceleration discontinuities. Those other drivers frustrated by the slow acceleration driver might get angry at the slowpoke and take untoward actions at that driver. Likewise, when there is a jackrabbit among other cars, there is likely a road rage that can emerge as other drivers try to cut off that Indy car or catch up and try to tell them off.

Now that we've covered a myriad of facets about car driving and acceleration, we might also contemplate how acceleration relates to stresses for the driver.

Do you think that while you are accelerating that you are under less stress or more stress than when driving along in general?

I suppose it is hard to say.

Some people get highly stressed by being in bumper-to-bumper traffic and for which there is minimal acceleration involved. You are going at a start-and-stop pace, crawling along. Some drivers get a bit of thrill by accelerating up an onramp onto a busy freeway since they know that once they get onto the freeway the traffic will be pretty much at a standstill and be agonizingly sluggish. They have a car, and cars can go fast, so they try to experience the fastness by zooming on the onramp. It is their only moment of glory at being behind the wheel of the vehicle while doing their daily commute.

Okay, so we can readily agree or at least acknowledge that acceleration can be a stress-inducing driving act, though we might also willingly concede that it is not the only driving act that can produce stress.

If you take a look at a newbie teenage driver, you can oftentimes see them sweating profusely while learning to drive a car. They grip the steering wheel like a vise. Facial expressions clearly show concentration, consternation, fear, etc. This can readily occur throughout an entire driving journey. As such, there isn't any singular driving act or driving chore that they relax with, and the moment they start the engine until they turn off the car is filled with angst and dread.

Envision that you wanted to perform an analysis of how much stress a driver might be having throughout their driving journey. You could ask the person about their perceived stress levels. You could try to hook the person to a device that could attempt to physiologically calculate their stress. You could study the face of the person to see what facial expressions they make. And so on, including that the sweatiness of the person could be a consideration too.

Let's focus on sweating.

One means of trying to quantify the degree or magnitude of stress involves measuring the amount of perinasal perspiration (known as PP) that a person is showcasing.

We typically think of having sweaty palms as an indicator of potential stress and will often wipe off our hands to try and get rid of the perspiration, especially if about to shake someone else's hands. PP signals are typically commensurate with this palm-sweating, a form of electrodermal (EDA) activity.

You could potentially seek to detect the perinasal perspiration of a person by using a thermal imaging sensor that took readings via heat radiating from the face of a driver (akin to modern-day thermometers that let you point and detect if a person might have a fever or heightened temperature). Some parts of the face will be cooler and some parts of the face would be hotter. The abject temperature along with temperature differences can be readily measured and analyzed. An added advantage to this approach is that you don't need to hook up the person to any particular device and nor do you have to ask them directly about their stress.

All told, the PP can serve as a surrogate for how much stress a person is seemingly experiencing. This is more formally cast as a stress-induced neurophysiological response that manifests as a transient form of perspiration taking place in the perinasal area.

Say that last sentence twice, fast, as it is quite the tongue twister.

Let's bring together all of these topics into a nice tidy package.

An interesting new research study entitled "Arousal Responses To Regular Acceleration Events Divide Drivers Into High And Low Groups" was undertaken by researchers Tung Huynh (University of Houston), Mike Manser (Texas A&M), and Ioannis Pavlidis (University of Houston) to explore stress levels of drivers and made use of PP in doing so, closely examining acceleration events. Their paper was published in the ACM CHI Conference on Human Factors in Computing Systems Extended Abstracts, May 8–13, 2021.

In their study, they asked a selected sample of drivers to go ahead and drive an everyday route in a city setting that consisted of relatively light traffic and fair-weather conditions. Each driver drove the same route under roughly the same or similar circumstances. The driving effort could be characterized as relatively straightforward, pretty easy overall, and more like a mild driving romp than a maddening crowd-coping dog-eat-dog drive.

This is worth noting since the driving route and the manner of what kind of driving is required were able to be construed as a stable and consistent environment. If each driver had driven an entirely different route or in radically varying levels of traffic, it would make trying to contrast the stress-inducing moments and journey characteristics harder to compare. Likewise, if the driving had been snowy for some drivers and dry and sunny for others, this would have ostensibly significantly altered the driving practices and therefore variously prodded the stress exhibited during the driving task per each driver.

The occasions for acceleration were of the ordinary type that would be encountered in such a setting and are customarily referred to as naturalistic driving.

In contrast, if we put drivers onto a closed-off racetrack and asked them to drive in a spirited way, the odds are that you would witness quite a lot of rather strenuous acceleration efforts. This would be a somewhat artificially contrived setting that was unlike the natural or conventional driving chores that most of us face daily. For this study, the acceleration occurred in the ways we all are accustomed to doing so, such as when entering into a fast-moving stream of daily traffic, when proceeding from a red light that has turned green, etc.

The main research questions being addressed in the study were stated this way: "How do arousal responses of normal drivers relate to acceleration and other driving variables in the context of a standard commute? Is there any underlying grouping in these responses?"

Notice the use of the phrase "arousal responses" which simply connotes how reactive someone might be to a stimulus of some kind (this is the usual technical jargon common amongst such studies). The researchers had reviewed prior studies and identified the insight that there is apparently "a category of normal drivers who are hyperaroused during routine acceleration events - a phenomenon we call accelarousal, and which carries behavioral and design implications."

In brief, the research results indicated: "A key contribution of this study is the clustering result that reveals an underlying high and low arousal grouping of normal drivers with respect to acceleration. The finding bears implications for certain categories of the driving population." The implication is that some drivers are more likely to be accelarousal-prone versus other drivers (referred to as non-acceleration-prone drivers). Those drivers that are accelarousal-prone could especially be incurring greater levels of stress which over a lengthy spate of driving might have particularly adverse health effects.

Imagine for example that we have two drivers, both serving as ridesharing or ride-hailing drivers. Assume that one of them is accelarousal-prone and the other is not. They serve as drivers for many months, perhaps years, and doing so in equivalent terms of the number of hours driven and in the same city areas. Of course, it might be hard to compare them because of other varying factors, but let's stick with this scenario for the moment.

It could be that the accelarousal-prone driver ends up with various stress-related ailments and suffers ergo from commensurate health consequences. Meanwhile, the other driver seems just fine, and the stress has washed off their back like a duck in water. If we didn't realize that one was more prone to this acceleration stress, there might be quite a mystery as to why one was more adversely impacted by the driving than the other. Again, as a caution, we must be careful to not overinflate this example and need to consider a slew of additional factors that might come to play.

Which do you think that you are, the type of driver that is accelarousal-prone or the non-acceleration-prone driver?

I'll let you ponder that for a moment. Maybe ask a friend or family member whether you are of one type or the other. That will certainly garner quite a bit of heated discussion and likely engage all in a lively discussion on the topic, that's for sure.

Shifting gears, consider that the future of cars consists of self-driving cars. Self-driving cars are driven via an AI driving system. There isn't a need for a human driver at the wheel, and nor is there a provision for a human to drive the vehicle.

Here's an intriguing question that has arisen: *What impacts if any will the accelarousal-prone aspects have in an era of AI-based true self-driving cars?*

Before jumping into the details, I'd like to clarify what is meant when referring to true self-driving cars.

Self-Driving Cars And Acceleration Stress

For Level 4 and Level 5 true self-driving vehicles, there won't be a human driver involved in the driving task.

All occupants will be passengers.

The AI is doing the driving.

One aspect to immediately discuss entails the fact that the AI involved in today's AI driving systems is not sentient. In other words, the AI is altogether a collective of computer-based programming and algorithms, and most assuredly not able to reason in the same manner that humans can.

Why this added emphasis about the AI not being sentient?

Because I want to underscore that when discussing the role of the AI driving system, I am not ascribing human qualities to the AI. Please be aware that there is an ongoing and dangerous tendency these days to anthropomorphize AI. In essence, people are assigning human-like sentience to today's AI, despite the undeniable and inarguable fact that no such AI exists as yet.

With that clarification, you can envision that the AI driving system won't natively somehow "know" about the facets of driving. Driving and all that it entails will need to be programmed as part of the hardware and software of the self-driving car.

Let's dive into the myriad of aspects that come to play on this topic.

First, as mentioned, Level 4 and Level 5 won't make use of a human driver and will instead be driven by an AI driving system. This means that whether a human driver is accelarousal-prone or not is no longer applicable since there isn't a human driver at the wheel. That would seem to summarily close off any further discussion on the matter and we can go home now.

Au contraire, mon ami (on the contrary, my friend)!

There is the matter of putting some strident attention towards the *passengers* that are inside a self-driving car.

Perhaps the passengers are subject to being accelarousal-prone. This makes indubitable sense. When you are driving a car, and if you have someone in the vehicle with you, the manner in which you accelerate is likely to impact any such passenger too. I'm sure you've had moments whereby you slammed your foot onto the accelerator pedal and your passenger looked at you with shock or concern, likely not aware of what the roadway situation is and why you have opted to rocketship forward.

You can ostensibly argue that the passenger is potentially *less* impacted because they aren't driving the car and therefore do not carry the burden of the driving task. The logic is that the driver has both the acceleration to be confronted with and the grave responsibility of controlling the vehicle, incurring a double whammy of potential stress. The passenger is sometimes characterized as a compliant and otherwise relatively docile occupant that has no direct means of controlling the car, no more than a lump of clay.

Well, two can play at that game. You can make an additional argument that perhaps the stress on the passenger could actually be *worse* than for the driver.

How so?

The passenger is bereft of a direct means to control the vehicle and ergo entirely at the whim of the driver. You could make the case that this is even more stressful than being the driver. The passenger is going along for the ride and the use of acceleration can make that ride seem even more perilous and stressful. Meanwhile, the driver is calling the shots, as it were. When a person has no avenue of control over their destiny, there can be a tremendous amount of stress.

Let's though for now not get mired into an endless debate about which has more stress, the driver versus the passenger, and instead be willing to agree that the passenger can have stress as a result of acceleration events. You would be hard-pressed to argue to the contrary.

To clarify, not all passengers would necessarily be subject to acceleration-induced stress. This brings us to a notable point. There is presumably the potential of having two types of passengers, those that are accelarousal-prone ones and those that are not accelarousal-prone.

Aha, this provides some valuable insight into the ongoing and future design, development, and use of self-driving cars.

AI driving systems of AI-based true self-driving cars ought to be devised to detect the different types of passengers and drive the vehicle differently depending upon the type present in the vehicle. For example, suppose there is a passenger alone in a self-driving car and the AI driving system has somehow ascertained that the person is accelarousal-prone. In that case, the AI driving system could purposely accelerate in rather steady ways and do so at a measured pace. No fast starts. No quick and startling moments of sudden acceleration.

This driving action of being sensitive to the accelarousal-prone nature of the passenger would need to be tempered by the driving situation at hand. Imagine that a big truck is about to swerve into the path of the self-driving car and the only viable escape requires the self-driving car to rapidly accelerate out of the way. The overall safety of the passenger and the vehicle would outweigh the otherwise preferred mode of doing acceleration in a more subdued fashion.

Self-driving cars are anticipated to contain inward-facing sensors such as video cameras and onboard microphones. This provision is used for a multitude of purposes. Passengers can use Zoom-like interactive sessions while traveling inside a self-driving car and take remote education courses. Another use would be for the AI driving system to monitor the occupants and try to determine if they might be marking graffiti or marring the interior of the vehicle. That might seem a bit gloomy as a reason, so we can also include that the mechanisms could detect when someone is having a sudden heart attack or other emergency and needs assistance.

Presumably, a thermal imaging sensor could be used too. This device could try to measure the PP and in a real-time attempt to ascertain the accelarousal-prone nature of the passenger. Based on that calculated analysis, the AI driving system would adjust the acceleration process accordingly.

Some might say that seems overly convoluted as an approach to determining the accelarousal-prone nature and it might be simpler to ask the passenger what they want. AI driving systems are likely to include a Natural Language Processing (NLP) system that is used to interact with passengers. A passenger could be asked what levels of acceleration they prefer. This is an abundantly easy form of interaction and akin to the capabilities of a contemporary Siri or Alexa.

Conclusion

There are a variety of additional twists and turns involved.

Briefly, for Level 2 and Level 3 conventional human-driven cars, there is an ongoing consideration about the handoff of the driving task, doing so in two ways. There is the driving system that requests the human driver to engage in the driving task, and there is the case of the human driver seeking to engage the driving system to undertake the driving task. To some degree, it might be useful for the handoff to incorporate whether the human driver is accelarousal-prone or not. Akin to the earlier discussion, this determination might be done via a thermal imaging sensor, via other sensors, or by using an NLP.

There is a subtle but important undercurrent in mentioning the Level 2 and Level 3 conventional human-driven cars.

The odds are that we are going to have a mixture of human-driven cars and AI-based true self-driving cars for quite a long time, likely decades or longer. There is not going to be an overnight magical switch from human-driven cars to all self-driving cars. Indeed, debates will become fierce about whether human drivers will have to entirely give up the driving task, for which some fervently vow they will not do so until you pry their cold dead hands from the wheel.

Assume for sake of discussion that there is going to be a mixture of human-driven cars and AI-based true self-driving cars on our streets, byways, highways, and freeways. One interesting question is whether acceleration as a standard practice will change due to this mixture.

For example, pundits emphasize that self-driving cars will be programmed to always drive cautiously and fully legally abide strictly by the rules of the road. I've repeatedly pointed out that this already is having an "unintended adverse consequence" on human drivers that are nearby to self-driving cars (see my column for discussions on these matters).

In short, human drivers get frustrated by the poking along with self-driving cars and are apt to try and accelerate around the seeming slowpoke vehicles. You see, oddly enough, the advent of self-driving cars could indirectly prod human drivers into doing more acceleration, including drivers that prior had not particularly done so. Just imagine how accelarousal-prone human drivers might react.

As they say, the best-laid plans of mice and humankind can oftentimes go astraydriving a ca

CHAPTER 5
CORNER CASES AND SELF-DRIVING CARS

Get ready to go on a seemingly endless loop of sorts.

Imagine that you are driving your car and perchance come upon a dog that has suddenly darted into the roadway.

Most of us have had this happen. You hopefully were able to take evasive action. Assuming that all went well, the pooch was fine and nobody in your car got hurt either.

In a kind of *Groundhog Day* movie manner, let's repeat the scenario. We will though make a small change.

Are you ready?

Imagine that you are driving your car and perchance come upon a deer that has suddenly darted into the roadway.

Fewer of us have had this happen, though nonetheless, it is a somewhat common occurrence for those that live in a region that has deer aplenty.

In any case, would you perform the same evasive actions when coming upon a deer as you would in the case of the dog that was in the middle of the road?

We can debate this open question and derive potential differences.

Some might claim that a deer is more likely to be trying to get out of the street and be more inclined to sprint toward the side of the road. The dog might decide to stay in the street and run around in circles. With that being said, that kind of blanket statement will rankle either dog lovers or deer lovers, or both. It is hard to say whether there would be any pronounced difference in behavior.

Let's anyway iterate this once again and make another change.

Imagine that you are driving your car and perchance come upon a chicken that has suddenly darted into the roadway.

What do you do?

For some drivers, a chicken is a whole different matter than a deer or a dog. If you were going fast while in the car and there wasn't much latitude to readily avoid the chicken, it is conceivable that you would make the tough decision to go ahead and ram the chicken. The logic being that we generally accept the aspect of having chicken as part of our everyday meals, thus one less chicken is ostensibly okay, especially in comparison to the risk of possibly rolling your car or veering into a ditch upon sudden braking.

Essentially, you might be more risk-prone if the animal was a deer or a dog and be willing to put yourself at greater risk to save the deer or the dog. But when the situation involves a chicken, you might decide that the personal risk versus the harming of the intruding creature is differently balanced. Of course, some would vehemently argue that the chicken, the deer, and the dog are all equal and drivers should not try to split hairs by saying that one animal is more precious than the other.

We'll move on.

Let's make another change. This change is about something that wasn't explicitly discussed earlier.

Without having said so, it was likely that you assumed that the weather for these scenarios of the animal crossing into the street was relatively neutral. Perhaps it was a sunny day and the road conditions were rather plain or uneventful.

Change that assumption about the conditions and imagine that there have been gobs of rain, including that you in the midst of a heavy downpour. Your windshield wiper blades can barely keep up with the sheets of water and you are straining mightily to see the road ahead. The roadway is completely soaked and extremely slick.

Do your driving choices alter now that the weather is adverse?

Any reasonable person would say so.

Whereas you might have earlier opted to radically steer around the animal, any such maneuver now, while in the rain, is a lot dicier. The tires might not stick to the roadway due to the coating of water. Your visibility is reduced and you might not be able to properly judge where the animal is and nor what else might be near to the street. All in all, the bad weather makes this become an even worse situation.

The point of this varying scenario is that the nature of the driving scene and the overall situation can significantly impact what actions you might opt to take as a driver.

We can keep going with this scenario.

For example, pretend that it is nighttime rather than being daytime. That certainly changes things. Another facet would be the surrounding traffic. Imagine that the setting involves no other traffic for miles. After you've given that situation some careful thought, reimagine things and pretend that there is traffic all around you, cars and trucks abundantly, and also there is heavy traffic on the opposing side of the roadway.

How many such twists and turns can we concoct?

In one sense, you might claim that there is an endless variety. We can continue to add or adjust the elements, doing so over and over. Each new instance becomes its own particular consideration. You would presumably need to mentally recalculate what to do as the driver. Some of the story adjustments might reduce your viable options, while other of the adjustments might widen the number of feasible options.

The combination and permutations can be dizzying.

A newbie teenage driver is oftentimes taken aback by the variability of driving. They encounter one situation that they've not encountered before and go into a bit of a momentary panic mode. What to do? Much of the time, they muddle their way through and do so without any scrape or calamity. Hopefully, they learn what to do the next time that a similar setting presents itself and thus be less caught off-guard.

Experienced drivers seem to have seen it all and therefore are able to usually react as needed. That vastness of knowledge about driving situations does have its limits. You would be unduly tempting fate to contend that you have seen it all.

As an example, there was a news report about a plane that landed on a highway because of in-flight engine troubles. I ask you, how many of us have seen a plane land on the roadway in front of them? A rarity, for sure.

These examples bring up a debate about the so-called edge or corner cases that can occur when driving a car. An edge or corner case is a reference to the instance of something that is considered rare or unusual. These are events that tend to happen once in a blue moon. They are usually coined as outliers.

A plane landing on the roadway amidst car traffic would be a candidate for consideration as an edge or corner case. A dog or deer or chicken that wanders into the roadway would be less likely construed as an edge or corner case. The former instance is extraordinary, while the latter instance being somewhat commonplace.

Another way to define an edge or corner case entails the somewhat apparent aspect that those are instances beyond the core or crux of whatever our focus is. As an analogy, envision that we have a large-sized card table and we are going to try putting together a jigsaw puzzle. We will place all of the jigsaw pieces onto the table, initially splaying them here and there. Our next task entails arranging the scattered pieces.

The mainstay of the table will have the core set of puzzle pieces.

Toward the corners or edge of the table, we will put the pieces that seem out of sorts. To put together the puzzle, we will aim to deal with the core or crux first, now residing in the middle of the table. Once we get that core work done, we will turn our attention to those pesky edges or corner pieces.

I had mentioned that there is a debate about edge or corner cases.

Here's the rub.

How do we decide what is on the edge or corner, rather than being classified as in the core?

This can get very nebulous and be subject to acrimonious discourse. Those instances that someone claims are edge or corner cases might be more appropriately tagged as part of the core. Meanwhile, instances tossed into the core could be potentially argued as more rightfully be placed into the edge or corner cases category. If you've ever done a jigsaw puzzle with someone else, you must know what it is like to have heated discussions on such matters.

One aspect that escapes attention oftentimes is that the core does not necessarily have to be larger than the number or size of the edges. We just assume that would be the logical arrangement. Yet it could be that we have a very small core and a tremendously large set of edges or corner cases.

The whole thing gets especially mushy if you don't have any definitive concordance on what constitutes a core versus an edge. Those debating about whether something is considered core or considered an edge can readily talk past one another. They do not realize that they are going to be arguing until the cows come home since they each have hidden assumptions about which is which.

We can add more fuel to this fire by bringing up the concept of having a *long tail* (not per se the kind of tail as on the wagging tail of a dog).

People use the catchphrase "long tail" to generally refer to circumstances of having a preponderance of something as a constituted central or core and then in a presumed ancillary sense have a lot of other elements that tail off. You can mentally make a picture of a large bunched area on a graph and then have a narrow offshoot that goes on and on, becoming a veritable tail to the bunched-up portion.

This notion is borrowed from the field of statistics. There is a somewhat more precise meaning in a purely statistical sense, but that's not how most people make use of the phrase. The informal meaning is that you might have lots of less noticeable aspects that are in the tail of whatever else you are doing.

A company might have a core product that is considered it's blockbuster or main seller. Perhaps they sell only a relative few of those but do so at a hefty price each and it gives them prominence in the marketplace. Turns out the company has a lot of other products too. Those aren't as well-known. When you add up the total revenue from the sales of their products, it could be that all of those itty-bitty products bring in more dough than do the blockbuster products.

Based on that description, I trust that you realize that the long tail can be quite important, even if it doesn't get much overt attention. The long tail can be the basis for a company and be extremely important. If the firm only keeps its eye on the blockbuster, it could end up in ruin if they ignore or undervalue the long tail.

That doesn't always have to be the case. It could be that the long tail is holding back the company. Maybe they have a slew of smaller products that just aren't worth keeping around. Those long-tail products might be losing money and draining away from the blockbuster end.

On a lighter note, you could say that sometimes the dog wags the tail, and other times the tail wags the dog. And since I've gotten the mention of dogs repeatedly into this saga, allow me to recast that last sentence. You could say that sometimes the cat wags the tail, and other times the tail wags the cat. This should appease dog and also cat lovers.

Overall, the long tail ought to get its due and be given proper scrutiny. Combining the concept of the long tail with the concept of the edge or corner cases, we could suggest that the edge or corner cases are lumped into that long tail.

Getting back to driving a car, the dog or even a deer that ran into the street proffers a driving incident or event that we probably would agree is somewhere in the core of driving. It seems that you would be hard-pressed to argue that there is something highly unlikely about such an occurrence.

In terms of a chicken entering into the roadway, well, unless you live near a farm, this would seem a bit more extreme. On a daily drive in a typical city setting, you probably will not see many chickens charging into the street.

Speaking of drivers and driving, the future of cars consists of self-driving cars.

Self-driving cars are driven via an AI driving system. There isn't a need for a human driver at the wheel, and nor is there a provision for a human to drive the vehicle.

Some pundits fervently state that we will never attain true self-driving cars because of the long tail problem. The argument is that there are zillions of edge or corner cases that will continually arise unexpectedly, and the AI driving system won't be prepared to handle those instances. This in turn means that self-driving cars will be ill-prepared to adequately perform on our public roadways.

Furthermore, those pundits assert that no matter how tenaciously those heads-down all-out AI developers keep trying to program the AI driving systems, they will always fall short of the mark. There will be yet another new edge or corner case to be had. It is like a game of whack-a-mole, wherein another mole will pop up.

The thing is, this is not simply a game, it is a life-or-death matter since whatever a driver does at the wheel of a car can spell life or possibly death for the driver, and the passengers, and for drivers of nearby cars, and pedestrians, etc.

Here's an intriguing question that is worth pondering: *Are AI-based true self-driving cars doomed to never be capable on our roadways due to the endless possibilities of edge or corner cases and the infamous long-tail conundrum?*

Before jumping into the details, I'd like to clarify what is meant when referring to true self-driving cars.

Self-Driving Cars And The Long Tail

For Level 4 and Level 5 true self-driving vehicles, there won't be a human driver involved in the driving task.

All occupants will be passengers.

The AI is doing the driving.

One aspect to immediately discuss entails the fact that the AI involved in today's AI driving systems is not sentient. In other words, the AI is altogether a collective of computer-based programming and algorithms, and most assuredly not able to reason in the same manner that humans can.

Why this added emphasis about the AI not being sentient?

Because I want to underscore that when discussing the role of the AI driving system, I am not ascribing human qualities to the AI. Please be aware that there is an ongoing and dangerous tendency these days to anthropomorphize AI. In essence, people are assigning human-like sentience to today's AI, despite the undeniable and inarguable fact that no such AI exists as yet.

With that clarification, you can envision that the AI driving system won't natively somehow "know" about the facets of driving. Driving and all that it entails will need to be programmed as part of the hardware and software of the self-driving car.

Let's dive into the myriad of aspects that come to play on this topic.

First, it would seem nearly self-evident that the number of combinations and permutations of potential driving situations is going to be enormous. We can quibble whether this is an infinite number or a finite number, though in practical terms this is one of those counting dilemmas akin to the number of grains of sand on all of the beaches throughout the entire globe. In brief, it is a very, very, very big number.

If you were to try and program an AI driving system based on each possible instance, this indeed would be a laborious task. Even if you added a veritable herd of ace AI software developers, you can certainly expect this would take years upon years to undertake, likely many decades or perhaps centuries, and still be faced with the fact that there is one more unaccounted edge or corner case remaining.

The pragmatic view is that there would always be that last one that evades being preestablished.

Some are quick to offer that perhaps simulations would solve this quandary.

Most of the automakers and self-driving tech firms are using computer-based simulations to try and ferret out driving situations and get their AI driving systems ready for whatever might arise. The belief by some is that if enough simulations are run, the totality of whatever will occur in the real world will have already been surfaced and dealt with before entering self-driving cars into the real world.

The other side of that coin is the contention that simulations are based on what humans believe might occur. As such, the real world can be surprising in comparison to what humans might normally envision will occur. Those computer-based simulations will always then fall short and not end up covering all the possibilities, say those critics.

Amid the heated debates about the use of simulations, do not get lost among the fray and somehow reach a conclusion that simulations are either the final silver bullet or fall into the trap that simulations won't reach the highest bar and ergo they should be utterly disregarded.

Make no mistake, simulations are essential and a crucial tool in the pursuit of AI-based true self-driving cars.

There is a floating argument that there ought not to be any public roadway trials taking place of true self-driving cars until the proper completion of extensive and apparently exhaustive simulations. The counterargument is that this is impractical in that it would delay roadway testing on an indefinite basis, and that the delay means more lives lost due to everyday human driving. There is a lot more to these vital imbroglios, which I've covered in my prior columns (see **the link here**), and I suggest that readers interested further should consult those analyses.

An allied topic entails the use of closed tracks that are purposely set up for the testing of self-driving cars. By being off the public roadways, a proving ground ensures that the public at large is not endangered by whatever waywardness might emerge during driverless testing. The same arguments surrounding the closed track or proving grounds approach are similar to the tradeoffs mentioned when discussing the use of simulations (again, see my remarks posted in my columns).

This has taken us full circle and returned us back to the angst over an endless supply of edge or corner cases. It has also brought us squarely back to the dilemma of what constitutes an edge or corner case in the context of driving a car. The long tail for self-driving cars is frequently referred to in a handwaving manner. This ambiguity is spurred or sparked due to the lack of a definitive agreement about what is indeed in the long tail versus what is in the core.

This squishiness has another undesirable effect.

Whenever a self-driving car does something amiss, it is easy to excuse the matter by claiming that the act was merely in the long tail. This disarms anyone expressing concern about the misdeed. Here's how that goes. The contention is that any such concern or finger-pointing is misplaced since the edge case is only an edge case, implying a low-priority and less weighty aspect, and not significant in comparison to whatever the core contains.

There is also the haughtiness factor.

Those that blankly refer to the long-tail of self-driving cars can have the appearance of one-upmanship, holding court over those that do not know what the long-tail is or what it contains. With the right kind of indignation and tonal inflection, the haughty speaker can make others feel incomplete or ignorant when they "naively" try to refute the legendary (and notorious) long-tail.

Conclusion

There are a lot more twists and turns on this topic.

Due to space constraints, I'll offer just a few more snippets to further whet your appetite.

One perspective is that it makes little sense to try and enumerate all the possible edge cases. Presumably, human drivers do not know all the possibilities and despite this lack of awareness are able to drive a car and do so safely the preponderance of the time. You could argue that humans lump together edge cases into more macroscopic collectives and treat the edge cases as particular instances of those larger conceptualizations.

You sit at the steering wheel with those macroscopic mental templates and invoke them when a specific instance arises, even if the specifics are somewhat surprising or unexpected. If you've dealt with a dog that was loose in the street, you likely have formed a template for when nearly any kind of animal is loose in the street, including deer, chickens, turtles, and so on. You didn't need to beforehand prepare for every animal on the planet.

The developers of AI driving systems can presumably try to leverage a similar approach.

Some also believe that the emerging ontologies for self-driving cars will aid in this endeavor.

You see, for Level 4 self-driving cars, the developers are supposed to indicate the Operational Design Domain (ODD) in which the AI driving system is capable of driving the vehicle. Perhaps the ontologies being crafted toward a more definitive semblance of ODDs would give rise to the types of driving action templates needed.

The other kicker is the matter of common-sense reasoning.

One viewpoint is that humans fill in the gaps of what they might know by exploiting their capability of performing common-sense reasoning. This acts as the always-ready contender for coping with unexpected circumstances. Today's AI efforts have not yet been able to crack open how common-sense reasoning seems to occur and thus we cannot, for now, rely upon this presumed essential backstop (for my coverage about AI and common-sense reasoning, see my columns).

Doomsayers would indicate that self-driving cars are not going to successfully be readied for public roadway use until all edge or corner cases have been conquered. In that vein, that future nirvana can be construed as the day and moment when we have completely emptied out and covered all the bases that furtively reside in the imperious long-tail of autonomous driving.

That's a tall order and a tale that might be telling, or it could be a tail that is wagging the dog and we can find other ways to cope with those vexing edges and corners.

CHAPTER 6
MOUNTAIN LION AND SELF-DRIVING CARS

What would you do?

A woman in California heard her beloved pet dog barking frantically outside of her home and wondered what in the heck was going on in her backyard. It was the kind of frenetic yapping that only happens when something terrible is transpiring.

Upon looking out the window of her domicile, she saw a mountain lion that was going toe-to-toe with her cherished pooch. As an indication of how fierce the mountain lion must be, it had seemingly scaled a towering six-foot deer fence that surrounded the perimeter of the property.

Imagine the stout determination of that mountain lion.

Yikes!

The woman had to take action immediately.

Her canine was getting off-and-on mauled by the mountain lion. It was an entirely frightening and gut-wrenching spectacle. The courageous dog was doing whatever it could to defend itself, possibly also wanting to defend the property and the family therein from this dangerous intruder.

You could try opening the backdoor of the house and attempt vigorously to summon the pooch to quickly come indoors. This though might invite the mountain lion in too. It was also doubtful that the dog would give much consideration to such an escape and was entirely focused on doing battle with the mountain lion. One supposes that if the dog veered from the confrontation, the mountain lion would merely pounce mercilessly onto the innocent animal and the hound would have little chance of scampering into the house anyway.

There wasn't any obvious way to scare off the mountain lion. Yelling at it would be ineffective. The beast was focused on making a kill. For all intents and purposes, the mountain lion had gotten a taste of the dog and likely believed that victory was within grasp. All aspects suggested that this mountain lion was unstoppable and had become possessed with the intent of taking her much-loved doggy.

Unstoppable except for the overpowering force of a moving car.

The woman darted into your side yard, jumped into the seat of her car, started the engine hurriedly, and drove directly toward the mountain lion. With a lot of horn honking and the menacing threat of a several thousand-pound automotive steamrolling car coming at the trespasser, the mountain lion took off.

Victory for humanity and dog lovers.

Defeat for a menacing mountain lion.

The dog was taken to a veterinarian and was expected to make a full recovery from the bodily injuries suffered during the brawl with the mountain lion. Some extra dog food and treats were well-earned by this brave defender. The mountain lion was being sought by the California Department of Fish and Wildlife.

A generally happy ending to the daunting ordeal.

The saga is interesting here because of the use of a car to defend against the attacking mountain lion.

Perhaps most of us think of our cars when we mainly are already in them, such that if you were seated in the driver's seat and you saw that a mountain lion was on the attack that you would straightaway use your car to scare off the unwanted brute. I dare say that we would probably be less inclined to consider using your car when we aren't even inside the automotive wonder.

Going through your mind instead might be things that you could readily pick up and use as a weapon against the mountain lion. Possibly you might grab a shovel from your garage or select a large wooden post that might perchance be laying around. Of course, brandishing such a weapon will nonetheless put you in potential grave danger. The mountain lion might decide you are more savory than going after your dog or at least decide that diverting attention toward you makes the most sense since you are presumably trying to attack it (the notion of only trying to shoo away the animal might not enter into the animal's mindset).

Think about what you have to do to use a car in this setting.

In the case of using a conventional car, you need to make sure that you have the keys to the car. You need to open the door of the car and get into the car. You need to fumble around and use the keys to start the car (hopefully it starts). You need to put the car into gear. You need to drive the car to where the scuffle is taking place. You then need to aim toward the transgressor.

You want to be careful and not accidentally strike your dog. You need to keep your cool, at least enough to be able to drive the car without wrecking or rolling the vehicle. In your haste as a driver, it could be that an attempt to use your car ends up worsening the situation. There are lots of things that could go wrong.

On the other side of the ledger is that the mountain lion will be unlikely able to harm you. Even if the animal charges at the car, this would seem marginally risky to you. Suppose the mountain lion leaps to the hood of the car? Well, that's quite a trick, but the odds of the angry beast breaking through the front windshield and bursting into the vehicle are extremely low. Pretty much unimaginable.

The good luck or smartness in selecting the car is that you are in a veritable protected shell. We can all reasonably agree that the mountain lion cannot get at you. As stated earlier, the bigger downside is that you panic at the driving controls. One can envision a highly stressed driver inadvertently hitting the gas and barreling into their own home or backyard property. Besides possibly damaging those items, it is conceivable that you might find yourself in a car crash of your own making.

One hates when that happens.

In this case, it seems that the woman had enough presence of mind that she did not apparently try to run over the mountain lion per se. She might have merely wanted to get it to change course and skedaddle. The focus was saving her treasured pooch. It could also be that the dog and the mountain lion were so closely battling each other that it was too risky to try and ram solely the unwelcome wrongdoer. Another possible notion is that the mountain lion was just doing what mountain lions do, potentially starving for a meal. How far does one go to stop an everyday animal that is doing what nature drives it to do?

Anyway, the main point about the car is that it was a bit of an unusual selection for this particular circumstance. Unusual or not, you have to admit that the choice worked.

Speaking of cars, the future of cars consists of AI-based true self-driving cars. Self-driving cars are driven via an AI driving system. There isn't a need for a human driver at the wheel, and nor is there a provision for a human to drive the vehicle.

Here's an intriguing question that is worth pondering: *Would you have been able to use an AI-based true self-driving car in this kind of dire or ostensibly dreadful situation?*

Before jumping into the details, I'd like to clarify what is meant when referring to true self-driving cars.

Self-Driving Cars And Confronting Mountain Lions

For Level 4 and Level 5 true self-driving vehicles, there won't be a human driver involved in the driving task.

All occupants will be passengers.

The AI is doing the driving.

One aspect to immediately discuss entails the fact that the AI involved in today's AI driving systems is not sentient. In other words, the AI is altogether a collective of computer-based programming and algorithms, and most assuredly not able to reason in the same manner that humans can.

Why this added emphasis about the AI not being sentient?

Because I want to underscore that when discussing the role of the AI driving system, I am not ascribing human qualities to the AI. Please be aware that there is an ongoing and dangerous tendency these days to anthropomorphize AI. In essence, people are assigning human-like sentience to today's AI, despite the undeniable and inarguable fact that no such AI exists as yet.

With that clarification, you can envision that the AI driving system won't natively somehow "know" about the facets of driving. Driving and all that it entails will need to be programmed as part of the hardware and software of the self-driving car.

Let's dive into the myriad of aspects that come to play on this topic.

First, regarding using your vehicle to dissuade a mountain lion, you might have to discard the notion that you would have a car at all.

Say what?

Some pundits keep exhorting that we will not individually be able to own self-driving cars. This lack of ownership is often couched as based on the projected high price associated with purchasing a self-driving car. I've debunked this contention.

Another claim is that only large companies will own and operate self-driving cars, doing so in fleets, partially to ensure that proper care and maintenance takes place. I've debunked that argument too.

Okay, so I contend that individual ownership of self-driving cars will indeed occur. In that case, you would have available your self-driving car sitting in your driveway and waiting to be used to scare off a mountain lion. The only catch is that your self-driving car might be out and about, rather than being parked and doing nothing.

You see, conventional cars are idle and parked for around 95% or more of their available usage time. They sit around, waiting for us to use them. The key to this idleness is that a human driver is needed. The car is nothing more than a large paperweight until a human driver hops into the driver's seat.

A self-driving car will be able to drive without a human driver. This means that you can potentially have your self-driving car doing errands for you, such as going over to the grocery store to pick up groceries for you (a grocery store employee would load the bags into your trunk, and the autonomous vehicle would then return to your home). You can also use your self-driving car for ridesharing or ride-hailing purposes. All you need to do is make it available for that aim, perhaps posting it as available on a popular ride-hailing network, and your car is now making money while you do other chores or do nothing whatsoever.

That is a bit of a rub.

It will be tempting to have your self-driving car running around and doing all sorts of things. Meanwhile, you won't have it right next to you and ready for your use. There is a tradeoff involved, that's for sure. Would you feel better or safer to have your self-driving car parked and waiting for you, or is it okay to have it roaming around and performing errands or earning money for you?

Tough call.

Let's assume for sake of discussion that your self-driving car was perchance there in your driveway when the mountain lion came a calling.

You run out to your self-driving car and want to get into it. But wait, do you need to actually be inside the self-driving car to have it become operational?

Some argue that you should be able to control your self-driving car while outside of the vehicle. This might be done via an app on your smartphone. It could also be conceivably done by a voice recognition capability of the vehicle whereby it has microphones aimed outward and picks up voice commands that are spoken to it. You presumably could yell out to the self-driving car that it should startup and go after that threatening mountain lion.

A counterargument is that we are going to be getting into some pretty dicey situations if we allow people to remotely control their self-driving cars. The person controlling the vehicle might decide to do something dastardly, and since they are not inside the vehicle, they are going to avoid any direct adverse consequences from their commands. Some assert that we are opening Pandora's box by allowing remote control of a multi-ton vehicle, a far cry from the remote control of a toy racing car.

Let's assume for sake of discussion that you can give remote commands but only to the degree that you are allowed to give the AI driving system an indicated destination. You can for example tell the self-driving car to drive to the grocery store or over to Aunt Betties' house. You cannot specifically guide the vehicle such as telling it to proceed ahead twenty feet or anything that seems to be an open-ended type of instruction.

In the mountain lion scenario, you can probably sense that we are heading toward a bit of a problem about trying to use a self-driving car to intimidate the beast that is attacking your prized pooch.

About the only way to go after that mountain lion will involve a likely circuitous route. This could include driving onto your grass and avoiding any bushes, trees, or other items in your backyard. A human at the wheel would be eyeing the mountain lion and generally be heading in the direction of the animal. It is unlikely that the self-driving car has been programmed to do this.

I mention that the AI probably wasn't programmed to take that kind of action. I say this because some would insist a self-driving car ought to never ever do anything such as aiming to strike a living creature. I've covered this in my discussion about Asimov's three laws of robotics and how they pertain to and might not be quite fitting for the advent of self-driving cars.

If an automaker or self-driving tech firm decided to include a module or program code to allow for trying to go after an animal, the self-driving car could certainly proceed in that manner. At this time, the aspect of having that kind of programming is highly doubtful. Imagine the backlash.

You might be thinking that this type of capability would be handy in the case of the attacking mountain lion. Yes, that would seem to be the case. Unfortunately, suppose the person inadvertently instructed the AI driving system to go after the dog. Unsettling. Or, suppose the mountain lion was the stated target, but the AI driving system become confounded and went toward the dog or was seeking the mountain lion but then struck the dog.

This is a horrible can of worms.

The easiest answer is to make clear that the AI driving system should not try to hit any living creature. That seems to make abundant sense. On the other hand, you've now taken your self-driving car out of the picture in terms of being able to use it to fight off the mountain lion. In short, the self-driving car will not be a viable tool for your defense or the defense of saving your precious canine.

All in all, this suggests that the woman in California would have had to find some other means to distract or repel the mountain lion, assuming that she owned a self-driving car and that it was parked and ready to be used.

Conclusion

Some numerous additional twists and turns could be considered.

One twist is that self-driving cars are right now being developed primarily for on-road use rather than off-road use. The existing standard that stipulates the levels of self-driving cars encompasses only on-road activities and intentionally excludes any off-road transit (see my columns for an explanation about the standard).

For the mountain lion scenario, the self-driving car would likely "refuse" to go into the backyard since it is not a paved road and not readily navigable in the normal semblance of on-road driving (by suggesting that the system "refused' you, this is not intended to be a sentience marker, and only that the programming would probably emit a message stating that the AI driving system is unable to navigate in an off-roading situation).

Consider another twist, which some of you might have already been contemplating. Could you contact the fleet operator and ask them to drive the car toward the mountain lion? The idea is that self-driving cars will have a provision to access a remote human agent that can potentially do something with your self-driving car.

I've repeatedly warned that we ought to not allow remote agents the ability to actively drive a self-driving car. This takes us back to the qualms about the possibility of untoward actions. A remote agent can provide overall suggested guidance to the AI driving system of the self-driving car, such as proffering to slow down or speed up, or take a right turn soon, that kind of thing, but this is to be construed simply as guidance only. The AI driving system still has to ascertain what driving actions are "reasonable" and sensible at any point in time of the driving task.

To some extent, most AI developers are not particularly sitting around thinking about mountain lions and wondering what the AI driving system should be programmed to do. At this time, there is a tremendous amount of energy and angst going toward the straightforward goal of getting self-driving cars to safely drive from point A to point B. The mountain lion conundrum is at best an edge or corner case, meaning that this instance and others akin to it are something that someday they might worry about covering.

Though we can eventually anticipate that self-driving cars will routinely be transporting our beloved pets, taking them to see grandma or grandpa, or going on a visit to the veterinarian, doing so without you having to accompany the animal, we have a number of other incremental steps to go before that day readily arrives.

There is one lucky dog that is likely happy that a conventional car was at the ready and able to turn the tide in the battle with the mountain lion. One wonders, do you think the dog though is to this day insisting that it could have won the skirmish all on its own and that the car was not needed to intervene?

That's those brave, brash, and brazen dogs for you.

CHAPTER 7
MARS HELICOPTER AND SELF-DRIVING CARS

Have you ever glanced at a snapshot and asked someone when they took that photo?

I'm sure that you have.

You undoubtedly wanted to place the picture into a context of date and time. Maybe the photo was snapped years ago and showcases the past. Or perhaps the picture is quite recent and displays the way things are today. All in all, knowing when a photo was taken can be useful and at times essential.

In the computer field, we often refer to timestamping things.

When a computer is hooked up to a camera, the taking of a picture is usually accompanied by adding a timestamp to the collected image. The timestamp merely indicates the date and time of the picture. This can be stuffed inside the data that contains the actual image or might be added as a supplemental piece of metadata that otherwise describes or indexes the photo.

If a series of photos are being taken, the timestamp begins extremely important.

Let's explore why.

Imagine that you own a car that has a camera mounted on the dashboard and is pointed at the roadway. You opt to go on a driving journey and decide to have the camera periodically take pictures of the road ahead. Picture after picture is being snapped. No big deal, easy-peasy.

During the drive, you at one point are in a residential neighborhood and a dog perchance wanders across the street. Fortunately, you see the dog and come to a stop to let it proceed safely. Shortly thereafter, a toddler runs across the street. Since you already had come to a halt, the child is able to dart through the street without incident. There was nothing especially untoward about the event and you might chalk it up to just an everyday driving trek.

A few weeks later you tell someone generally about the driving experience. As you begin to explain the travails, you suddenly cannot remember whether the dog appeared first and then the child came afterward, or possibly that the child was the first to come through the street and the dog was following the toddler. It would be easy to have muddled the relatively uneventful matter and particular sequence in your mind.

Aha, you have those pictures stored in your dashboard camera!

You download the pictures to your laptop.

While pulling up each of the images, suppose that there wasn't an apparent timestamp. This means that each picture was without any definitive indication of the date and time they were taken. You can plainly see each picture and you can attest that they are accurate portrayals of what you saw during your driving effort. Unfortunately, they are lacking timestamps.

It would almost be as though you scattered the pictures around on a tabletop and had to figure out which came before which other one. This can a tricky puzzle to solve.

Sure enough, you find the picture that shows the dog that was in the street, and you find the picture that shows the toddler that was in the street. But you do not know for sure which photo is first in order. Darn, this does not aid in solving your quest to remember the sequence of those events.

As mentioned, timestamps can be crucial.

If you were earnestly determined, you could closely inspect each of the two photos. There is a chance that there could be a sighting of the child in the photo that has the dog in the middle of the street. If the child is off to the side and running away from the street, you could infer that the child likely proceeded first and the dog followed. Likewise, if the photo of the child in the middle of the street showcases the dog, either heading toward or away from the street, you can try to infer the sequence that must have occurred.

It sure would be a lot simpler to have the timestamps.

Well, you dig around and discover that there is a timestamp embedded into the metadata of the image. You use a special program to ferret out the timestamp. The issue of ascertaining the sequence seems to be solved.

Life is never that easy, of course, and you suddenly notice that the timestamp has a date of June 31, 1777, which makes absolutely no sense at all. You know that cannot be right. The times shown on each of the pictures indicate an evening time period, though you know for sure that you encountered the dog and the toddler during the daytime hours.

Yikes, the timestamps are messed up.

How far are you willing to trust the timestamps?

For example, you could discard the date and assume that the date was just somehow improperly preset. You could ignore that the time stated was in the evening and go with the assumption that the clock was not properly set to begin with. At least you can see whether the timestamp via the time listed on each photo will reveal which photo was taken first.

Are you willing to accept the notion that this will be irrefutable evidence as an indication of which photo was taken first and therefore whether the dog or the child was first to enter into the street?

Seems like you would be on shaky ground. The fact that the date is wrong would be worrisome. The fact that the times are apparently wrong in terms of an accurate rendering of the time of day is also troubling. At this juncture, you are going to presume that at least the sequence is right due to the timestamp showing one time on the dog photo and another time on the photo containing the toddler.

If you were only doing this quest out of innate curiosity, it might not matter much whether you were willing to accept that the timestamp time was presumably apt and you now knew which event happened first. Would you be quite so sanguine if the matter was vitally important? Envision that for some reason this is a top-stakes issue and needs to be seriously resolved.

I guess we could play that ever-popular kid's game of asking whether you would be willing to bet your life on it. Kind of sketchy and not something that a life-or-death decision would seem solidly viable to rely upon. The photos appear to clearly demonstrate that you did indeed see a dog and you did indeed see a child, this is something nearly indisputable. The incontrovertible sequence is regrettably still somewhat up in the air.

Speaking of being up in the air, let's shift our attention to the topic of autonomous helicopters. We'll swing back around to the whole matter about photos and timestamps after covering this added ground.

You might be aware that NASA has put an autonomous helicopter on Mars. The helicopter is part of the overall Mars 2020 Perseverance rover mission. With the catchy name of Ingenuity, the autonomous helicopter has already established new records based on its flights on Mars, and the NASA teams should deservedly be proud of the accomplishments so undertaken.

The reason that the helicopter is referred to as being autonomous entails the aspect that it has to fend for itself when flying around. If human controllers here on earth were to try and fly the craft directly, the time delay due to the distances and transmission times would not be adequate. By the time that the human pilot here saw what was taking place there, and then issued a driving or piloting command, which then had to be transmitted and received, the helicopter could have encountered a problem that utterly ruined the faraway craft.

By having developed an autonomous piloting system, Ingenuity can pretty much fly around on its own.

That being said, this does not imply that the craft is willy-nilly going wherever it wants to go. NASA and the Jet Propulsion Laboratory (JPL) have established predetermined missions and each such mission has been carefully planned and prepared for.

A series of missions are being performed. Each mission has particular goals of what is to be accomplished. As the missions proceed, they are getting a bit more complex each time, almost like starting by crawling and then proceeding to walk and then running (or, in the case of a helicopter, short up and down vertical flights that are followed by longer distance and multi-pathed horizontal flights).

This brings us to Flight Six and an interesting in-flight anomaly that could have led to the autonomous helicopter nosediving into the Mars surface. If that were to occur at any point during the Mars excursion, you can likely assume the helicopter is out for the count. There would be no ready means to repair the craft. Alone it would sit, having done its part for science, and be a silent marker saying that humans have been here.

What happened with Ingenuity?

I'll start by emphasizing that it was able to complete the assigned mission and exists, still intact, and ready for the next mission (well, with some tweaking to be done remotely).

Partway through the sixth mission, the craft began to unnervingly roll and pitch in an undesirable manner. This rapid tilting and adjustments in velocity can be seen in the video recorded on Mars. Anyone watching the recorded video has to feel their heartstrings being pulled since the autonomous helicopter looks like it has gone crazy and appears to be flying erratically. You would likely assume that something awful has happened to Ingenuity and that its demise (of sorts) is imminent.

The basis for wild flying is somewhat complicated.

There is one word though that sums up the overarching issue: *Timestamps.*

Whoa, you must be saying to yourself, weren't we just discussing timestamps a moment ago? How fortuitous! Actually, the point of that earlier saga about timestamps was to get you ready for identifying what happened to Ingenuity on Mars during its Flight Six.

Strap yourself in and let's jump into the fray.

When the autonomous helicopter is flying, it tends to use a downward-facing camera that is usually being aimed at the Mars surface. About every thirty seconds, a picture is taken. Each picture is computationally analyzed by an onboard computer image processing system. Over time, a series of pictures can aid in ascertaining where the craft is, along with changes being made in velocity, altitude, attitude, position, and the like.

Notably, this encompasses comparing one photo versus another photo.

Hint: Remember the earlier tale of the photos captured about the toddler in the street and the dog in the street. This will come in handy in a moment.

This particular camera on Ingenuity is generically referred to as a *navcam*, meaning that it is a camera that primarily has to do with aiding the navigation of the craft. The computer that is autonomously piloting the system uses the images and the analyses of the images to help figure out where it is, where it is heading, etc. This analysis is matched with other navigational capabilities, including the use of an Inertial Measurement Unit (IMU).

With a bit of a drum roll, I now present you with the official statement about the anomaly (as per the NASA website): "Approximately 54 seconds into the flight, a glitch occurred in the pipeline of images being delivered by the navigation camera. This glitch caused a single image to be lost, but more importantly, it resulted in all later navigation images being delivered with inaccurate timestamps. From this point on, each time the navigation algorithm performed a correction based on a navigation image, it was operating based on incorrect information about when the image was taken. The resulting inconsistencies significantly degraded the information used to fly the helicopter, leading to estimates being constantly 'corrected' to account for phantom errors. Large oscillations ensued."

I hope you can see how the analogous discussion about your using a car dashcam and having to figure out whether you saw a dog and then a toddler, or whether it was the toddler and then the dog, applies to this circumstance.

According to the official description of what Ingenuity did, it seems that somehow an image was "lost" during the capture or processing stages, and this somehow prompted or stoked the rest of the pictures to get assigned "inaccurate" timestamps. This caused the rest of the autonomous piloting to get confounded about the navigational aspects of the craft. It doesn't seem yet fully clear cut as to what the timestamps were and how they got misassigned or misaligned, but we'll just take this as it is for now and go with it.

You might be wondering why the craft didn't go so haywire that it crash-landed.

Glad that you asked.

One separate but integral aspect of the Ingenuity autonomous piloting is that it apparently tries to keep the craft within some preferred or reasonable thresholds of operation.

This is oftentimes a kind of failsafe mechanism for Autonomous Vehicles (AVs).

If everything else is going berserk, at least the core driving or piloting component is usually supposed to keep the vehicle from veering radically from normally expected parameters. The programmers usually include stated thresholds that indicate to stay within those boundaries, and even if there is some other internal component trying to force the vehicle to stray outside those limits, the core piloting system refuses to do so and tries to counter the actions by blocking or counterbalancing what is taking place.

As per NASA's explanation about how Ingenuity overcame the timestamp snafu: "One reason it was able to do so is the considerable effort that has gone into ensuring that the helicopter's flight control system has ample 'stability margin': We designed Ingenuity to tolerate significant errors without becoming unstable, including errors in timing. This built-in margin was not fully needed in Ingenuity's previous flights, because the vehicle's behavior was in-family with our expectations, but this margin came to the rescue in Flight Six."

There was also a lucky rabbit's foot that helped out too.

When Ingenuity reaches the final phase of a flight and is starting into its descent, the navcam is no longer actively used for navigational purposes. This makes sense due to the likelihood of dust being tossed up when the autonomous helicopter gets closer to the Mars surface and would obscure or make the images unusable or unreliable. The NASA description is stated this way: "That design decision also paid off during Flight Six: Ingenuity ignored the camera images in the final moments of flight, stopped oscillating, leveled its attitude, and touched down at the speed as designed."

You could quibble somewhat on this latter aspect. As suggested, this might be more a matter of luck rather than a purposeful design basis. It seems highly unlikely that an envisioned situation was that the navcam itself might be generating difficulties and therefore upon landing that it would ergo make indubitable sense to switch away from using it. Instead, in this case, the other reason for no longer using the navcam when the landing stage began became unintended and yet an altogether welcomed helping hand.

Let's pause there and take a short breath of relief about Ingenuity.

Also, a notable rule of thumb about any engineering effort arises from the immortal words of Thomas Jefferson, of which he stated that he was a great believer in luck and the harder he worked, the more of it he seemed to have.

Some succinctly assert that good luck is the result of good planning.

Now that we've covered the matter of an autonomous helicopter operating on Mars, let's shift our attention down to earth. There are going to be all sorts of autonomous vehicles here on earth, including autonomous helicopters, autonomous drones, autonomous trucks, autonomous ships, autonomous cars, and so on. For ease of reference, consider those autonomous vehicles to be self-driving.

I'd like to see what lessons we can learn from the Ingenuity situation and apply those to the advent of AI-based true self-driving cars.

Self-driving cars are driven via an AI driving system. There isn't a need for a human driver at the wheel, and nor is there a provision for a human to drive the vehicle.

Here's an intriguing question that is worth pondering: *How do timestamps and image processing apply to AI-based true self-driving cars and could something akin to the Ingenuity anomaly happen to a self-driving car?*

Before jumping into the details, I'd like to clarify what is meant when referring to true self-driving cars.

Self-Driving Cars And Timestamps Issues

For Level 4 and Level 5 true self-driving vehicles, there won't be a human driver involved in the driving task.

All occupants will be passengers.

The AI is doing the driving.

One aspect to immediately discuss entails the fact that the AI involved in today's AI driving systems is not sentient. In other words, the AI is altogether a collective of computer-based programming and algorithms, and most assuredly not able to reason in the same manner that humans can.

Why this added emphasis about the AI not being sentient?

Because I want to underscore that when discussing the role of the AI driving system, I am not ascribing human qualities to the AI. Please be aware that there is an ongoing and dangerous tendency these days to anthropomorphize AI. In essence, people are assigning human-like sentience to today's AI, despite the undeniable and inarguable fact that no such AI exists as yet.

With that clarification, you can envision that the AI driving system won't natively somehow "know" about the facets of driving. Driving and all that it entails will need to be programmed as part of the hardware and software of the self-driving car.

Let's dive into the myriad of aspects that come to play on this topic.

A suitable place to start involves the appearance of an anomaly while an autonomous vehicle is in the field and essentially underway. That's a bad time for things to go awry.

In the case of a Mars autonomous helicopter, there had likely been a vast amount of careful design, building, and testing long before the AV was sent along to Mars. Yet, despite rigorous efforts to identify beforehand potential issues that might arise, a quite serious issue nonetheless did arise.

Some might have heartburn referring to the issue as a so-called "anomaly" which perhaps uses some queasy or loose semantics to overshadow the aspect that this seems to be an outright error or bug in the system. The phrasing of the less alarming wording via the innocuous "anomaly" seems to soften the bruising qualm that the developers, leadership, and development process let the flaw slip through and eventually arise while the craft was at least a long-distant 34 million miles away from home and in the midst of its mission.

Questions that certainly on a debriefing basis would seem to be warranted include how did a dropped image lead to the consequent series of dysfunctional outcomes? Wouldn't a dropped image be considered part of the foundational design and have been anticipated? If not, at least this ought to have seemingly been a test case. If it was a test case, what happened during the test? Did it not reveal the subsequent problems associated with the timestamp? Maybe it did but wasn't noticed, for which that alone is cause for concern. What provision did the design have about the verification or validation of timestamps? Were there not tests involved that purposely messed with the timestamps to see how the rest of the system would react? And so on.

In any case, fortunately, the AV was able to remain aloft and landed without damage or being destroyed. We can be thankful for that.

This though seems to have happened by the reliance on an overall failsafe rather than having some distinct formulated provision to cope with this specific error or bug. A catchall saved the day. As did a separate feature that had no particular relation to the bug and perchance by the skin of one's teeth provided some (unintended) protective cover.

The thing is, the depth and intensity of design and testing that takes place for a craft like Ingenuity are some of the most impressive and robust work done on any AVs of any kind. In contrast, for some of the existing self-driving car development efforts, the quality and intensity of design and testing are not nearly as thorough and exhaustive.

In short, if this type of bug can skip through and end up in the final system of an especially meticulously devised AV, we ought to be keeping a keen eye on the everyday efforts of developing self-driving cars.

We can also ponder the consequences aspects in the case of a self-driving car. A downed autonomous helicopter on Mars as a trial experiment would ostensibly be bad, sad, and disappointing, but no one would be dead. A self-driving car here on earth that experiences a serious bug or error while on the public roadways could spell disaster in terms of the possibility of getting into a fatal car crash, harming the occupants of the self-driving car, along with the possibility of injuring or killing pedestrians and other riders in other nearby cars.

That covers the somewhat generic matter about hidden bugs or errors and the need to surface them beforehand and excise them or at least have purpose-built targeted provisions to cope with them (in addition to, and not in lieu of overall failsafe capabilities too).

That being said, is there any chance of dropped images from the video cameras that are being used on self-driving cars?

You might be wondering about that. Perhaps there is zero chance of a similar error arising for self-driving cars.

No such luck.

Sorry to say that there is a non-zero chance of this happening, or more clearly there is indeed a chance of this happening. One might readily argue there is a strong chance of this occurring, arising due to a variety of reasons (due to space constraints here, I'll not go into the details herein, though am likely to cover this in later columns).

Is there any chance of the timestamps utilized in self-driving cars going awry in one manner or another?

Absolutely.

But that doesn't necessarily imply that the various self-driving car efforts are all mindfully focusing on those specific potential issues and ergo devoting substantive resources toward those particular types of errors or bugs.

Keep in mind that many of the AI development teams are already thinly stretched with just trying to get their self-driving car project to successfully go from point A to point B, doing so safely and without incident. If there are qualms about dropped images or a snafu with timestamps, it is likely at a considered low-chance possibility right now and not acutely getting outsized attention at this time.

Perhaps the Ingenuity snafu will be a helpful wake-up call.

Conclusion

Some insist that self-driving cars should be entirely tested on private closed tracks or proving grounds before they are allowed onto public roadways. Some similarly insist that self-driving cars should entirely be tested via computer-based simulations, doing so before being allowed on public roadways. Presumably, a combination of simulation and proving grounds would seem relatively satisfactory to those camps (I've discussed this overall topic at length, see my columns).

Will whatever catchall failsafe provisions that each automaker or self-driving tech firm is selectively devising be sufficient to overcome any unforeseen errors or bugs?

Don't know. Can't say for sure.

We know this much, namely that the lives of that dog and toddler running into the street might depend on it.

Go ahead and put an indisputable timestamp on that solemn thought).

CHAPTER 8
CYBER SECURITY
AND
SELF-DRIVING CARS

Those darned possums were determined to break into my house.

Have you ever had a similar problem?

I was beset or in a siege by a seemingly endless supply of possums. I first discovered that they had opted to invade my domicile when I heard a scampering sound in the attic. Upon my daring to take a peek, I saw an adult-aged possum staring directly at me, doing so as I shone my bright flashlight at the creature that was using my attic as a veritable second home.

Rent-free, I might add.

I was luckily able to motivate the scampering beast to leave the attic. This wasn't an easy task, let's leave it at that. Anyway, the possum left the same way it got in. Turns out that one of my small screens that allowed ventilation into the attic had deteriorated and was easily pushed aside by the determined animal. I repaired the screen. In my mind, that was the last I would ever see of the possum.

I underestimated my crafty foe.

After having initially gotten into the attic, it is my guess that the possum sized up the situation and decided that this would be an ideal place to raise a family. The attic was normally relatively dark. There was plenty of cushy insulation for a comfortable form of bedding. The temperatures in the attic were usually not overly hot and nor overly cold. The attic provided protection from predators and was otherwise vacant, except for some boxes of old books and papers.

Seems like this Goldilocks-like possum had found the just-so-right locale to settle down.

I left for a few days on a business trip and when I returned to my home the possum was not at all on my mind. Well, until I heard noises once again in the attic. What the heck? I figured that maybe some other wild beast had decided to take a look around. Perhaps a skunk or a raccoon. Seemed like the possum might have left an odor behind that could allure other creatures to come and see what all the fun was about. I secretly hoped it was a squirrel. That would be generally okay with me, though I nonetheless would still shepherd it out of my attic.

As I slowly lifted up my attic door, I shined my flashlight into the darkness and saw not just one pair of eyes, but several pairs of eyes. The possum had returned with all the kids (can I refer to the offspring or joeys that way?). I assumed the ventilation screen had given way again. Nope, the possum had somehow pried loose a shingle on the roof and made a damaging hole directly into the attic.

A determined house crasher and party goer.

Over the course of several weeks, I went to battle with the possums.

I would manage to get them out of the attic. They would find some other means to get back in. At one point, they became outrageously courageous. For example, one evening I went outside to move a bicycle off my driveway and left the front door ajar as I did so. As I made my way back to the slightly open door, a possum was nearing the doorway and seemed to be thinking that it was nice of me to entirely leave a passageway open, reducing the otherwise burdensome chore of trying to find a feasible break-in spot.

If you had asked me beforehand about the sanctity of my house and its overall security, I would have readily asserted that my house was ostensibly secure. All the doors had locks and included deadbolt locks too. All the windows had locks and also had screens that were snug and well-fitting. There was a gated fence around the perimeter of the property. We were very careful to lock up whenever we were at home and when we left on trips. We didn't even put in a doggie door for our beloved pooch, since we figured it might allow for a stranger to squeeze into the residence (maybe that was due to watching the movie *Home Alone* too many times).

It really got my goat that the possums turned upside down my perception of the successful lock-down of our treasured abode.

Why all this talk about possums and household security?

Because I want to bring up the topic of cybersecurity, especially as it pertains to AI-based true self-driving cars.

It might seem puzzling that there is any semblance of a connection between those pesky possums and the topic of cybersecurity and self-driving cars. As will soon be apparent, the parade of possums that you could suggest "attacked" my house is somewhat analogous to those dastardly human hackers that try to break into computer systems. And when you give this matter some careful thought, it is relatively apparent that a self-driving car is really a computer on wheels.

Self-driving cars are chockfull of computers.

There are the computers that underpin the AI driving system. These are typically specialized processors that are especially souped-up to perform lots of computations, something sorely needed to sufficiently be able to autonomously drive a car. By and large, the computer processing onboard a self-driving car is awe-inspiring and rivals the kind of supercomputers that we used to call supercomputers back in the olden days (to clarify, today's supercomputers are still many times faster than the computers put into a self-driving car, so my comparison is to the prior eras of supercomputers).

But the computers for self-driving purposes are just one instance of computing that is found inside a modern car.

You see, conventional cars are also chockful of computers. There are a whole bunch of other computers in contemporary cars regardless of whether they are yet capable to be a self-driving or driverless vehicle (also referred to as an AV or autonomous vehicle).

If you mindfully ponder the many ECUs (engine control units) and ECMs (engine control modules) that are jampacked into a car, you can find yourself quickly losing count of the number of computers involved. The number of microprocessors varies by brand and model of vehicle, though you could reasonably estimate that there are at least fifty to possibly one hundred processors thereabouts, and the count keeps going up as we expect our cars to do more and more fancy acts.

Your first thought might be that the more the merrier seems to be an appropriate mantra.

We all want our cars to get better at what they do. If it takes a bunch more computers to get there, so be it. Most of us only care about the potential cost involved. As long as automakers can ensure that cars are still affordable, toss as many processors into the vehicle as might be useful for assuring our enjoyable driving journeys. Go at it, we say, and boost the computing power as much as you want.

There is a rub.

In brief, for each computer that you decide to add to a car, you are essentially putting another possible window or door in place (not literally, that's a metaphor). Each computer becomes a potential portal or invitation to hacking. The cybersecurity "threat surface" or exposure realm for cars is getting higher and higher. All those microprocessors become a tantalizing target. They increase the risk of cyberhacking.

In a sense, those possums (hackers) are delighted that there are more ways to get in.

I'm sure you are protesting that getting into a house is a lot easier than sneaking into a computer. Yes, perhaps, but this all depends upon how well protected those computers are. Similar to my story about the possum that found a deteriorating ventilation screen and easily popped it to get into the attic, there are some computers in a car that are akin to that kind of vulnerability.

Just as I thought that my home was a veritable Fort Knox, so too might you assume that your car is an impenetrable fortress. That assumption is full of holes.

Speaking of conventional cars, the future of cars consists of AI-based true self-driving cars. Debate ensues as to whether or not we will soon be able to achieve true self-driving cars. Some skeptics assert we might not ever attain the vaunted goal of fully autonomous self-driving cars.

Keep in mind that self-driving cars are driven via an AI driving system. There isn't a need for a human driver at the wheel, and nor is there a provision for a human to drive the vehicle.

Here's an intriguing question that is worth pondering: *What is the cybersecurity threat surface for modern computer-infused cars and especially for the emerging AI-based true self-driving cars?*

Before jumping into the details, I'd like to further clarify what is meant when referring to true self-driving cars.

Self-Driving Cars And Cybersecurity Holes

For Level 4 and Level 5 true self-driving vehicles, there won't be a human driver involved in the driving task.

All occupants will be passengers.

The AI is doing the driving.

One aspect to immediately discuss entails the fact that the AI involved in today's AI driving systems is not sentient. In other words, the AI is altogether a collective of computer-based programming and algorithms, and most assuredly not able to reason in the same manner that humans can.

Why this added emphasis about the AI not being sentient?

Because I want to underscore that when discussing the role of the AI driving system, I am not ascribing human qualities to the AI. Please be aware that there is an ongoing and dangerous tendency these days to anthropomorphize AI. In essence, people are assigning human-like sentience to today's AI, despite the undeniable and inarguable fact that no such AI exists as yet.

With that clarification, you can envision that the AI driving system won't natively somehow "know" about the facets of driving. Driving and all that it entails will need to be programmed as part of the hardware and software of the self-driving car.

Let's dive into the myriad of aspects that come to play on this topic.

Before I share some cybersecurity insights, allow me a moment to bring up some related points.

Whenever I write about cyber-security, there are some that right away complain that by doing so the indications proffered are allowing cyber-hackers to gauge what kinds of cyber protections are being devised and what kinds of cyber vulnerabilities exist.

The worry is that writing about these topics, helps the cyber-hackers, arming them accordingly.

Please realize that this is the now-classic head-in-the-sand posturing regarding discussing cyber-security and related matters. Some believe that we should not talk about, nor write about, and not in any manner even whisper the nature and avenues of cyber-security and cyber-hacking, since it tips a hand to the evildoers.

This is a misguided and ill-informed notion, though one can certainly sympathize with their logic.

Here's the conundrum.

It is plainly the case that cyber-hackers are going to figure out these same facets, one way or another, and by trying to hide such discussions it does little good, including that it tends to undercut the preparations for and awareness about being on the hunt to stop and prevent cyber-hacking.

A head in the sand translates into getting kicked in the rear, as the old saying goes.

Meanwhile, there is another stated reason to not discuss such matters, namely that doing so, will cause mass hysteria. Again, the logic for this is certainly understandable.

When those writing about cyber-security and cyber-hacking do so irresponsibly, attempting merely to fan the flames of angst, there is no question that such shoddy and perhaps even iniquitous efforts are sad, hurtful, and do not advance sensibly the battle between cyber-security and cyber-hacking.

It is vital that discussions about cyber-crime be taken seriously, somberly, factually, and portray matters in a balanced and rational way. As an example of how these topics are indeed publicly being discussed, you might wish to refer to a handy U.S. Congressional Research Service (CRS) report labeled as R45985 and entitled "Issues in Autonomous Vehicle Testing and Deployment" written by Bill Canis.

Having covered the preceding caveats, let's dive into some background and context of how cyber-security and cyber-hacking come to play related to AI-based true self-driving cars.

The OBD Portal

The first potential point of entry worthy of attention entails the OBD (on-board diagnostics) portal.

You might already vaguely be familiar with the OBD portal in your conventional car. This is the place that an electronic diagnostic code can be sourced about the vehicle status. If you've ever gotten the so-called "idiot light" or dashboard indicator telling you that something is amiss in your car, another means to find out the details of the problem consists of accessing the OBD portal. A handheld device can be used to plug into the OBD portal and there are smaller USB-memory sticks that are available to do likewise.

The OBD portal is usually just slightly under the dashboard, openly accessible, down kind of where you might see your parking brake release or hood release. It isn't usually obvious to the eye and is purposely positioned somewhat out of view. You need to look for it. Any car mechanic or gearhead that tinkers with cars is certainly familiar with the OBD portal. This digital communications port can provide essential real-time data about internal issues of the vehicle, normally conveyed via a standardized set of DTCs (diagnostic trouble codes).

Okay, you might be pondering, so there is this OBD portal that allows you to read the car status. Not a big deal, it would seem.

Well, it is a big deal.

The OBD portal generally allows you to connect to a wide array of embedded systems within the vehicle. Furthermore, the OBD portal can be used to send instructions or data into the various connected systems and does not need to solely be acting on a read-only basis. In some cases, the OBD portal can be used to flash new firmware into the connected embedded systems, thus potentially allowing for reprogramming of what those systems are to do.

Anyone that knows anything about OBD knows that this is a vulnerability that is oftentimes treated as though it is inconsequential.

The logic seems to be that since you would need to get into the vehicle to access the OBD, this aspect alone is a sufficient form of protection. The thing is, if let's say the car door is inadvertently left unlocked, a savvy thief can potentially start the vehicle via using the OBD portal and yet be absent of the car key (or take other untoward actions regarding the vehicle).

Another claim is that the OBD is relatively unknown among the masses and therefore is protected via the classic notion of security through obscurity. In short, if nobody particularly realizes that this exposed point of entry exists, it will silently sit there and remain unused for any nefarious purposes. That might be the case for the masses, but any savvy cybersecurity car thief or bad hacker would readily know about it.

From the perspective of AI-based true self-driving cars, the availability of the OBD portal presents qualms, that's for sure.

A cyber hacker could try to use the OBD portal to confound or overtake the AI driving system. A counterargument is that the AI driving system is hopefully protected by its own layer of systems security and cannot be breached via the OBD pathway. That might or might not be the case, though this also tends to overlook the crucial aspect that the AI driving system relies upon the other vast number of connected embedded car subsystems, for which those might get cyber hijacked or distorted via a cybersecurity attack.

Probably the biggest saving grace about the OBD portal for self-driving cars is that it is a physical connection and pretty much requires physically being inside the car. The emphasis is that you would only be able to mess with one self-driving car at a time. This would limit how widespread you could carry out a dedicated cyberattack on an entire fleet of self-driving cars. As will next be discussed, there are much more pervasive ways to perform such evil deeds.

The Vaunted OTA

The most notable Achilles' heel for self-driving cars is going to be the OTA (Over-The-Air) electronic communications capability.

Some consider the OTA to be the best thing since sliced bread. Self-driving cars will have a communications device that allows for making a connection to a cloud computing platform that is presumably maintained by a fleet operator or the automaker or similar. Patches and various software updates for the AI driving system can readily be downloaded and installed. This allows for rapid changes while self-driving cars are in the field and avoids having to bring the vehicle to a local dealer or repair shop to merely make system changes.

The OTA will also provide a means to upload data from the self-driving car. Self-driving cars will be collecting gobs of data via their onboard sensor suite. This data can be pushed up into the cloud. Some uses will be to improve the AI driving system capabilities by analyzing driving journeys. There is also the likely monetization that will be quite profitable for those operating a fleet. I've referred to this as the "roving eye" and indicated that though it has some goodness possibilities, it also portends for worries about privacy intrusion and like concerns.

It is perhaps plainly apparent that the OTA is a huge potential hole for any cyber hackers or possums that might want to make their way into the AI driving system. As an analogy to a house, you could suggest that this is the front door and is nearly begging to be usurped.

What makes the OTA especially beguiling is that a cyber crook could potentially do rather widespread damage via sending out say patches to an entire fleet of self-driving cars. Whereas the OBD portal was a one-at-a-time trick pony, the OTA is a salivating form of temptation because it holds forth the chance of intruding upon thousands, perhaps millions of deployed self-driving cars (when that day arrives).

Internet Of Things (IoT)

You undoubtedly use your smartphone while inside today's conventional cars. The smartphone might be operated in a completely unconnected manner related to the vehicle. On the other hand, automobiles are gradually providing for smartphones to be connectable to the vehicle, usually doing so to make use of an in-car entertainment or infotainment system.

We are all aware that there are going to be a lot of devices with Internet connectivity, referred to as the Internet of Things (IoT). A smartwatch will make use of IoT. Jewelry is starting to make use of IoT. Soon enough, your clothing will make use of IoT, such as your shoes being able to connect to the Internet and retrieve and report data about your foot-related travails. And so on.

When a rider gets into a self-driving car, they are going to be wearing a plethora of IoT devices. Each of those IoT devices is potentially going to want to access something related to the vehicle. This is like inviting a herd of possums (known as a passel) into your yard. They are close enough to try and poke around, hoping to find a weakness to get into your home.

Those ECUs And Other

As earlier mentioned, there are many ECUs embedded within a modern vehicle, including for self-driving cars too.

There is likely to be an ECU for the engine, an ECU for the steering controls, an ECU for the braking capabilities, etc. You might be surprised to realize that there is likely an ECU for the airbags and the seatbelts, an ECU for the lighting system of the vehicle, an ECU for the power windows, and so on. Today's cars also have allied systems such as a TPMS (tire pressure monitoring system).

All of these ECUs and other embedded subsystems present vulnerabilities.

One concern is that a cyber hacker could overtake a particular ECU and it would no longer respond as it would otherwise normally act. If the AI driving system was unaware that an ECU had been overtaken, you can imagine how the ECU could detrimentally affect the driving of the vehicle. The AI driving system might remain untouched, but a crucial element of operating the self-driving car is now a potential ticking time clock of danger.

An additional devious ploy would be to use the granted access of the ECU, which normally has relatively unfettered access to the rest of the vehicle, as a means of trying to carry out other assorted cyberattacks. This could be a divide and conquer tactic. Start with the most innocuous of ECUs and then gradually attempt to take over more and more of them. This includes ultimately aiming to overtake the AI driving system.

In my house, at one point a possum not only got into the attic, but this access was also then used to get into a closet that had a small attic doorway of an auxiliary nature. The possum pushed down hard on the flimsy attic doorway and fell into the rest of the closet. I don't think the possum knew beforehand where it was going, and merely was trying to see what might be beyond the hatchway. In any case, the idea is that if you can get into one area or element, perhaps this can be profitably used to get into more areas (a common technique by cyber hackers).

The CAN Internal Network

Cars typically have an internal electronic network that enables the various systems and subsystems to electronically communicate with each other. Rather than having to wire each system to each other system, which would be a potential nightmare to try and undertake and maintain, instead a convenient overarching digital pathway is established.

Electronic messages and data flow back and forth on this internal network. Think of it as a river that runs throughout the vehicle and for which any device connected to the river can partake in tasting the water or can also place items into the water for purposes of floating downstream or upstream to others along the river.

The technical parlance is that this is the CAN (controller area network). It is usually referred to as a CAN "bus" in that it is a type of passageway for messaging.

Envision that an AI driving system is trying to electronically communicate to the ECU used for the brakes. If a cyberhacker has found a means to intrude upon the CAN bus, let's say in our river-related analogy the evildoer is floating along with a conniving piece of code that can intercept messages, this is a classic man-in-the-middle security breach. Not good.

Since I keep mentioning the possums, it is noteworthy that they decided that the air conditioning ducts in my home would be a handy means to get from one place in the house to another. They infiltrated the (shall we say) network of piping and were able to traverse wherever they wished to. This also led them to try to chew through the grates of the A/C ducts that led into the various rooms of the residence.

V2V and V2X

I've written extensively that a boon to self-driving cars will be the use of V2V (vehicle-to-vehicle) electronic communications (see my columns). This might be undertaken via DSRC (dedicate short-range communications) capabilities. The notion is that a self-driving car could send a message to another nearby self-driving car, doing so to perhaps forewarn about debris in the roadway up ahead.

There will also be V2I (vehicle-to-infrastructure) electronic communications. Think about traffic signals that can send out electronic messages to let self-driving cars know that the traffic light is not working or that it is turned to a full-stop red because of a traffic incident nearby. There are going to be a variety of these kinds of vehicle-related communications avenues, which all told is referred to as V2X (vehicle-to-everything).

An AI driving system is likely to rely significantly upon the V2X. If cyber hackers could fool the V2X, they have a chance of tricking the AI driving system.

Conclusion

You might be puzzled that if self-driving cars are potentially a leaking sieve of cybersecurity holes, why haven't those despicable cyberhackers already been going after self-driving cars in droves.

The straightforward answer is that it hasn't been worth their time. There are only a small set of tryout self-driving cars underway today. Attacking an experimental self-driving car is not especially profitable right now. Going after large companies like banks, hospitals, gas pipelines, and the like are today a much more attractive target.

Other than trying to glean some bragging rights, it just isn't especially worthwhile at this time to cyber hack self-driving cars. Furthermore, the attack can be readily downplayed as nothing more than an annoyance and had little or no demonstrative impacts. This claim can be strengthened by the assertion that the tightened security hasn't been put in place yet, and will happen once self-driving cars are widely employed. All told, finding ways to cyberattack self-driving cars is not on the priority list of things that can gain fame or fortune.

Right now.

You can bet your bottom dollar that once self-driving cars avidly being used and widespread, the attention of the cyber crooks will indubitably turn toward self-driving cars.

Just as I had to take special precautions to keep out the possums, automakers and self-driving tech firms cannot let themselves fall asleep at the wheel when it comes to bolstering cybersecurity protections. It is easy to fall into such a trap when there isn't any overwhelming menacing indication at this time.

Be expecting that possums are going to quietly first perhaps occupy the attic, and the next thing you know, the entire house will be in their destructible hands (marsupial feet.

CHAPTER 9
CONGRESSIONAL REGULATIONS AND SELF-DRIVING CARS

Regulatory enigma.

You might be surprised to learn that there is a regulatory enigma of sorts that surrounds and engulfs the advent of AI-based self-driving cars.

How so?

Nobody is quite sure what to make of the beast, as it were, in terms of what size and shape of regulatory rules and legal oversight is best warranted for the emergence of self-driving cars.

Some emphatically insist that we should live and let live, meaning that the marketplace should decide how, where, when, why, and other crucial elements about the deployment of self-driving cars. Others exhort that this is a high-tech innovation that abundantly needs and altogether requires demonstrative legislative controls and strict guidance (it is, after all, akin to a computer on wheels).

Some reside at nearly polar opposites of what should be done.

In addition, some sit somewhere in between and are trying to find some agreeable middle ground. One thing that most everyone acknowledges is that self-driving cars are important, and they are especially notable since they involve clear-cut life-or-death kinds of considerations.

Cars by their very nature are intertwined with life and death.

We ought to acknowledge that right upfront. We make use of cars on our public roadways. They are an essential form of transportation. Plus, our society has culturally ingrained itself into cars as more than simply a transit option. Car driving is depicted in our movies and TV shows. People discuss cars and the driving of cars as regularly and routinely as they discuss the clothes they wear or what kind of food they eat.

Teenagers see the driving of a car as a key step toward adulthood and bask in the freedom they can inure by being able to drive a car. For teens, possessing a driver's license is a huge source of personal identity and illuminates their rights of passage into the world as independent beings. There has been a tad bit of waning on this heretofore life monumental heralding as some newbie drivers decide to wait to drive, but the preponderance is still in effect.

Adults are likewise culturally wrapped into the semblance of cars, either owning cars or riding in cars. Though there are many efforts to bolster mass transit, there is nonetheless a kind of loyalty stickiness that cars are conveniently able to get you from point A to point B, directly so. That's a tough advantage to somehow undercut or convince is unworthy.

The costs associated with cars are of course tremendous. Not just the cost of buying a car or maintaining a car. Via our cars, in the United States alone there are about 40,000 annual car crash-related fatalities and about 2.5 million associated injuries. This is how the catchphrase of life-or-death enters into the equation.

Each time that you get behind the wheel of a car, you are about to enter into a driving journey that might end badly. We don't think about driving in those kinds of terms. It would be perhaps overly dreadful. The base assumption is that you will presumably make your driving trek safely, doing so entirely absent of getting struck by another car and likewise avert plowing into a nearby car.

Okay, cars are readily at the top of mind. That seems apparent. Self-driving cars are gradually getting to that same pinnacle, though they are more so a curiosity right now than a real-world consideration per se by most. You see ongoing news stories about self-driving cars. If you perchance live in one of a select few places in the country, you can likely witness self-driving cars going down the street.

All in all, realistically, you probably have much greater odds encountering face-to-face a horse or a zebra than you do a self-driving car right now.

That's not to suggest that anticipating the advent of self-driving cars should be something on the backburner. Heck no. There are occasions when an innovation has been unleashed and there was insufficient preparation involved, allowing rather untoward results that could have been prevented beforehand. This is the proverbial problem of waiting until the horse is out of the barn that we always should be mindful of.

Counterbalancing the desire to make sure that all is readied would be the qualm that the preparations themselves could put a crimp on progress. If an innovation isn't given sufficient room to breathe, it could either never see the light of day or at least might be summarily delayed. And, in the case of self-driving cars, since the assumption portends that self-driving cars will likely reduce the annual number of car crash fatalities, each day of potential *undue* delay is a costly price to pay.

Notice that the word "undue" was intentionally utilized. It is easy to claim that any delay is too much. The rub is that there is possibly a Goldilocks level of delay. This means that there is a likely tradeoff between potentially enabling or stoking car crash fatalities versus reducing or eliminating car crash fatalities (see my columns for in-depth discussions on this).

We return to the matter at hand which is what about the regulations as they might pertain to self-driving cars.

There are plenty of regulations about cars.

There are plenty of regulations about car drivers.

You might certainly be tempted to assume that we must already have more than enough regulations to cover the matter of cars that drive. This just seems to make sense in the face of things.

Where the confusion enters into this picture is the notion that self-driving cars are a two-in-one combo deal. That's not how regulations have been previously devised.

You see, a true self-driving car is not just a car. It is also in a sense a driver. You have a car that drives itself. As such, we are apt to find that existing regulations about cars are not on par with such a seemingly oddball creation.

Regulations about cars as strictly being an automobile, namely a thing that can carry us around, do not particularly veer into the realm of being a car driver. Regulations about car driving do not particularly roam in the realm of what a car or automobile is or must provide.

Self-driving cars have brought together those two otherwise somewhat disparate topics (they are absolutely related topics, but so far treated ostensibly separately in a manner of speaking). This ends up becoming a kind of loophole in existing regulations. As mentioned earlier, some are adamant that we must close those loopholes immediately. Others say that we ought to wait and see.

The added twist is that the federal government aims at dealing with the aspects of the car, while the states tend to focus on the car drivers.

If the states were to branch further out from their attention to encompass the nature of cars themselves, going ergo beyond the role of car drivers, they would be on a slippery slope of usurping the federal regulations, it would so seem. Meanwhile, you could similarly contend that if the federal government opts to dive into the particulars about car drivers, this would seem to stray into regulatory territory typically reserved for the states.

Yes, believe it or not, the emergence of self-driving cars brings forth a conundrum of the classic push and pull of federal rights versus states rights. Kind of shocking to think that simply automating the driving task would get into such a thorny patch, but it most certainly does.

Here is an intriguing question that is worth pondering: *What are the top four Congressional issues when it comes to the advent of AI-based true self-driving cars?*

I'm limiting this discussion to just the four most prominent issues. There are literally dozens of issues that could be debated and the resulting dialogue undoubtedly would go far beyond the space limits for this piece.

You might quibble with the four that I have chosen for discussion. I'll explain in a moment how I boiled down the whole kit and caboodle into just four of the major issues. And, for those of you interested in further knowing about those other issues not addressed herein, I've covered or will be covering the myriad of relevant issues in my ongoing columns.

Before jumping into the details, I'd like to clarify what is meant when referring to true self-driving cars.

Self-Driving Cars And Congressional Top Issues

For Level 4 and Level 5 true self-driving vehicles, there won't be a human driver involved in the driving task.

All occupants will be passengers.

The AI is doing the driving.

One aspect to immediately discuss entails the fact that the AI involved in today's AI driving systems is not sentient. In other words, the AI is altogether a collective of computer-based programming and algorithms, and most assuredly not able to reason in the same manner that humans can.

Why this added emphasis about the AI not being sentient?

Because I want to underscore that when discussing the role of the AI driving system, I am not ascribing human qualities to the AI. Please be aware that there is an ongoing and dangerous tendency these days to anthropomorphize AI. In essence, people are assigning human-like sentience to today's AI, despite the undeniable and inarguable fact that no such AI exists as yet.

With that clarification, you can envision that the AI driving system won't natively somehow "know" about the facets of driving. Driving and all that it entails will need to be programmed as part of the hardware and software of the self-driving car.

Let's dive into the myriad of aspects that come to play on this topic.

I had earlier indicated that the Congressional issues underlying the advent of self-driving cars would be culled down into four key major aspects. The four do not represent the entirety of the many topics confounding and confronting the many questions we have yet to resolve about self-driving cars. But these four are certainly paramount and are plentifully worthwhile for devoted attention.

The four aspects are:

- **Feds v. States:** *Congressional regulatory scope versus the states when it comes to self-driving cars*
- **Exemptions Latitude:** *Deciding how far existing regulatory provisions should be stretched for self-driving car testing on public roadways*
- **Cybersecurity Requirements:** *To what degree should regulations mandate cybersecurity of self-driving cars*
- **Roving Eye Data Rights:** *Figuring out the regulatory landscape encompassing stakeholder data rights of the self-driving car roving-eye*

I'll briefly share with you the nature of the regulatory challenges underpinning each of the four aspects.

Hopefully, doing so will inspire you to become further interested in and possibly get directly involved in trying to resolve these controversial issues. While discussing the four areas, there is a handy U.S. Congressional Research Service (CRS) report labeled as R45985 and entitled "Issues in Autonomous Vehicle Testing and Deployment" written by Bill Canis that I will be quoting from time to time and serves to aid in highlighting the wrangling involved in these matters.

You might also find noteworthy that the nearest that Congress has come to potentially establishing regulations specifically about self-driving cars has been the House of Representatives H.R. 3388 known as the SAFE DRIVE ACT that is dated September 2017, and a separate effort by the Senate S. 1885 known as the AV START ACT that is dated November 2107 (see my columns for coverage). Neither of those was passed into law. There have been other Congressional efforts since then that have either sought to resuscitate those proposed regulations or that have somewhat tried to go a different route, but such efforts have not been (shall we say) as pronounced as the H.R. 3388 and the S. 1885.

In terms of regulations by the states, there are approximately 30 states that now have specific regulations on the books about self-driving cars. Most of the other states are either in the midst of grappling with draft regulatory provisions or have had strident discussions about what might be warranted. See my columns for coverage.

Okay, now we can leap into the fray and examine each of the four major aspects. Please fasten your seatbelt.

Feds v. States

Issue: *Congressional regulatory scope versus the states when it comes to self-driving cars*

I already tipped my hand about this topic. As earlier stated, one of the most vexing questions is who is the boss. Traditionally, Congress and the federal government focus on the nature of the vehicle. The states tend to handle the driver and elements entailing driver registration and suitability for being behind the wheel.

A self-driving car is an all-in-one combination.

It is a car.

And it is a driver.

Some would suggest that this means that you cannot readily have two bosses anymore. One boss needs to oversee both the car and the driver. It would be hard to cope with continuing to allow the states to deal with the AI driving system while the feds stay occupied with just the car. You can't split the baby like that (a perhaps crude but illustrative saying).

One obvious answer is that you might anoint the federal government to be solely responsible for regulating self-driving cars.

This is said to make sense due to the notion that there would be one overarching scheme that would encompass the entire country. Without that kind of universal role, you would seemingly have a byzantine series of state-by-state differences. That could be a potential nightmare for the automakers and self-driving tech firms, having to make sure that their self-driving cars are able to fulfill a potential muddled patchwork of idiosyncratic state-derived laws.

Imagine that a self-driving car comes up to the border between one state and another state, coming to a screeching halt because it is not considered suitable under the regulations of that other state. Passengers would not be enthralled. A farfetched scenario is that you would have the self-driving car stop at the hub set up at the border of the two states. You would get out of one self-driving car and get into a different self-driving car that was properly approved for use in that other state.

So much for interstate commerce.

This all seems to point out that Congress does have the primary seat in all of this. Ouch, those are fighting words, exclaim the states.

The states would argue vehemently that they ought to be able to decide what happens regarding self-driving cars within their state borders. Congress might not be as tuned to the needs of each specific state and therefore provide a bland generic regulatory approach that overrides the desires and concerns of specific states. Our country works satisfactorily now with the states deciding on the car driver elements and there is no reason to assume that they cannot handle the same when it comes to self-driving cars.

Round and round we go.

Here's a quick summary of the debate: "The extent to which Congress should alter the traditional division of vehicle regulation, with the federal government being responsible for vehicle safety and states for driver-related aspects such as licensing and registration, as the roles of driver and vehicle merge" (per CRS R45985).

Exemptions Latitude

Issue: *Deciding how far existing regulatory provisions should be stretched for self-driving car testing on public roadways*

Based on existing regulations, the spate of self-driving cars rolling around on public roadways will likely need to seek various exemptions from prevailing federal standards. Those federal standards were crafted based on the assumption that there would be a human driver at the steering wheel and operating the driving controls.

One anticipated overhaul of car design will be those self-driving cars will not have any human-accessible driving controls. Out goes the steering wheel. Out go the pedals. They aren't needed. This frees up the interior space of a car. Numerous car designs have been proposed that would make use of this newly freed up roominess.

Perhaps there will be swivel chairs in self-driving cars, allowing the passengers to turn this way and that way during a driving journey. They don't need to always be facing forward anymore. We might also find ourselves taking naps or getting an entire snooze while riding in a self-driving car. In that case, the seats might be reclinable or be replaced with beds of some kind.

Anyway, cars today are supposed to have driving controls. Furthermore, the driving controls must meet distinctly specified guidelines. That's why you can pretty much go up to any car, get in, and instantly start to drive it. Without those guidelines, presumably, each car would have some proprietary form of driving controls and you would expend a lot of concentration on just trying to master how to drive the darned thing.

You might be thinking that the feds ought to go ahead and provide as many exemptions as are requested. Any holdup on exemptions would delay those self-driving car testing efforts. Do not let paperwork get in the way of progress, some urge.

Well, that is a pretty risky way to do things, the counterargument goes. You are letting these unproven self-driving cars zip around on our public roadways. The willy-nilly approval for those exemptions is bound to mean that unsound self-driving cars are cruising next to you on your local highways and byways.

Do you really want to take a chance like this?

They would fervently caution that we might be opening Pandora's box. Have the self-driving car get fully tested on proving grounds and closed tracks, long before being placed onto our streets and given exemptions. Likewise, compel the automakers and self-driving tech firms to first showcase via computer-based simulations that their self-driving cars are ready and able to handle the harsh and dangerous real-world of public roadway driving.

The counter to that counterargument is that we won't see the attainment of self-driving cars for a very long time if those exemptions aren't allowed.

As an aside, and as steadfast readers know, I have repeatedly warned that we are going to have some attempts at trying to use the exemption granting as a kind of boogieman, seeking to make the feds into a seeming bureaucratic boondoggle and ostensibly preventing progress. There will be cases that this indeed might be true, but there are going to be other cases where this prevention is worthy and yet will be cast as though it is untoward.

Anyway, round and round we go.

Here's a quick summary of the debate: "The number of autonomous vehicles that NHTSA should permit to be tested on highways by granting exemptions to federal safety standards, and which specific safety standards, such as those requiring steering wheels and brake pedals, can be relaxed to permit thorough testing" (per CRS R45985).

Cybersecurity Requirements

Issue: *To what degree should regulations mandate cybersecurity of self-driving cars*

The computer inside your laptop is a target for cybercrooks. You already know that.

Self-driving cars are computers on wheels. There are a lot of computers onboard.

The obvious computer is the one that runs the AI driving system (to clarify, there are likely numerous onboard computers devoted to the driving task). In addition, there are typically going to be fifty to a hundred other microprocessors involved in the numerous vehicular ECU (engine control unit) systems and subsystems. This entails the computers that keep the engine running, computers that control the brakes, computers that deal with the airbags, and so on.

All of this makes the car go.

Sadly, all of this also makes the car a really tempting target for cyber hacking.

The cybersecurity "threat surface" of a self-driving car is immense. Lots and lots of ways can be tried to break into a self-driving car by an evildoer. I've previously and extensively covered the cybersecurity aspects of self-driving cars. The opportunities for doing really bad things are rife and the whole topic will make the hairs stand on the back of your head.

The crucial question in this discussion focuses on how much regulatory action should there be about the cybersecurity provisions of self-driving cars. We can also toss into the mess that we need to ascertain the federal attention to the matter and how that fits into or conflicts with or compliments what the states want to do on this hefty matter.

Round and round we go.

Here's a quick summary of the debate: "How much detail legislation should contain related to addressing cybersecurity threats, including whether federal standards should require vehicle technology that could report and stop hacking of critical vehicle software and how much information car buyers should be given about these issues" (per CRS R45985).

Roving Eye Data Rights

Issue: *Figuring out the regulatory landscape encompassing stakeholder data rights of the self-driving car roving-eye*

Self-driving cars will have a communications device that allows for making a connection to a cloud computing platform that is presumably maintained by a fleet operator or the automaker or similar. This device is usually referred to as the OTA (Over-The-Air) electronic communications.

Patches and various software updates for the AI driving system can readily be downloaded and installed via the OTA. This allows for rapid changes while self-driving cars are in the field and avoids having to bring the vehicle to a local dealer or repair shop to merely make system changes.

The OTA will also provide a means to upload data from the self-driving car. Self-driving cars will be collecting gobs of data via their onboard sensor suite. This data can be pushed up into the cloud. Some uses will be to improve the AI driving system capabilities by analyzing driving journeys. There is also the likely monetization that will be quite profitable for those operating a fleet. I've referred to this as the "roving eye" and indicated that though it has some goodness possibilities, it also portends for worries about privacy intrusion and like concern.

The data collected by a self-driving car could reveal where you went, how long you stayed at your destination, etc. Inward-facing video cameras could capture your entire time while inside the self-driving car. The outward-facing video cameras would capture you walking up to the self-driving car and walking away from it. Whenever a self-driving car goes down a neighborhood street, it will be collecting data that showcases the people standing in front of their homes, walking their dogs, playing ball with their kids.

I ask you this, who owns or can decide what happens with that captured data?

That is assuredly a whopping big can of worms.

You might argue that the passenger ought to decide what happens with the data. There is an equally powerful argument that the owner of the self-driving car ought to make that decision. Perhaps the fleet operator should be able to decide.

Round and round we go.

Here's a quick summary of the debate: "The extent to which vehicle owners, operators, manufacturers, insurers, and other parties have access to data that is generated by autonomous vehicles, and the rights of various parties to sell vehicle-related data to others" (per CRS R45985).

Conclusion

You are now primed and ready to engage in discussions and debates on these meaty topics.

What are the right answers, you might be mulling?

That's up to all of us to decide.

Start your engines and get engaged in the self-driving cars regulatory enigma.

CHAPTER 10
RANSOMWARE AND SELF-DRIVING CARS

Ransomware is being continually mentioned in the daily news and appears to be a seemingly unstoppable fiendish craze.

Perhaps the recent attack of ransomware on the Colonial Pipeline received the most rapt attention since it led to concerns over gasoline shortages and caused quite a stir amongst the general public. When ransomware is used against a particular bank or hospital or school, this normally doesn't have quite the same widespread disruption as did the fuel pipeline incident.

The thing is, we are probably going to see a lot more ransomware being fielded and doing so against all manner of businesses and governmental entities. Some would assert that we are only so far at the tip of the iceberg when it comes to ransomware hacks.

Part of the reason why you can expect more use of ransomware is that it is relatively easy for an evildoer or crook to deploy the computer hacking scourge. Whereas the perpetrator used to need to have some keen computer nerdish skills, that's pretty much not the case anymore. Sadly, the ease of attempting to infect computer systems with ransomware has become nearly easy-peasy and has opened the floodgates to just about any determined villain to try (ransomware programs can be cheaply purchased online via the so-called *dark web*). There are now plentiful Ransomware-as-a-Service (RaaS) capabilities available that will do most of the heavy lifting for those that prefer a hands-off chauffeured form of ransomware cyberattacks.

As a point of clarification, not every use of ransomware is successful.

There are innumerable attempts that get rebuffed by cybersecurity protections or that are otherwise caught by alert computer security specialists. The rub is that the ransomware ploy only has to succeed one time, in the sense that if a malicious hacker tries a hundred different attempts at various entities, and only one of those takes hold, the crook still wins and the gambit was successful.

This is reminiscent of a popular catchphrase in the cybersecurity field, namely that the system protective measures need to be right all of the time, while the intrusion approaches only need to be "right" one time (as in being able to get past any safeguards and do the nefarious act intended).

You might vaguely be aware that law enforcement authorities tend to assert that the entities snagged by a foul dose of ransomware should refuse to pay any ransom. The logic is pretty straightforward. If ransoms are not paid, there won't be any money or profiteering by those employing ransomware as a form of attack. Once the dough dries up, presumably the preference to use ransomware will accordingly evaporate.

It is a money thing, after all.

Some would contend that the ransomware attackers are not solely about the money. Some evildoers simply relish doing evil acts. Some like to get publicity and notoriety for what they have fiendishly accomplished. You could argue quite stridently that even if there was no payment at all, there are going to be those that will use ransomware anyway, joyfully seeing the resultant chaos.

And, there is the possibility too of wanting to showcase a prowess in being a computer system hacker that can break into places when they want to do so. In essence, if a ransomware attack is successful regardless of gaining money, the person or group responsible has shown their hand or proffered their calling card. In theory, they could switch to other forms of cyberattacks and attempt to get monies via other means, such as siphoning off funds from companies, and so on.

Up until now, much of the ransomware attack has been done on a kind of Goldilocks basis.

The notion is to go after entities that will be more inclined to pay the ransom. If there is a tremendous amount of public attention to a ransomware attack, this can stiffen the resolve by the entity to not pay the ransom. Meanwhile, if the ransomware attack is relatively unheralded and only the entity knows about it, this can allow for a quietly paid ransom that isn't especially burdensome to the entity. By carefully picking the intended targets, there is a bit of a sweet spot of entities that are bound to pay.

If a criminal is going to launch a hundred different attempts (referred to as "spray and pray" or some suggest "spray and prey" is more applicable), they might as well seek to maximize the chances of that ransomware shots-in-the-dark to be moneymakers. Avoiding the highly visible instances, such as a fuel pipeline, would generally make more sense in terms of increasing the probability of achieving the ransom. Once a high-profile target of ransomware gets outed as being infected, tremendous pressures are exerted to avoid paying the ransom, though this is somewhat counterbalanced by the outrage that ensues and the desperate need to rectify the ransomware attack at the soonest moment and in whatever manner might well do so.

That's why the paying of ransom by the newsworthy instances is especially telling and sends a signal of sorts to the ransomware fiends. Rather than trolling after lots of quieter ransomware targets, maybe the big fish, the whales as it were, could be profitable.

The problem for the ransomware attackers is that the notable instances also tend to draw more cybersecurity sheriffs to town, meaning that there will be a more determined and intense effort to find and bust the cyberhackers.

For those that decry the paying of the ransom when an entity is struck by ransomware, there are potential countervailing arguments loosely supporting the ransom payer. First, the held hostage entity is usually presented with a ransom amount that is relatively minuscule in comparison to the size of the entity, meanwhile the cost of the ongoing losses by being jammed up are all mounting too (and facing severe reputational loss as well). Thus, the decision to expend the money versus the admittedly unassured chances of resuming operations is a proposition that is hard to mindfully calculate and is altogether tempting.

Second, those stakeholders that are dependent upon the entity are likely to apply outstretched pressure that the entity ought to "do whatever it can" including the option of paying up to ostensibly get itself out of the jam (even though the reality is that the ransom payment might not provide such a result, but that isn't necessarily in the minds of those exhorting to get the matter hurriedly resolved).

And another factor that comes to play is whether the ransom payment itself might also possibly lead to catching the cyber crooks. As recent cases have shown, the tracing of the ransom payment can at times take place, even in the use of cryptocurrencies. This provides some potential solace for the entity that chooses to pay the ransom, namely that doing so could be a trick upon the tricksters as to providing a trail to their identities and whereabouts. There is also the chance that the ransom might be recovered, which is a double whammy of sorts against the ransomware attacker (the ransom might get them nabbed, plus the ransom might ultimately be stripped from them).

Undoubtedly, many of the cyber hackers put little stock in getting caught, so this idea that a dangling sword hangs over their heads if they seek to disrupt a larger target is not something they typically give much credence toward. They are often self-assured in their belief that they cannot be tracked down. It is an ongoing cat and mouse game, for which the mouse does indeed at times get caught, though it might think it won't.

In a moment, I'll be discussing how ransomware is going to inevitably target a realm that to date has seen little attention for this form of cyber hacking. I wish it weren't so, but the reality is that eventually, you can expect that the advent of AI-based true self-driving cars is going to be disrupted via the ransomware blight.

That exciting and state-of-the-art self-driving or driverless cars that we are hoping will someday be cruising all of our highways and byways are going to, lamentably, get in the gunsights of ransomware.

Yikes!

Before I share some cybersecurity insights on this hefty and quite somber topic, allow me a moment to bring up some related points.

Whenever I write about cyber-security, there are some that right away complain that by doing so the indications proffered are allowing cyber-hackers to gauge what kinds of cyber protections are being devised and what kinds of cyber vulnerabilities exist.

The worry is that writing about these topics, helps the cyber-hackers, arming them accordingly.

Please realize that this is the now-classic head-in-the-sand posturing regarding discussing cyber-security and related matters. Some believe that we should not talk about, nor write about, and not in any manner even whisper the nature and avenues of cyber-security and cyber-hacking, since it tips a hand to the evildoers.

This is a misguided and ill-informed notion, though one can certainly sympathize with their logic.

Here's the conundrum.

It is plainly the case that cyber-hackers are going to figure out these same facets, one way or another, and by trying to hide such discussions it does little good, including that it tends to undercut the preparations for and awareness about being on the hunt to stop and prevent cyber-hacking.

A head in the sand translates into getting kicked in the rear, as the old saying goes.

Meanwhile, there is another stated reason to not discuss such matters, namely that doing so, will cause mass hysteria. Again, the logic for this is certainly understandable. When those writing about cyber-security and cyber-hacking do so irresponsibly, attempting merely to fan the flames of angst, there is no question that such shoddy and perhaps even iniquitous efforts are sad, hurtful, and do not advance sensibly the battle between cyber-security and cyber-hacking.

With that crucial contextual indication, let's next take a serious and measured close look at what ransomware is about. After doing so, we can explore how ransomware will be used against AI-based self-driving cars.

Ransomware And Assorted Details

The term "ransomware" comes from a mash-up of the words ransom and malware and denotes a circumstance wherein a computer malware (a type of computer virus) is used to infect a computer so that the extorter can then try to extort something from the victim.

As you will shortly see, it is sometimes also called scareware, since it tries to scare the victim into paying a ransom. Sometimes the ransomware is more puffery than harmful, but it tries to scare a business into paying, either because the business does not realize that the ransomware really hasn't done much but they fear that it has, or the business wants to keep hidden that it got attacked and so is willing to pay hush money.

Unlike the more commonly known destructive computer viruses that we all dread and hate, a ransomware infection is not particularly used for destructive purposes as much as it is used for obstructive purposes. Obstructions include making various business files and data unusable (but with the chance of turning them back into being usable) or obstructing access to a series or a set of computer systems.
Ransomware will typically undertake one of two attacks.

Either it will try to lock up the computers being infected and take them hostage from access by the business or entity, or the ransomware will try to encrypt the data on the computer system and take the data hostage so that even if accessed by the business or entity it will be unusable (essentially scrambled and for which only a special key will unscramble the mess).

Usually, trying to lock up the computer is not going to be very effective and can be more readily overcome by cybersecurity specialists. Indeed, the lock-up attack is usually more scare than serious per se, and it is an attempt to intimidate those that rely upon that computer. The hope by the extortionist is that the entity will get frightened and then be amenable to paying a ransom as a preventive measure and avoid suffering additional attacks.

Often, in lieu of the lock-up attack, the other form of ransomware attack involves encrypting the data that resides on the computer systems. The ransomware program usually uses a relatively standardized form of encryption to encode the data, and the key that could decode the encoded data is presumably known only by the extorter. A ransom is then sought to purchase the key that will decode the data.

Notice that the extortionist is usually not "stealing" the data per se, and instead is just locking it up. Stealing the data would involve "taking it" (or, perhaps more like copying it), which either involves making a copy and then threatening to release it or distribute it or making a copy and then deleting the data from the original location so that you then no longer have that data available. The extorter could certainly seek to steal the data, but more often they just lock it in place.

You might wonder why the extorter would not always want to steal it.

One reason is that trying to copy the data would usually involve pulling lots of data across a computer network and this could take a lot of time, increasing the chances of the infecting program getting detected and stopped, and it could also reveal the infecting program by detection mechanisms that would realize the computers are sending out a huge chunk of data.

Do not though be misled into thinking that ransomware cannot be destructive.

It can be.

Sometimes the ransomware deletes some of the files and data, perhaps inadvertently at times, or even intended as a show of strength by the extorter to impress the victim about what power the extorter has over the situation. You might think of this as a variant of kidnapping and the extorter decides to harm the kidnapped hostage by wounding the leg to prove they are willing to play rough.

The extorter might even provide a snippet of the data to you, doing so to prove that they have it or can unlock it, which might be analogous to say taking a picture of a kidnapped victim while holding today's newspaper, essentially proving that they have the hostage currently in their possession and for pressuring to get a ransom.

You might be puzzled as to why anti-virus software doesn't right away detect ransomware and stop it cold before it can take hold.

Some anti-virus software packages don't look extensively to find ransomware. Some ransomware is so well hidden or masked that anti-virus fails to detect it. In fact, ransomware programs are continually being updated and modified by the perpetrators so that the anti-virus community has a hard time keeping up with the ransomware signature hide-and-seek (there is a field of study known as cryptoviology that focuses on computer viruses).

You might think that businesses and other entities would be a hard target to breach. Alas, you would tend to be wrong in your assumption since many organizations are sadly often ill-prepared for ransomware. As the old saying goes, an ounce of prevention is worth a pound of cure. If you get your business in shape to prevent becoming a victim of ransomware, you can save a ton of headaches and potential loss of company money, data, and reputation.

Most businesses sadly won't undertake the right precautions upfront and only after the fact will they devote the needed resources toward computer security that can reduce their chances of a ransomware infection. It is like earthquakes and not doing anything to prepare for one, but after one hits and causes damage and havoc that only then will precaution be put in place for the next earthquake that comes along.

Of course, at that point, the horse was already let out of the barn.

The ransom demand by the extorter will usually start high. They shoot for the moon as a negotiating tactic, knowing that they will likely settle for a lot less.

To push along the negotiations, most extorters will provide a time limit. They will say that if you don't pay within 48 hours that they will never provide you the key. Or, they might say that after 24 hours the price doubles for each next 12 hours. Similar to what you have seen in movies and TV shows, this is old-fashioned extortion at this point. The digital part of it is the new twist in terms of taking a hostage, but the rest of it is the same sort of blackmail tactics that have plagued mankind forever.

Of course, even if the extorter says they will provide the key when paid for, you have no assurance that they will ever provide the key. Some firms have made a payment that the extorter assured would get them the key, and then the extorter made a second demand saying that they now wanted more money.

Suppose you do get the key?

This does not guarantee that you can fully decrypt your data and nor that all of your data is still there.

During the infection process, some of your data might have been deleted or changed by the infecting program, and so the key only decrypts some of your data or there isn't even your data left to be decrypted. It is doubtful that the extortionist will provide you any guarantee that the key will work and that your data still exists (sometimes this provides a ploy for follow-up ransom demands, in a never-ending cycle).

Overall, I think you get the idea that once you've been infected by ransomware, all bets are off as to whether you will be able to reclaim your data. The allure or illusion that the cyber hacker will enable you to do so is quite enchanting. This again is a tradeoff practice. Some ransomware attackers believe that if they don't provide the proper key, subsequent entities that are attacked will realize that paying the ransom is useless. As such, it might make sense to gain a reputation as a *reasonable* ransomware purveyor (a rather outlandish calling!), to try and increase the odds of getting paid ransoms later on.

Let's next shift our attention to how ransomware is going to adversely impact the advent of AI-based true self-driving cars. Keep in mind that self-driving cars are driven via an AI driving system. There isn't a need for a human driver at the wheel, and nor is there a provision for a human to drive the vehicle.

Here's an intriguing question that is worth pondering: *In what ways will ransomware be used against AI-based true self-driving cars and how can we all be prepared to try and avert such dastardly cyber threats?*

Before jumping into the details, I'd like to further clarify what is meant when referring to true self-driving cars.

Self-Driving Cars And Ransomware

For Level 4 and Level 5 true self-driving vehicles, there won't be a human driver involved in the driving task.

All occupants will be passengers.

The AI is doing the driving.

One aspect to immediately discuss entails the fact that the AI involved in today's AI driving systems is not sentient. In other words, the AI is altogether a collective of computer-based programming and algorithms, and most assuredly not able to reason in the same manner that humans can.

Why this added emphasis about the AI not being sentient?

Because I want to underscore that when discussing the role of the

AI driving system, I am not ascribing human qualities to the AI. Please be aware that there is an ongoing and dangerous tendency these days to anthropomorphize AI. In essence, people are assigning human-like sentience to today's AI, despite the undeniable and inarguable fact that no such AI exists as yet.

With that clarification, you can envision that the AI driving system won't natively somehow "know" about the facets of driving. Driving and all that it entails will need to be programmed as part of the hardware and software of the self-driving car.

Let's dive into the myriad of aspects that come to play on this topic.

The two primary cybersecurity threat vectors underpinning AI-based true self-driving cars consist of the onboard computer systems and also via the cloud.

The onboard computers are within the autonomous vehicle and provide the computing resources needed to run or perform the AI driving system software. Outside of the self-driving car and connected remotely would be various cloud-oriented computing systems that are allied to the operational aspects for making active use of a self-driving car.

From a cloud perspective, self-driving cars will likely be connecting with a cloud-based service for purposes of scheduling and the dispatch for providing rides.

It is generally assumed that most self-driving cars will be used on ridesharing or ride-hailing basis. This does not necessarily have to be the case, though it does make sense. If you individually owned a self-driving car, you might be tempted to have it make money for you while you are at work or home sleeping at night. Rather than sitting idly parked in your driveway, you could list the autonomous vehicle on a ridesharing network and it would go back and forth providing money-making rides for you.

The same can be said for fleet operators that decide to make use of self-driving cars for large-scale ridesharing activities. Some argue that only fleet operators will own self-driving cars and there won't be any individual ownership taking place. I disagree. My viewpoint is that there will indeed be an individual ownership, along with large fleets too (see my column for in-depth debates on this matter).

In any case, for a self-driving car to be used on a ride-hailing basis means that there have to be some means for the AI driving system to become informed about where to pick up a ride and where to drop off a ride. This is likely going to be done via electronically connecting to a ridesharing network.

Another use of the cloud entails employing an OTA (Over-The-Air) electronic communications capability for self-driving cars.

When software updates are needed for the AI driving system, the OTA can be utilized to download and then install the patches from the cloud. In addition, the self-driving car can upload data into the cloud via the OTA. For example, there will be data uploaded that has been temporarily stored onboard the vehicle such as recently captured video camera data, radar data, LIDAR data, and so on. The type of cloud being used for this purpose is sometimes referred to as a DevOps cloud, a mashup of the development efforts for the self-driving car and the operational aspects.

With those background setting indications, we can consider the highest vulnerability exposures for ransomware attacks.

Ransomware in the Scheduling/Dispatch Cloud

A ransomware attack might be focused on the scheduling/dispatch cloud.

Envision that the ransomware has locked up the data underpinning the scheduling and dispatching of self-driving cars. Pretend that the data is scrambled and essentially unusable.

This suggests that this particular cloud will no longer have viable data accessible about the registered riders that are using the ridesharing network. Nor will the data about which self-driving cars are registered be available. The locations of the self-driving cars would no longer be readily ascertained due to the data about their geographic positions being unreadable. And so on.

In short, the ability to schedule and dispatch self-driving cars is pretty much frozen.

Keep in mind that none of the self-driving cars are directly affected.

The ransomware has not touched the AI driving systems. The self-driving cars could presumably still be driving around just fine. Of course, the question arises as to where they are going, since they would no longer be actively able to use the scheduling/dispatching cloud for purposes of getting assigned rides.

In theory, passengers could directly tell the AI driving system where to go. If a self-driving car is being used for ridesharing, perhaps the AI driving system would proceed as requested by a passenger and merely record that a ride was provided (which later on would be uploaded for purposes of charging the rider for the ride). On the other hand, if the scheduling/dispatch cloud isn't able to confirm taking on the ride, the AI driving system might simply emit a message to the passenger that the cloud system is currently unavailable and therefore no further rides will be allowed (until the scheduling/dispatch cloud becomes properly available once again).

This use of ransomware would disrupt the ridesharing use of whatever set of self-driving cars are listed on this particular cloud-based ridesharing network. The money possibly lost due to the self-driving cars being idled and awaiting ride assignments could be relatively significant. But this is not likely an especially onerous use of ransomware, since it could be that the self-driving cars might relatively readily be switched over to another clean cloud and continue working while the ransomware inflicted cloud is rectified.

Ransomware in the DevOps Cloud

A ransomware attack might be focused on the DevOps cloud.

Envision that the ransomware has locked up the data and some of the source code underpinning the development and operations aspects of self-driving cars. Pretend that the data is scrambled and essentially unusable.

This means that any pending patches or software fixes that were supposed to be downloaded into the self-driving cars are no longer readily available. Likewise, the data being collected onboard the self-driving car such as video camera data, radar data, LIDAR data, and the like is not able to be uploaded at that time.

If there were pending patches that were urgently needed for ensuring the ongoing safety and use of self-driving cars, this disruption could be significant. It could undermine the safety of self-driving cars.

The odds though are that the existing software that was already installed is doing fine and the patches are more akin to improvements or minor corrections, and otherwise, the self-driving cars are okay while awaiting eventually to get the fixes. This is logically the case much of the time, especially since doing the OTA updates is a matter usually done after-hours and when the self-driving cars are not otherwise actively booked for rides.

In terms of being blocked from uploading data that is onboard the self-driving cars, it could be that the data can sit onboard for a while. Usually, self-driving cars are equipped with sufficient disk storage to keep on-hand the data, doing so until a convenient time arises to use the OTA for uploading purposes. One supposes that this could eventually be exceeded as to the amount of onboard disk storage, which would suggest that some of the data might be "lost" due to not being able to either store it locally and nor upload it to the cloud.

Generally, none of this would stop self-driving cars from continuing to drive. The odds are that this use of ransomware would have a greater scare tactic effect than actually undercutting the use of self-driving cars.

That being said, if the DevOps cloud is the only place that the developers are storing the source code and patches (yikes!), they are in for a lot of trouble and would be unable to appropriately maintain the AI driving systems. That would be more than a scare, that's for sure. As well, if the uploaded data is being monetized, this use of ransomware could sorely cut into the money-making use of that data.

Ransomware in the Onboard AI Driving System

This is the most chilling and doomsday-like portrayal of self-driving cars, consisting of the ransomware somehow attacking the onboard AI driving systems.

Presumably, this would render the impacted self-driving cars useless and they would become no more than a hefty doorstop or multi-ton paperweight.

One would hope that at least the AI driving system was able to get the vehicle into what is known as a Minimal Risk Condition (MRC) posture before the ransomware took hold. The MRC is usually associated with coming to a safe stop and doing so in a manner and place that is considered relatively prudent.

This type of ransomware would certainly be the most worrisome and the height of danger for these scenarios. Note that ransomware is not trying to take over the control of the AI driving systems. It is just locking up the AI driving system, which of course is still a bad thing, for sure. Worryingly, there are other kinds of computer viruses that are being targeted toward taking over the driving controls (see my discussions about this in my columns on cybersecurity and self-driving cars).

Conclusion

You might be wondering why there haven't been significant ransomware attacks against self-driving cars already.

First, we don't know that there haven't been. Would an automaker or self-driving tech firm want the world to know about it? Likely not.

Also, there are undoubtedly lots of ongoing attempts to use ransomware attacks, which have been variously mentioned or rumored amongst those in the cybersecurity and self-driving cars arena. There are ongoing debates taking place about whether the makers and operators of self-driving cars will be required by regulation or law to report cybersecurity intrusions, including the use of ransomware.

The other somewhat obvious aspect is that self-driving cars are not yet pervasive. You could argue that the money to be made from ransomware at this time in this market space is too little. Only once self-driving cars become more pronounced would it seem they are a worthy target for the fiends that exploit ransomware uses.

Bottom-line is that the automakers and self-driving tech firms need to be on their toes. The silence that they might hear right now from the ransomware striking thugs is not to be taken as a sign that self-driving cars are not on the hit list. Self-driving cars assuredly are.

Make a serious-minded note right now, avoid ever getting a ransom note by making sure that your systems are ransomware resilient or impervious. Those are words to live by.

CHAPTER 11
FBI POSSIBLE USE AND SELF-DRIVING CARS

Gotcha!

You might have seen the recent headlines blaring that the FBI secretly duped hundreds of alleged criminals by providing in the open marketplace one of those seemingly secure communications apps akin to a WhatsApp, Signal, Wickr Me, Viber, or similar encryption messaging platforms. Would-be and actual crooks apparently could not resist the allure of using a form of communication that they apparently thought was completely safeguarded from the authorities and altogether foolproof.

Those caught in the sting are likely feeling quite foolish now.

The very mechanism that was intended to protect them from getting caught was their actual downfall of, in fact, getting nabbed.

Ironic.

Clever.

An enthralling plot that is certainly worthy of a movie or TV drama about ways that crooks shoot their own foot, as it were.

The FBI artfully carried out these sting operations by co-opting the Anom system, a somewhat popular encrypted mobile device and network service that had already become relatively prevalent for criminal activities. According to the FBI, the big bust took place worldwide and netted hundreds upon hundreds of arrests. The claim is that these were criminal participants in narcotics trafficking, organized crime, and a slew of illegal and dastardly activities.

Some have heralded this sly ploy of providing a type of honeypot to get potential evildoers on the hook.

The voluminous communique of those using the secure app was essentially secure to the rest of the world but completely unsecure and readily readable by the FBI. One can imagine the puzzlement of the nabbed users as they likely had already ascertained that their communications were seemingly encrypted and secure. They must have felt comfortable and confident that the encryption would rebuff any attempts by the police or law enforcement, stopping those authorities cold and leaving no trail and no means of knowing what clandestine efforts were afoot.

Law enforcement was reportedly monitoring over 12,000 users that were globally spread across over one hundred countries. Encrypted messages were easily decrypted since the FBI had all the keys that were being used by the communications app. If the communications had not been encrypted, surely the presumed thieves would not have been using the app. The false sense of security that the messages were encrypted had to be a feeling of relief that they could carry on whatever bad deeds they wished to discuss via the app.

Not everyone thinks this is a decidedly good thing. Some have expressed qualms that there might very easily be innocent users that have gotten swept into the large fishnet. Also, the question arises as to whether users that had no criminal activity underway were being screened and their messages examined, routinely, even though they were simply using the app for personal privacy purposes. Did this eagerness to get the bad actors inadvertently overextend into invading the privacy of others? This will all certainly play out as the cases are brought to court and the matter gets additional coverage.

Interestingly, some say that this might scare other criminals into avoiding the use of secure communications apps. Perhaps the lesson to be learned by potential crooks is do not to trust any encrypted messaging platform. A retort to that contention is that this might simply shift the criminals toward using the most well-known platforms and deny the startups from getting any air time. In other words, the evildoers might assume that the prominent platforms would not be run by the FBI, while the FBI might try again to co-opt some smaller and less known platform in a future similar sting.

Makes your head spin.

In any case, let's leverage the concept of having law enforcement decide to co-opt some form of technological innovation and make use of it to try and nab the baddies of this planet.

What other type of high-tech could the FBI choose to use for such a crimefighting purpose?

The answer: *Self-driving cars.*

Say what?

Yes, you could envision a scenario in which the FBI or essentially any law enforcement agency might co-opt the use of AI-based true self-driving cars and use those AVs (autonomous vehicles) to track and arrest wrongdoers.

Keep in mind that self-driving cars are driven via an AI driving system. There isn't a need for a human driver at the wheel, and nor is there a provision for a human to drive the vehicle.

Here's an intriguing question that is worth pondering: *In what ways could law enforcement run a fleet of AI-based true self-driving cars to ensnare criminals?*

Before jumping into the details, I'd like to further clarify what is meant when referring to true self-driving cars.

Self-Driving Cars And Snagging Crooks

For Level 4 and Level 5 true self-driving vehicles, there won't be a human driver involved in the driving task.

All occupants will be passengers.

The AI is doing the driving.

One aspect to immediately discuss entails the fact that the AI involved in today's AI driving systems is not sentient. In other words, the AI is altogether a collective of computer-based programming and algorithms, and most assuredly not able to reason in the same manner that humans can.

Why this added emphasis about the AI not being sentient?

Because I want to underscore that when discussing the role of the AI driving system, I am not ascribing human qualities to the AI. Please be aware that there is an ongoing and dangerous tendency these days to anthropomorphize AI. In essence, people are assigning human-like sentience to today's AI, despite the undeniable and inarguable fact that no such AI exists as yet.

With that clarification, you can envision that the AI driving system won't natively somehow "know" about the facets of driving. Driving and all that it entails will need to be programmed as part of the hardware and software of the self-driving car.

Let's dive into the myriad of aspects that come to play on this topic.

I've previously provided insights about the use of self-driving cars for solving murder cases and other unsolved crimes, see **the link here**. That type of crime-solving approach would be an aboveboard use of self-driving cars as an aid in crimefighting. There isn't anything especially sneaky or behind-the-scenes going on.

There is also the possibility of using self-driving cars as *bait cars*, namely having the AVs sitting around to see if a would-be car thieve will take the bait and try to steal the car (see **the link here**). This admittedly is a slyer use of self-driving cars by law enforcement.

Our attention in this discussion is the overarching notion that law enforcement might run a fleet of self-driving cars, doing so without telling anyone that the fleet is operated by law enforcement.

The underlying rationale would be to try and track and eventually arrest lawbreakers (without their awareness that this is happening). Once the big bust occurs of nabbing alleged criminals, the gig would be up and the odds of running another similar sting would be likely diminished.

It is somewhat a one-trick pony, akin to the encryption messaging sting.

To see how this might be undertaken, let's sketch the key facets of this scenario.

First, the odds are that self-driving cars will be deployed in fleets. A large company that wants to get into ridesharing or ride-hailing might purchase a bunch of self-driving cars and operate them as a collective. Some pundits assert that rental car companies will do this, along with other firms that see a profitable opportunity by making money from the ridesharing of self-driving cars.

We will still have human-driven cars available for ridesharing purposes. There is a false narrative by some that we would have only self-driving cars on our roadways and completely do away with all human-driven cars. That is quite a wild stretch of the imagination. Besides the obvious aspect that the replacement or excising of all conventionally driven cars would take many decades to gradually take place, some human drivers insist they won't give up their driving until the day that their cold dead hands are pried from the steering wheel.

Okay, so we will gradually witness the emergence of self-driving cars and they will oftentimes be organized into fleets. Self-driving cars will typically be listed on ridesharing networks. A person needing a ridesharing lift will use the desired network and see that there are human-driven ridesharing cars and there are also self-driving ridesharing cars available.

The self-driving cars might be listed on popular ridesharing networks or could be utilized exclusively by using a specialized app that the company operating the fleet makes available.

You won't especially care which self-driving car is available for ridesharing. The odds are that you will mainly be interested in using either a human-driven car versus a self-driving car and will not focus on which brand or model of a self-driving car is being proffered. The exception to this rule-of-thumb will be that the size of the vehicle and where it is able to go will be the key determiner of selecting a specific self-driving car offering.

A perceived advantage to using a self-driving car will be that it might be considered a safer driver than using a human-driven ridesharing car. In theory, self-driving cars will always be driving in a legal manner, obeying the speed limits and other driving rules. The AI driving system will not get drunk, will not drive while distracted, and so on. The hope is that self-driving cars will overall be safer at driving than human drivers.

Another perceived advantage would be that human drivers can sometimes be a pain in the neck, while an AI driving system is ostensibly quiet and unintrusive. As a passenger, you don't need to carry on a pleasant conversation with an AI driving system.

From a crooks' perspective, a human driver is a bit of a potential problem. The human driver could be a witness to the fact that a crook took a ride. This presumably would include an indication of where the crook was picked up, what they looked like, and where they were dropped off. In addition, the human driver could, later on, attest to what the crook did while inside the self-driving car, perhaps overhearing snippets of conversation.

In that sense, the perceived beauty of using an AI self-driving car would be that a crook would not have to worry about that overly curious human driver that seems to be sticking their nose where it does not belong. There won't be a human driver inside a self-driving car. The crook would be able to ride along and not be observed by a nosey human driver.

You might be thinking that the crook could just enlist the human driver into whatever criminal enterprise is taking place. Sure, that's a possibility. The problem is that using a human driver can be a loose end. Will the human driver keep their mouth shut? Suppose the human driver turns and becomes a state witness? Worse still, what if the human driver is an undercover law enforcement officer.

Using a self-driving car cuts out all of those apprehensive misgivings about having a human driver.

Seems pretty convincing. Law abiding people will be attracted to using self-driving cars. Criminals will be attracted to using self-driving cars too. A perfect convergence to possibly get the criminals to let down their guard. The self-driving car fleet operator would normally not be differentiating one type of rider from another. As long as the riders are paying to ride, that's what counts. People will go where they want. People will do whatever they want while inside the autonomous vehicle (well, within limits, see my discussion at **this link here**).

In a manner of speaking, crooks might perceive self-driving cars in the same light as using a secure encrypted messaging platform. Self-driving cars would seem to provide a criminally handy form of transportation. No human driver. No human witnesses. Conduct your criminal activity while inside the self-driving car, having private discussions with your fellow lawbreakers.

No one would ever be the wiser.

Maybe yes, maybe no.

Imagine that the FBI realizes that self-driving cars could be a means to ensnare riders that are criminals such as organized crime participants, narcotics traffickers, etc.

One approach would be to try and convince an existing fleet operator to let the FBI be immersed in the fleet deployment. This could be dicey as a secretive arrangement and might end up tipping the hand of law enforcement since an insider of the fleet operator might spill the beans to the crooks.

It might be sounder for the FBI to put together its own fleet. This could be done from scratch. They go out and buy a slew of self-driving cars and then start listing them for use. Things are a bit more complicated due to the need to keep the self-driving cars properly maintained, properly serviced, updated with needed AI driving system patches, and the like. In any case, it is all doable.

One supposes that an alternative would be to approach a fledgling startup that is operating a fleet of self-driving cars and do a co-opt deal with that firm. This might be handier since the cover story is already established and this might lessen suspicions by any potential crooks that might decide to use those particular self-driving cars.

What could the FBI use those self-driving cars for?

The obvious aspect would be to keep track of where the riders are picked up and where they are dropped off. This would include the date of the travels made, the times of the traveling, and other facets.

But that's not all, by a long shot.

Self-driving cars have a host of sensors that are used to detect the driving scene. This encompasses devices such as video cameras, radar, LIDAR, ultrasonic units, thermal imagining, and other data capturing sensors. Though the purpose of those sensors is presumably for discerning the driving environment, they are collecting widely a lot of data that has little to do with the driving act per se.

I've described this as the "roving eye" problem.

When a self-driving car is driving down a normal neighborhood street, there is more than just video imagery about the roadway itself. The camera is also capturing the activities taking place such as someone mowing their lawn, a house that has kids playing outside, and pretty much anything that is within visual range. Companies that are deploying fleets of self-driving cars can attempt to monetize this data. For example, potentially selling the data to real estate firms that want to know what the status of the housing units is in a given community.

This can be a potential privacy intrusion nightmare. Given that self-driving cars will be going back and forth throughout your community, it would be feasible to play back the collected data and start to piece together the daily activities of us all. Open questions exist about the ownership and use of this data.

For the FBI, the data from a self-driving car could be golden.

A criminal is picked up by a self-driving car being run by the FBI. Imagine that other allied crooks are there chatting with the criminal when the person gets into the self-driving car. This would be captured on video. When the crook arrives at the designated destination, the person gets out of the self-driving car and is met by other people. All of them are now captured on video. If you multiply out this type of video capturing, over time you could piece together the entire network of crooks involved in whatever lawless acts they are doing.

There is more fuel to be placed on this fire.

Self-driving cars will have inward-facing cameras too. This is to allow for catching riders that might decide to mar the interior of the vehicle by writing graffiti or tearing up the seats. A more positive-minded use would be for taking online courses and being able to do Zoom-like discussions while riding along in a self-driving car.

The conversations inside a self-driving car could entirely be captured on video. Think of the treasure trove of info. If the criminal has a fellow crook inside the self-driving car, their conversation would be entirely recorded. Even if the person is alone inside the self-driving car, their use of a personal smartphone could be detected and recorded.

Of course, all of this presumes that the criminals are lulled into believing that self-driving cars are secure and not being used to surveil them. Here's how that would possibly be cleverly staged to hoodwink the baddies.

The odds are that once self-driving cars become prevalent, the general public will wise up that self-driving cars have this intrinsic capability of being a tattletale. You can bet that many people will refuse to ride in self-driving cars for that very reason. There is even a chance that communities might try to ban the use of self-driving cars or put hefty restrictions on what they can record when inside their locale.

So, expect that there will be some self-driving car fleets that will advertise and pledge that you won't have your privacy intruded if you use their particular fleet. This might be a key differentiator for prospective riders. They will look at any listed self-driving cars on a ridesharing network and seek to use only the ones that have made that kind of promise.

Does this mean that the FBI is therefore fouled out by that kind of preference?

Nope.

They could presumably tout that their fleet is indeed the type that averts using the non-driving related data.

Similar to how Anom was touting that their encrypted messaging platform was secure, the FBI could ostensibly make the same kind of claim about the secretly run fleet of self-driving cars.

There might be additional under-the-table ways to especially allure the crooks they are targeting.

For example, possibly allow payment for the rides via some shady cryptocurrency. The FBI wouldn't care whether the rides were paid for or were using an unreliable form of payment, since the subterfuge is a pretext to catch the baddies. The prices for the rides could also be set extremely low, below the prices of other competing self-driving car fleets.

The best dream for law enforcement would be that the criminals involved would somehow generally agree to use that specific fleet, more so than any other self-driving car. Get the evil masterminds to standardize on a seemingly secure and well-guarded fleet of self-driving cars. Perhaps the undercover agents operating the fleet could offer a sweetly priced deal that also includes top-priority riding privileges and any other bells and whistles associated with using self-driving cars.

And then nab them.

Case closed.

Conclusion

All of this isn't going to happen if we don't have self-driving cars in any large-scale way. Thus, until there is ongoing and booming growth in the adoption of self-driving cars, the law enforcement gambit is not especially viable. Eventually, the FBI or some akin law enforcement agency running a secretly arranged sting operation is a possibility.

One last parting thought on this mind-bending topic.

When it comes time to bust the crooks, you could potentially have the self-driving cars go pick them up, acting in a normal fashion as though nothing untoward is about to happen. Those criminals would gladly get into the self-driving cars that they have been using routinely for months or years.

The next thing they know, the self-driving fleet all at once takes the unsuspecting rubes to a local FBI branch office, handing them directly over to the eagerly awaiting law enforcement agents.

Now that's a form of special delivery.

CHAPTER 12
KITTEN HIDING AND SELF-DRIVING CARS

Something adorable could have been a heap of unpleasant trouble.

A kitten had decided to hide underneath a parked AI self-driving car.

I'm sure that you've seen or even personally witnessed having a cat or dog that opted to sneak under your conventional car and decided to hide out in this seemingly protective cove. Of course, we all know that once the vehicle starts up, things are going to get dicey for the cuddly pets if they don't quickly scramble out from their hiding spot. Worse still, the likely now startled animal could shockingly freeze up in place and be ominously in the path of the wheels and be at risk of getting (heaven forbid) run over.

Yikes!

In my neighborhood, there seems to be a slew of meandering cats. Thus, I always do a quick peek underneath my outdoor parked conventional car whenever I am going on a driving journey. More than once I've caught a blissful feline that was catnapping and unaware of the potential dangers involved.

Any street-savvy cat has probably already figured out that it is time to rapidly move on whenever a car engine gets started. I usually assume that the cats undertaking the under-the-car gambit are seasoned prowlers that are constantly on alert and ready to skedaddle with tremendous grace and speed.

A kitten might not yet have learned this crucial school-of-hard-knocks lesson.

I dare say that few people seem to put much thought toward looking underneath their vehicle before they begin to go for a drive. You might remember in your teens taking a driver training class that repeatedly emphasized the importance of doing a careful and plodding walk around your vehicle before you get into the car itself.

This was a type of pre-flight check.

The idea is that you might notice a flat tire, or maybe a ding or dent in the exterior, etc.

In short, it makes abundant sense to ensure that your car is ready for a road trip. Plus, you want to know what your car looked like beforehand, in case something untoward happens during a driving adventure. Upon going to say a grocery store, you might believe that someone carelessly allowed a shopping cart to skirt and scrape across the side of your car and scratch it up, though it could be that the scratch was there earlier, and you had lackadaisically not glanced around to see it.

The most vital reason to do a walk around of your vehicle would be to ascertain that the car is fully functional and ready to go.

If you just jump into the driver's seat first, you might not realize that your right rear tire is perilously low on air. Or maybe a nail or spike has somehow ended up on the gravel just where your right front tire sits, and for which the moment you pull forward there is going to be a bursting sound and a lot of angst and dismay on your part. Had you noticed the silently menacing piece of steel waiting to puncture your tire, you could have easily swept it out of the way beforehand.

Another reason to do a brief walk around your vehicle entails any otherwise unseen complications.

Here's what I mean.

When my children were toddlers, it seemed like they used to

regularly leave a toy behind my parked car. The car was usually seated on an outdoor pad in our front yard and was slightly on an incline. It was easy for the kids to inadvertently leave a toy laying here or there. It was equally easy for me to be in a hurry, rushing to work, and hastily back down the driveway without knowing that a toy was about to get summarily crushed.

To be clear about this, I would mindfully look to ensure that no humans and no animals were anywhere behind the vehicle. This was standard practice. That being said, a small toy could be laying flat on the ground, unmoving, and utterly blend into the pattern of the concrete pad. If that were the case, and assuming that the toy by a bad stroke of luck was in the path of the wheels, it was going to be a goner.

More than once I regrettably smashed such a toy. As a parent, your first thought seems to consist of chiding the kids for having left their toys in a vulnerable spot. One might even suggest that this is a valuable lesson for them, namely if you don't take good care of your things they will be at risk of getting lost or damaged. On the other hand, there is also the rule of thumb that the parent backing down a driveway ought to be inspecting the path and ensure that there isn't anything in the way.

I admit that I sometimes opted to get a replacement toy, explaining that the matter was unfortunate for all and yet we didn't need to go quite overboard about lessons learned. Some others thought that was merely proving that two wrongs make a right, and my kids would lead a life of confusion and misunderstanding about how the world really works.

No worries, things didn't play out that way and those theories were disproven.

Anyway, back to the kitten and the looming danger of resting underneath a car.

The thing about a conventional car is that a human driver might notice beforehand that a kitten or other animal is in fact hiding out and ought to be dissuaded from staying where they are. The person would undoubtedly try to shoo out the hiding intruder. It is possible too that you might hear the cat meowing or perhaps making some form of noise while moving around. All in all, there is some viable chance that you might detect the hidden trespasser (well, I guess you could assert that the cat has every right to be resting in that position, presumably protected from predators and for which you've allowed the opportunity to exist).

What about an AI-based true self-driving car?

You see, there isn't a human driver involved in a true self-driving car. Keep in mind that true self-driving cars are driven via an AI driving system. There isn't a need for a human driver at the wheel, and nor is there a provision for a human to drive the vehicle.

Here's an intriguing question that is worth pondering: *What will an AI-based true self-driving car do or fail to do when getting underway and seek to ensure that no objects or living creatures might be in immediate harm's way?*

Before jumping into the details, I'd like to further clarify what is meant when referring to true self-driving cars.

Self-Driving Cars And Hiding Kittens

For Level 4 and Level 5 true self-driving vehicles, there won't be a human driver involved in the driving task.

All occupants will be passengers.

The AI is doing the driving.

One aspect to immediately discuss entails the fact that the AI involved in today's AI driving systems is not sentient. In other words, the AI is altogether a collective of computer-based programming and algorithms, and most assuredly not able to reason in the same manner that humans can.

Why this added emphasis about the AI not being sentient?

Because I want to underscore that when discussing the role of the AI driving system, I am not ascribing human qualities to the AI. Please be aware that there is an ongoing and dangerous tendency these days to anthropomorphize AI. In essence, people are assigning human-like sentience to today's AI, despite the undeniable and inarguable fact that no such AI exists as yet.

With that clarification, you can envision that the AI driving system won't natively somehow "know" about the facets of driving. Driving and all that it entails will need to be programmed as part of the hardware and software of the self-driving car.

Let's dive into the myriad of aspects that come to play on this topic.

We can certainly expect that AI-based self-driving cars will attempt to examine the surroundings when first powered on and getting ready to undertake a driving journey.

Self-driving cars are usually outfitted with a sensor suite consisting of video cameras, radar, LIDAR, ultrasonic units, thermal imaging devices, and the like. Not all brands or models will necessarily have the same set of sensors, such that some automakers and self-driving tech firms are aiming to use only certain kinds of sensing devices and somewhat eschew other such types.

In any case, the sensors are likely to right away begin capturing data about the immediate surroundings the moment that a driving task is going to be initiated. Some self-driving cars will even be making use of some of their sensors while parked and not at all underway, doing so as a precaution to try and detect and dissuade car thieves or carry on other desired observations.

Let's assume that a driving mission has been given to the AI driving system and it is going to proceed with the assigned journey. Upon starting the engine and engaging the sensors, the programmed initial activity is assuredly going to be an assessment of where the self-driving car is, where it needs to go, and what might be directly within the starting path of the autonomous vehicle.

If the self-driving car is parked on a driveway and going to be backing down to the street, you can reasonably anticipate that the sensors on the rear of the vehicle will be trying to detect any obstructions that might be in the way. Perhaps a child has left a bicycle standing behind the self-driving car. Either the video cameras would pick up the image of the bicycle or possibly the radar would detect the bicycle. There could be a multitude of sensors that are able to simultaneously detect the presence of an object.

So far, so good.

Would a child's toy that was on the ground, sandwiched between the driveway and the right front tire, be readily detected?

The odds are against this being detected.

The position of the toy is probably not within the scope of the video cameras. You could say that this particular location is a blind spot of sorts. None of the other sensors are likely to detect the toy, especially if it is lying flat and entirely motionless. The same could be said of a nail or spike that perchance was laying in that general locale.

Would a kitten or other small animal hiding underneath the self-driving car be detected?

Highly unlikely.

Few self-driving cars have a video camera that is mounted or ostensibly positioned to see under the vehicle (likewise, you would not expect other externally attuned sensors to be there either).

Many AI developers either haven't considered putting a camera in that arrangement (the idea hasn't arisen), or they don't think it would be of much use. Plus, there is a cost associated with including yet another video camera in the self-driving car. All in all, the use of a costly video camera or other such sensors to be able to see what is under the car doesn't seem to be in the cards, for now (I have predicted that this attitude will change once self-driving cars become prevalent and are being used in everyday real-world driving settings).

You could categorize this scenario or use case into the large bucket of so-called edge or corner cases.

Those are situations and circumstances that are considered rare and ranked as low priority to be considered. Most of the AI driving systems and the AI developers making them are struggling to just get self-driving cars to go safely from point A to point B. Worrying about what is perhaps underneath the self-driving car is something well beyond the focus of attention at this time.

Just don't tell the kitten that they are ranked as low priority, you might get fervently cat scratched.

The bottom line is that most self-driving cars are generally blind (not set up to detect) whatever might be somewhere underneath the vehicle. Given that assertion, there is a bit of an escape hatch in that if the self-driving car were to detect an object before it ended up underneath the vehicle, this could aid the AI driving system in essentially calculating that the item has presumably gotten into that posture.

Consider how that might work.

Suppose that the sensors were active and detected a cat that was about ten feet in front of the vehicle and for which the feline was striding nonchalantly toward the front of the self-driving car. This is something that could be readily detected and tracked. Once the cat goes underneath the vehicle, the external sensors of the typical self-driving car are no longer able to detect the presence of the feline.

Meanwhile, the sensors that provide a 360-degree viewpoint around the vehicle would allow for detecting the cat once it comes out from underneath the self-driving car. If the cat does not appear on any of those sensory captures, it is reasonable to make the default assumption that the cat is still underneath the self-driving car. This is not a certainty, since perhaps there are some other means of the cat finding its way out, though we will not include that the cat has magical powers and nor that it is wearing an invisibility cloak.

Whenever a self-driving is underway, the AI driving system has the potential for figuring out what objects might have been driven over and perhaps be underneath the autonomous vehicle. This is due to detecting an object beforehand and then making calculated predictions about where the object might next be. For example, a discarded piece of splattered furniture on the freeway will at some point be underneath the self-driving car if the AI driving system opts to drive over the roadway object. Shortly thereafter, the object should be detectable as the self-driving car proceeds beyond the object and the strewn debris are now behind the vehicle and once again visible.

There are some dicey elements to this kind of computation.

Could the video camera image processing really account for all of the shattered remains of the furniture, or might some pieces still be underneath the vehicle and possibly stuck to the underframe in some fashion? The odds of being able to definitively make such a determination are rather slim.

Of course, this side tangent was based on the premise that the object of interest was detected before it went underneath the autonomous vehicle. If the self-driving car was parked on a driveway and entirely shut off, including all of the usual sensors, there would not be any "before" that could be relied upon to ascertain what might be underneath the vehicle.

Imagine two different variants of this scenario, whereby one instance consisted of the self-driving car going for a drive and doing so absent of having any passengers, while the other instance involves carrying one or more passengers.

In case you are wondering why a self-driving car would be getting underway without any passengers on board, that's a straightforward and altogether commonly expected aspect regarding the use of self-driving cars. You see, if someone requests a ride, the self-driving car might need to first drive to wherever that person is. As such, the self-driving car will be entirely empty until it reaches and has the passenger embark on the desired ride. Many are worried that we are going to have a lot of self-driving cars that are roaming here and there, doing so absent of passengers, and ergo might inadvertently clog up traffic accordingly (see my columns for analyses of this qualm).

The second use case of having a passenger at the outset is especially interesting because it introduces a potential "solution" related to finding that kitten that is hiding underneath the parked self-driving car.

Here's how that might happen.

A passenger comes up to a parked and inert self-driving car. The passenger rouses the AI driving system, either by using a smartphone to connect to it or possibly by speaking to the vehicle (a microphone is listening for a wake-up command, just like when you use Alexa or Siri).

The Natural Language Processing (NLP) component of the AI driving system might engage the human passenger in a brief dialogue. Besides asking where the person wants to go, the AI driving system might also ask the passenger to please glance around and underneath the autonomous vehicle. If the passenger notices anything out of the ordinary, the person could verbally alert the AI driving system accordingly. The AI driving system would have been programmed with some provision related to not getting underway until the matter is somehow properly resolved (that's an entirely different story, which will be covered in a later column).

Just as a human driver might normally be expected to look around their vehicle to do a pre-flight kind of check, an AI driving system could ask a human passenger to take on that role. It would be easy for passengers to do this, taking just a quick walk around and bending down to look underneath the self-driving car.

That seems to close this matter and we can go home now.

Not so!

First, we've already noted that this is just the use case when a passenger is involved. Therefore, we still have the gaping loophole of the use case for which there *isn't* a passenger at the get-go.

Second, mull over this notion of asking passengers to look around, and I think you'll quickly realize the folly of such an approach.

Some passengers will give only a cursory look-see. Their effort to examine what is underneath the vehicle is especially likely to be skimpy, at best (would you be willing to get down on the ground onto likely grimy asphalt, plus what if it is raining or some other adverse factor comes to play). The chances that a passenger will reliably spy on something is highly questionable.

I would bet too those passengers would feel as though they are being put upon by having to do "work" for the self-driving car. Why should a passenger have to be enlisted to do something that the AI driving system ought to be taking care of? When you get into a human-driven car, you don't usually expect the human driver to ask you to walk around and check out things. The response by passengers would probably be something like getting your lazy posterior out of the car and check around for yourself.

All told, asking passengers to look around seems misguided. It could be a temporary and half-baked way to momentarily deal with such issues but ultimately will need a more systemic solution.

Conclusion

If you are wondering what else could be done, other than mounting sensors that are oriented to inspect underneath the autonomous vehicle, there is in fact a potential additional solution.

Drones.

Yes, there are various efforts underway of pairing up drones with self-driving cars. A drone could be used for a variety of handy purposes. As mentioned in my columns, there are tests underway of using a drone to rapidly fly a fast-food meal to a moving self-driving car that has a hungry passenger inside.

Rather than simply providing some hamburgers and fries, let's consider how the drone helps to find that adorable kitten.

When a self-driving car begins a driving journey, it might directly launch its paired drone (which was sitting in a rooftop casing, the passageway of the casing is automatically opened and the drone is sent airborne). The drone briefly circles around the self-driving car. A video camera on the drone is beaming electronic signals to the AI driving system and showcasing the images being captured. The AI driving system mathematically examines the images and tries to determine if there are any objects in the way of the autonomous vehicle.

In addition, the drone is flown very close to the ground and immediately adjacent to the self-driving car. This allows the video camera of the drone to peer underneath the vehicle. If needed, the drone can be flown underneath the self-driving car to get a closer look at what might be there.

Kitten discovered!

That is the future and not something that you would find in today's self-driving cars.

You might be wondering what happened to the kitten that was snoozing underneath a contemporary self-driving car.

Turns out that the self-driving car had a human backup driver, sometimes referred to as a safety monitor, that was taking the autonomous vehicle for a test drive. This is frequently the case these days, namely that automakers and self-driving tech firms hire people to go along for a ride, watching to see what the AI driving system does. If there is something that the AI driving system appears to be amiss on, the human driver can disengage the AI driving system and take over the driving controls (for details about the nature of this role, see my column discussions).

Well, it turns out that upon approaching the self-driving car, the human backup driver startled the kitten.

Out darted the lively kitten!

I suppose you could say that this was all in a day's work for the human backup driver. They are intended to keep an AI self-driving car from going awry, and apparently able to save kittens from dangerous situations.

I wonder if the kitten used up any of its nine lives by surviving unscathed. This might be a necessity until self-driving cars are made kitten-proof..

CHAPTER 13
CONFIDENTIAL COMPUTING AND SELF-DRIVING CARS

Let's play a spying game.

A friend of yours wants to write down a secret and pass along the note to you. There is dire concern that an undesirable interloper might intercept the note. As such, the secret is first encrypted before being written down and thus will be inscrutable to anyone that perchance intervenes. All told, the message will look scrambled or seem like gobbledygook.

You have the password or key needed to decrypt the message.

After the note has passed through many hands, it finally reaches you. The fact that many others saw and ostensibly were able to read the note is of no consequence. They could not make head nor tails of what it said.

Upon receiving the encrypted message, you decide to decrypt it. Voila, you can now see what it says. The message successfully and with vital security has been appropriately received and deciphered. The world is saved and everyone can rejoice.

But wait for a second, when you decrypted the message, you wrote it down, and meanwhile, a dastardly spy was looking over your shoulder. The snoop has now seen the entire message, spying it in all its glory and while in plaintext. The gig is up. Sadly, after having gone from hand to hand and being protected that entire time, at this last moment the secret was revealed.

Maybe worse still, you are the one that revealed it (i.e., you being the intended receiver).

What went wrong?

Some might refer to this as the last-mile problem or perhaps more aptly coin it as the last-step problem in this instance.

You see, the catchphrases of last-mile or last-step are often used when describing a situation that has a kind of gap or arduous challenge at the very end of a task or activity. For example, in the telecommunications industry, there is the notion that the hardest and most costly part of providing high-speed networking to homes is the so-called last mile from the main trunk to the actual home of the consumer.

Envision a cable that runs down the middle of a neighborhood street and the last mile would be to make all the offshoot branches that need to extend from the centerline to each specific domicile. The number of such branches is high. It is one thing to simply lay down the center cable, while a hugely costly effort to then string out to each house. Even though the actual distance is not a mile long to get from the center to each house, the notion is that you've overall reached the proverbial last-mile or last step involved in the process.

This last-mile or last-step can be the weak link in a long chain of efforts.

Imagine expending an enormous amount of time and energy toward getting a slew of things done, and at the last stage, the matter is ultimately either untenable or somehow spoiled. This happened indeed in the scenario of you getting the purposely encrypted note. Once it got into your hands, you decrypted it and did not realize that you were being spied upon.

The classic line is to always make sure that you finish what you start. We might wish to definitively augment the line by adding that you need to finish fully and with the proper gusto, else the finish might be undermined and become the exasperating and disappointing point-of-weakness in a long series of otherwise careful steps.

In the cybersecurity field, there are three major ways that data such as the message on the note are usually intended to be protected or secured:

- Data at rest (standing still data)
- Data in transit (flowing data)
- Data in use (when being read or utilized)

Your friend's note to you was in transit when it was being passed along from person to person on its way to you. At some point, perhaps the note was sitting on someone's desk for a while, waiting for them to pick it up and continue the journey of the note to you. That would be data at rest.

That covers the data at rest and the data in transit instances.

When you opted to decrypt the note and take a look at what it said, the data was considered in use at that time. Per the saga, this is when things went awry and a despicable spy saw the message. Up until that moment, the message was relatively secret and secure. The last mile or last step exposed it.

I bring this up to highlight a hot new trend known as *confidential computing*.

We will use the tale of the encrypted note to help explore the nature of confidential computing. Admittedly, the parable per se is not wholly precisely on-target with the topic but you will soon see that it does offer a semblance of insightful parallels.

Confidential computing is usually associated with making use of cloud computing.

Cloud computing is the now familiar notion of using unseen computing resources that are available via remote access. Referring to this as cloud computing is an easy way to envision the matter and has fortuitously been an extremely catchy way to denote various computers as being "in the cloud" and available for use.

When your data is placed into a cloud-based computer, you likely want to feel comfortable that the data is well-protected. If the data is sitting in a database, perhaps a fiendish hacker might try to access the data. You want to prevent the cybercrook from being able to see your precious data, and ergo there are typically cybersecurity locks that seek to keep the bad hackers out of the database.

Suppose though the evildoer cracks through the locks. Aha, by encrypting the data, which is sitting at rest, the ability to do anything untoward with the data is greatly lessened. Though the hacker might be able to see the data, it is scrambled and generally unusable.

Imagine that there is a need to share the data and thus copy it to another database on a different computer. While the data is in this transit from one database to another, it is potentially vulnerable to prying eyes. If the data is encrypted while in transit, the interloper will presumably not gain much since the data is inscrutable.

We now are heading to the last mile or last step.

Assume that at some point the data will be needed for making calculations. The database with the encrypted data is accessed and the data while still encrypted is copied over to a computer that is doing the computations. All's good so far.

Upon the encrypted data being brought into the CPU (Central Processing Unit) of the computer, at this last-mile or last step, it is now necessary to decrypt it, else the data won't be of much use for making the desired calculations if otherwise remaining in an encrypted format.

Here is the potential loophole in all of this series of carefully encrypted steps. Now that the data is momentarily decrypted for use while inside the CPU, it becomes potentially open for a wrongdoer to peek at it. Akin to the saga of your having gotten the encrypted note into your hands, and then doing the decryption, there is a chance that someone might be spying and able to see the now in-the-clear message.

Your first thought might be that the idea of a cybercriminal hacking all the way into the inner guts of the CPU while it is processing seems nearly unimaginable.

Can they do really that?

The answer is yes, it is possible.

That being said, it is generally a quite difficult trick to pull off. Numerous system protections would have to be overcome. Nonetheless, a very determined and crafty cyber hacker could devise such a devilish scheme (especially when you include the nation-state's elements of cybersecurity).

This last-mile cybersecurity concern is being partially mitigated by the use of confidential computing.

Within the CPU of a confidential computing arranged computer, there is a special highly secure enclave setup. This is usually done via using a hardware-based environment that governs the execution of CPU running tasks. In industry parlance, this is known as a Trusted Execution Environment (TEE). Some keys or passwords are kept under added protection and used only when the last step occurs.

The enclave tries to hide from any other resources what is going on inside the enclave. Remember how you inadvertently allowed a spy to look over your shoulder? That is the type of intrusion that the enclave is fortress-like constructed to keep at bay.

Here's why this is especially relevant to cloud computing.

Suppose the cloud computer being used has somehow gotten malware on it. If there isn't a provided provision of confidential computing, the risks of the malware peeking at the CPU and also catching the data in an unencrypted format are heightened. Likewise, the OS or operating system of cloud computing could potentially take a peek (perhaps the OS then leaks it elsewhere), and even (sadly) there is a possibility that employees of the cloud provider might have access to take a look.

Via the use of the TEE and the enclave, the notion is that none of those other potential interlopers can see what is going on inside the CPU during the computational efforts. Furthermore, there is typically a feature of confidential computing that upon detecting that perhaps an interloper is trying to do something untoward, whatever CPU action might have been planned or underway is typically canceled and an alert is raised.

This could be likened to you having potentially noticed that a person was spying over your shoulder. I'd assume that had you realized the interloper was present, you would have stopped doing the decryption of the secret message. Of course, you might have already started to decrypt it, in which case maybe the interloper saw some of it, but at least you would curtail your activities at that juncture. Plus, you likely would have called for the cops to come and bust the reprehensible spy.

Most of the major cloud providers have made available various flavors of confidential computing, including the biggies such as IBM Cloud, Amazon AWS, Microsoft Azure, Google Cloud, Oracle Cloud, and others. The makers of CPUs are also integral to the confidential computing architecture and thus companies such as Intel, AMD, and the like are involved.

As eloquently stated in a paper by IBM Fellow and CTO for Cloud Security, Nataraj Nagaratnam: "As companies rely more and more on public and hybrid cloud services, data privacy in the cloud is imperative. The primary goal of confidential computing is to provide greater assurance to companies that their data in the cloud is protected and confidential, and to encourage them to move more of their sensitive data and computing workloads to public cloud services."

There is a well-known group called the Confidential Computing Consortium (CCC) that has banded together numerous cloud providers, hardware vendors, and software development outfits to focus on confidential computing. Per the posted CCC remarks of

Stephen Walli, Governing Board Chair: "The Confidential Computing Consortium is a community focused on open source licensed projects securing data in use and accelerating the adoption of confidential computing through open collaboration."

For those readers that are adept at programming, you likely know that your encrypted data while sitting on a database is usually decrypted once you bring the data into the internal memory of the computer system. This is done so that then the CPU can readily use the data for doing computations. In the confidential computing arrangement, the data is not decrypted until the final moment or last-mile or last-step of being placed into the CPU for use. Therefore, even while sitting in internal memory, the data is encrypted and less vulnerable to cyberattack.

One additional quick point is that this scheme for confidential computing does not guarantee that no one can ever hack it. The cybersecurity field is an ongoing game of cat and mouse. Each new protection that is devised will be deviously picked apart until some unforeseen hole or gotcha is discovered. The hole will usually get plugged. Meanwhile, the gambit continues as the cybercrooks try to find a means to undo or overcome the plug or look for other ways to break-in.

This is a never-ending cycle.

In that sense, the confidential computing approach is another added layer of cybersecurity. The more layers that you have, the odds are that it becomes increasingly harder for someone to crack through. At your home, you might have a gated fence around your property (a layer of protection), locks on your doors and windows (another layer of protection), and a motion detector inside the house (yet an additional layer). The belief is that by placing numerous hurdles in the way of a robber, they will be rebuffed in their intrusion efforts.

Having those added layers is not cost-free. For each layer, you need to ascertain the cost of the added protection versus the risks and consequences of someone breaking in. This is of course the same for confidential computing. Whether you require confidential computing is contingent on the type of computing activities you are undertaking, the magnitude of cybersecurity you are desirous of achieving, the risks and adverse consequences if a cyber breach occurs, etc.

Your car might also have various layers of security protection. There are locks on the car doors. The windows are made of materials that are hard to smash. Any motion immediately next to the vehicle might be detected and cause the horn to sound. And so on.

Speaking of cars, the future of cars consists of AI-based true self-driving cars.

Allow me to briefly elaborate on this point and then tie things to the topic of confidential computing.

There isn't a human driver involved in a true self-driving car. Keep in mind that true self-driving cars are driven via an AI driving system. There isn't a need for a human driver at the wheel, and nor is there a provision for a human to drive the vehicle.

Here's an intriguing question that is worth pondering: *Will confidential computing be useful for the advent of AI systems all told, and particularly for the advent of AI-based true self-driving cars?*

Before jumping into the details, I'd like to further clarify what is meant when referring to true self-driving cars.

AI And Self-Driving Cars And Confidential Computing

For Level 4 and Level 5 true self-driving vehicles, there won't be a human driver involved in the driving task.

All occupants will be passengers.

The AI is doing the driving.

One aspect to immediately discuss entails the fact that the AI involved in today's AI driving systems is not sentient. In other words, the AI is altogether a collective of computer-based programming and algorithms, and most assuredly not able to reason in the same manner that humans can.

Why this added emphasis about the AI not being sentient?

Because I want to underscore that when discussing the role of the AI driving system, I am not ascribing human qualities to the AI. Please be aware that there is an ongoing and dangerous tendency these days to anthropomorphize AI. In essence, people are assigning human-like sentience to today's AI, despite the undeniable and inarguable fact that no such AI exists as yet.

With that clarification, you can envision that the AI driving system won't natively somehow "know" about the facets of driving. Driving and all that it entails will need to be programmed as part of the hardware and software of the self-driving car.

Let's dive into the myriad of aspects that come to play on this topic.

One overarching point that is worthy of particular attention is that any AI system and especially ones running in the cloud should be potentially making use of confidential computing.

This is regrettably not a top-of-mind consideration for many AI developers.

The typical focus for AI software engineers is primarily on the underlying AI capabilities such as employing advanced uses of Machine Learning (ML) and Deep Learning (DL). Once the AI system is ready to be fielded, the AI builders tend to be less attentive to what happens when the program is placed into operational use. The assumption is that whatever existent cybersecurity is already available in the execution environment will probably be sufficient.

The average AI developer usually wants to get back to their AI bag-of-tricks and continue tweaking the AI-related elements of the system, or perhaps move onward to some other new development that requires their honed skills at crafting AI systems. Concerns about whether or not the prevailing execution environment for their budding AI system is highly secure does not explicitly enter into their mindset and nor is found in their usual toolset.

Some will exhort, hey, I'm not a darned cybersecurity expert, I'm an AI developer (that line is a heartfelt homage to the classic indication in *Star Trek* that hey, I'm a doctor, darn it, not an engineer).

The thing is, the best AI systems can be readily brought to their knees if the cybersecurity is not topnotch and using all available layers of protection. Up until recently, many AI systems were not necessarily aimed at domains that entailed potentially high risks and pronounced adverse consequences if the AI was undermined at execution.

Nowadays, with AI becoming pervasive across all manner of applications, the idea of treating AI systems as merely experimental or prototypes is now long gone.

Simply stated, any AI developer worth their salt should be seriously giving due consideration to how their AI systems will be deployed, including what kinds of cyberattacks might be launched to undercut the AI system processing. Since the AI developer ought to know what portends for especially vulnerable weaknesses in their AI while executing, they should take a close look at confidential computing as a potential countermeasure and gauge whether this added layer of security is warranted.

I'm not saying that it will always be a necessity, just that with AI systems of a sensitive nature running in the cloud, it is prudent and nearly obligatory to consider which of the numerous potential cybersecurity precautions should be undertaken.

Hopefully, that will be a useful call to arms for those AI developers that haven't yet taken into account the utility of confidential computing. And perhaps a startling wake-up blaring of trumpets for some.

Moving beyond the overall notion of all types of AI systems that are running in the cloud, let's next take a gander at the use of the cloud for the specific advent of AI-based true self-driving cars. The most commonly anticipated use of the cloud for self-driving cars encompasses the use of OTA (Over-The-Air) electronic communications capabilities.

Via OTA, various patches and updates stored in the cloud for a fleet of self-driving cars can be downloaded into each autonomous vehicle and accordingly installed, doing so automatically. This is handy to be able to remotely push out new features for the AI driving system or possibly provide bug fixes, plus avoiding having to bring the vehicles to a dealer site or some repair shop merely to do needed software updates.

The OTA will also enable the ease of uploading data from the self-driving cars into the fleet-provided cloud. Self-driving cars will have a sensor suite that includes video cameras, radar, LIDAR, ultrasonic units, thermal imagining, and other such devices. The data they collect can be usefully analyzed by collecting together the data across an entire fleet of self-driving cars and then conglomerating it while in the cloud.

So, you might be wondering, what does this have to do with confidential computing?

Think of it this way, if there are programs and data in the cloud that are going to potentially be downloaded and installed into the AI driving systems, this becomes a handy and sneaky path for a cyber attacker to get their malware into the self-driving cars. The cybercrook merely plants the evil-doing elements into the cloud and then patiently waits until the OTA mechanism does the rest of the work for the wrongdoer by broadcasting it out into the fleet.

Whereas most people tend to be thinking about how an AI driving system might get corrupted or undermined by someone physically accessing the autonomous vehicle, the likely greater threat comes from using the OTA to do so. The innocent beauty of the OTA is that it is an already assumed trusted avenue to directly get something inserted into the AI driving system, and this will happen across an entire fleet of self-driving cars. Imagine that there were hundreds, maybe thousands, perhaps hundreds of thousands of self-driving cars and all of them were using an OTA to get updates from a fleet cloud.

Okay, so we might want to put some devoted attention to what is happening in the fleet cloud. The more cybersecurity we put there, the lessened the chances that the OTA will become a specter of doom. It could be that the judicious use of confidential computing for the fleet cloud will curtail or at least make much harder the possibility of launching a cyberattack that might inevitably get carried out into the AI driving systems of the fleet.

Conclusion

Another potential use of confidential computing would be for the execution or processing that takes place inside self-driving cars.

When the AI driving system is being executed on the onboard computer processors, this execution obviously needs to be highly secure too. The tough tradeoff is that confidential computing tends to incur a performance hit on the processors and thus presents a somewhat complicated consideration when dealing with real-time systems. Keep in mind that real-time processing is controlling the actions of the self-driving car. Any substantive delay in processing times can be problematic.

Self-driving cars are real-time machines that also just so happen to involve life-or-death matters. You typically do not have that same life-or-death concern for an everyday cloud-based application. If the cloud processing has any modicum of delay, this might be of little consequence. In addition, because a cloud-based application resides in the cloud, you can readily toss more processors at the application or reallocate to using faster processors available in the cloud.

For a self-driving car, the processors installed into the autonomous vehicle are generally not as readily switched out, since that can be a very physical effort and logistically costly to undertake. Automakers and self-driving tech firms are pretty much stuck once they've decided which processors to put into their self-driving cars. They've got to hope that the choice will last a while.

CHAPTER 14
BIKE RIDERS AND SELF-DRIVING CARS

This happens in real life.

A bike rider was cruising along on a nice sunny day. Riding a bicycle while in city traffic is always a dicey proposition. Cars often inadvertently weave directly toward bike riders or veer precariously into reserved bike lanes and pinch or endanger the cyclists therein.

Most of the time, a cyclist is watching the cars that are in motion. That would seem the prudent focus of attention. A moving vehicle can quickly bear down toward a bike rider. All it takes is a split second and a horrific life-threatening collision can result.

There is though another menace awaiting the unsuspecting bike rider.

In one word: *Dooring.*

You've likely seen dooring depicted in movies and TV shows. Perhaps you've witnessed a dooring event or possibly encountered one directly.

Dooring is an abysmal situation when a car door is opened and a bike rider collides with the door or otherwise suffers a vehicular-related injury or worse as a result of the door-related incident. It could be that the bike rider rams into the open door and then goes flying off their bicycle. There are bound to be injuries due to the collision with the door and the subsequent smacking onto the street after being briefly airborne.

The potential for injury doesn't end with the initial collision itself. There is also a chance that the bike rider will end up stranded amid traffic. Thus, cars zipping along might run into or even run over the thrown bike rider. These secondary cascading effects can be just as bad or possibly even worse than whatever trauma occurred upon striking the open door.

Legally, here's an example of what the law typically says, in this case via the California DMV Vehicle Code section 22517: "No person shall open the door of a vehicle on the side available to moving traffic unless it is reasonably safe to do so and can be done without interfering with the movement of such traffic, nor shall any person leave a door open on the side of a vehicle available to moving traffic for a period of time longer than necessary to load or unload passengers."

It seems doubtful that most people would know word-for-word that particular law, but a semblance of common sense would seem to be sufficient to realize that you ought not to open a car door unless it is safe to do so. You would think that people would intrinsically know that seemingly obvious fact. If you open a car door and don't do so mindfully, bad things can happen.

Unfortunately, having such a rule of thumb in mind at all times when opening a car door is not necessarily in the cards. A passenger might be thinking of ten other things. Maybe they are late for an appointment. Perhaps they are thinking about work. The passenger could be eager to get out of the vehicle, doing so after a lengthy car trip. All in all, it is easy to swing open a car door and just do so without an iota of consideration for what might happen next.

Of course, the absent-minded door opening act could be done not just by passengers, but directly by the driver too. A driver might just as likely open their driver's side car door and do so without anticipating the traffic situation as would a passenger. We would normally assume that the driver should be more conscious of what the traffic is. As the driver, they presumably are alert to how traffic is flowing.

Nonetheless, a driver might open their door and produce a dooring incident. It can happen. It does happen. Statistics on such incidents are somewhat spotty on the specific instances of dooring and oftentimes simply get lumped into bicyclist-related car collision accidents. Some counts suggest that perhaps 10% to 15% of bike collisions encompass a dooring event.

Dooring is a worldwide problem.

On an international basis, the Vienna Convention provides this rule known as Article 24 which is similar to the California DMV language: "It shall be prohibited to open the door of a vehicle, to leave it open, or to alight from the vehicle without having made sure that to do so cannot endanger other road users."

One key aspect to keep in mind is that there is the sudden act of opening a car door, which is one type of dooring, and then there is the act of leaving a car door open for a prolonged period. It is easy to think that if a door is ajar for any sustained period of time, certainly a bike rider won't ram into it. The bike rider ought to presumably notice that the door is open and take preemptive maneuvers to avoid striking into it.

Yes, there might be more time available and the door might be earlier noticed, but the options of what to do might be without much viable recourse. The bike rider could consider jamming on their bike brakes and try to come to a halt before ramming into the open door. The effort to use your bike brakes in this manner is problematic and you might go flying off your bike in the very act of trying to avoid striking the open door.

Another presumed possibility is that the bike rider can swerve away from the open door. Consider though the potential options at hand. You can steer into moving traffic and take your chances that a car underway will run you over or you can proceed into the open car door and hope for a "better" outcome. This is one of those tough choices in life between the lesser of two evils.

Neither choice is desirable.

Bike riders are classified as VRUs (vulnerable roadway users). This is official terminology that reminds us of the dangers for anyone that perchance comes around or into contact with cars and other vehicles on our streets and highways. A pedestrian is also considered a VRU. VRUs are all at the potential mercy of our car-centric infrastructure. Dangers lurk at every nook and cranny.

This brings up an interesting point. We usually consider the person that opened the car door to be the one that is most at fault for what happens during a dooring event. Turns out there is likely plenty of faults to go around in such incidents.

Though the bike rider is rarely considered at fault, that is a possibility. I know that notion rankles most bike riders. They would assert that there is never an occasion where a dooring event could be construed as the fault of the cyclist. Without getting into that rather heated and acrimonious debate, let's just say that it is remotely possible that a bike rider could have been lax in their bike riding and ended up engulfed in a dooring event that they otherwise could have been averted.

As earlier mentioned, the car driver could be the one that opened their car door and thus led to the dooring incident. We can look at the car driver for having a different form of fault or responsibility in these matters. Perhaps the car driver has parked the vehicle in a place or situation that has increased the odds of a dooring circumstance.

For example, a driver of a ridesharing vehicle opts to come to a quick stop at a curb that is just at the corner of a busy street. In a sense, the driver is subtly and silently signaling to the passenger that this is the right spot to get out of the vehicle. The passenger assumes that the driver has chosen a safe place for a disembarking action. In that way of thinking, the passenger swings open their door.

Bang, a bicyclist that came around the corner rams into the wide-open door.

Was this the fault of the driver that led the passenger into a kind of hidden trap?

For my discussion about the difficulties of deciding upon suitable PUDO (pick-up, drop-off) selections.

You might fervently argue that no matter what the driver does or doesn't do, this in no way excuses the dolt of a passenger that opted to open their car door without first making sure the coast was clear. On the other hand, you could counterargue that the passenger was relying upon the skill and professionalism of the car driver to ensure that exiting from the vehicle could be done without any danger or harm.

One clever notion about opening car doors is to always make use of the so-called *Dutch reach*. As popularized by the Dutch, the idea is that you should form a habit of opening a car door via your other hand, the one furthest from the door itself. By grasping the internal door handle via your other arm and hand, you are forcing yourself into making a bodily twisting motion. In the midst of this twisting motion, you will hopefully be reminded to look over your shoulder before you open that potentially bike-rider colliding door.

It's a cool idea.

The practicality of it is somewhat less convincing. Will people that use this trick become used to it and therefore form a habit that fails to include the looking-outward part of the chore? You might argue that this clever ploy only should be used when the traffic conditions seem to spur such a precaution. This though then leaves the possibility that it isn't employed when the right moment, or shall we say the wrong moment, actually arises.

On top of that, we need to consider whether a passenger that opens a door is going to have a sufficient perspective to gauge whether the door opening is a free and clear act. Some passengers admittedly don't look at all. They just open that darned door, heck or high water. The next level of awareness entails making a quick peek at the traffic. I'd bet that most passengers are looking for any cars or trucks, more so than a cyclist. The general belief likely being that the passenger is watching for their own skin and they know that if they open the door and a car or truck sideswipes the door, it could be curtains for the passenger.

Only a tinier fraction of passengers is likely looking out for bike riders. Again, whether they are doing so for the sake of the cyclist or their own neck is somewhat in question. A passenger might swing open the door, realize they are endangering a bike rider, and decide not to close the door but instead just slump back into the car to avoid getting hit.

It would seem that a passenger that carefully scans for a bike rider and opts to open a car door, only after fully believing that there is no bike rider within eye distance, would be a somewhat rare bird. And, not wanting to seem gloomy, even that instance has a chance of still catching a bike rider into the door.

Why so?

Bike riders can be moving very fast.

They can also be hard to see.

A cyclist is relatively thin from a heads-on viewpoint and when coming at a vehicle on the side the cyclist is usually not easy to see. There is also a decided time factor involved in the effort of performing the door opening and getting out of the vehicle. You might while inside the car be able to glance and see that no bike riders seem to be nearby. You then take a second or two to go ahead and open the car door.

You then undo your seatbelt and start to swing your body to get out of the vehicle.

This could take a few additional seconds.

Let's suppose that the whole act of opening the car door and getting out of the vehicle is around five to maybe ten seconds in length. This doesn't even include the possible added time for perhaps saying some parting remarks to the driver, or for possibly reaching into the vehicle to grab your smartphone that has fallen out of your pocket while seated in the car. There are gobs of reasons that the timing of getting out of the car could be extended.

If we do some quick calculations, a bike rider that is proceeding at a modest speed of 10 miles per hour would go a distance of about 150 feet in roughly ten seconds. Let's use an approximation that an average car length is about 15 feet. This means that the bike rider would be potentially around 10 car lengths behind the vehicle that is in the act of having the door opened.

Could a passenger readily see outside the vehicle and a distance of about ten car lengths to detect whether a bike rider is approaching?

This is dubious in any kind of busy city setting. There are likely lots of other distractions and obstructions that render this kind of detection extremely arduous. Envision lots of cars and trucks streaming past the car that has this keenly observing passenger. Pedestrians are walking around and near the car. Parked cars are nearby. All in all, this is a very cluttered scene.

While we are still on the hunt for who might be at fault in dooring events, one supposes that we could include into the ragtag bunch the street planners and roadway engineers too. It is conceivable that the place that the car has stopped to allow for disembarking was not carefully designed or devised for this ancillary purpose. The driver might claim that they were enticed into stopping at that position. The passenger might insist they relied upon the driver and the roadway infrastructure design as a means to make a decision to open the car door.

Yikes!

One supposes that the best approach to avoiding dooring would consist of never getting out of a car toward any semblance of street traffic. For example, always slide over to the sidewalk side of the vehicle and get out there. This lamentably can be nearly impossible for car drivers in vehicles of today that pretty much always have bucket seats rather than bench-style seating.

Passengers need to be more aware of the dangers of dooring.

Trying to educate passengers is an uphill climb. Any awareness programs are usually in one ear and out the other (this is not dissing those attempts, only pointing out that there is a hefty decay rate of remembering to avoid dooring).

Car drivers need to be on their toes too. Do not park or stop in a place and time that might be conducive to a dooring incident, since this heightens the risks of such an occurrence. Furthermore, it would sure be nice if the car driver cautioned the passenger about getting out of the vehicle and proffered ways to do so as safely as feasible.

Bike riders have to be watching for all kinds of dangers, including dooring. Savvy cyclists tend to glance into the windows of cars up ahead of them that are parked and appear to be stationary. The hope is that you might see the head of someone in the vehicle or movement therein and deduce that they soon might abruptly open a door. In addition, you need to watch for the slightest movement of a car door, which will be an early clue that the door might be opening up.

Adding to this harsh burden, the cyclist should be continually analyzing the activities around them. Did a car just pull over to a stop, and if so, this could spell a dooring incident in the making? If a dooring begins to emerge, what options are available to avoid the collision? The sooner that the cyclist is cognizant of a dooring potential, the better their chances of taking evasive actions beforehand.

In terms of the roadway designers and street planners, the hope by urban mobility experts is that the cyclists and those ubiquitous cars ought to be kept apart as much as possible, doing so by the nature of the roadway infrastructure. This is easier said than done. Many of our cities are faced with a space crunch and a budget crunch that makes trying to separate bikers from cars a challenging proposal.

Speaking of cars, the future of cars consists of AI-based true self-driving cars.

Allow me to briefly elaborate on this point and then tie things to the topic of dooring.

There isn't a human driver involved in a true self-driving car. Keep in mind that true self-driving cars are driven via an AI driving system. There isn't a need for a human driver at the wheel, and nor is there a provision for a human to drive the vehicle.

Here's an intriguing question that is worth pondering: *Will dooring still occur in an era of AI-based true self-driving cars or will AI driving systems stridently ensure that dooring never happens again?*

A recent online posting of an interview with Waymo's Eric Deng, a product manager focused on autonomous driving in the context of cyclists and also micro-mobility devices, eloquently illuminates the importance of self-driving cars being infused with dooring awareness: "Dooring occurs when a vehicle is pulled over and ready to pull out back onto the road, and a cyclist is traveling on the road to the vehicle's left, passengers exiting the vehicle may not be aware of potential cyclists which could be coming from behind." And per his remarks: "At the end of the day, we are focused on helping to ensure that the cars we operate in the real world exhibit the right behaviors around cyclists and micro-mobility users."

Before jumping into some crucial overarching details about dooring, I'd like to further clarify what is meant when I refer to true self-driving cars.

Self-Driving Cars And Dooring Events

For Level 4 and Level 5 true self-driving vehicles, there won't be a human driver involved in the driving task.

All occupants will be passengers.

The AI is doing the driving.

One aspect to immediately discuss entails the fact that the AI involved in today's AI driving systems is not sentient. In other words, the AI is altogether a collective of computer-based programming and algorithms, and most assuredly not able to reason in the same manner that humans can.

Why this added emphasis about the AI not being sentient?

Because I want to underscore that when discussing the role of the AI driving system, I am not ascribing human qualities to the AI. Please be aware that there is an ongoing and dangerous tendency these days to anthropomorphize AI. In essence, people are assigning human-like sentience to today's AI, despite the undeniable and inarguable fact that no such AI exists as yet.

With that clarification, you can envision that the AI driving system won't natively somehow "know" about the facets of driving. Driving and all that it entails will need to be programmed as part of the hardware and software of the self-driving car.

Let's dive into the myriad of aspects that come to play on this topic.

First, an important clarification about the *gradual* advent of self-driving cars would be insightful for this discussion. Some pundits seem to suggest that there will be an overnight switchover from conventional human-driven cars to self-driving cars. This is portrayed as a seamless activity that miraculously somehow does away with conventional cars and replaces them with self-driving cars.

Seems like nonsense.

There are about 275 million conventional cars in the United States alone and they are not going anywhere. Do not visualize them as elephants that will disappear off the stage akin to a magic show.

The odds are that a build-up toward using self-driving cars will take many years to occur, on the order of likely decades. Inch by inch, conventional cars will be gradually retired or junked. Inch by inch, the proportion of self-driving cars on public roadways will rise in comparison to the number of conventional cars.

We don't know that conventional cars will entirely be tossed aside, even after a lengthy time period of transition from human driving to autonomous driving. Exhortations by some drivers are that you will take away their driving privileges only when you pry their cold dead hands from the steering wheel. A counterargument about that kind of stubbornness is that if self-driving cars do away with the foibles of human driving, and ergo the number of car crashes and fatalities can be lowered, perhaps human driving will be revoked and no humans will be permitted to drive in public lands (being allowed to drive presumably on private lands, for sake of hobbies, general interest, etc.).

Anyway, the main point here is that in terms of dooring events, there are still going to be human-driven cars on the roadway. You cannot dreamily wish them to vanish into thin air. This also means that those human drivers, when getting out of their cars when they come to a halt will potentially still invoke a dooring situation. It will happen.

In addition, this also means that passengers riding in a human-driven car will still be able to do a dooring event. Regardless of whether it is the driver's fault or the passenger's fault, the same status we have today could pretty much take place in an era of self-driving car prevalence.

Okay, but maybe we can have solace in the notion that the AI driving systems will not incur the dooring events.

One obvious piece of logic is that if there isn't a human driver, there isn't a chance of the driver opening the door and conking a cyclist.

Well, maybe yes, maybe no.

Here's the rub.

Some AI self-driving cars are anticipated to have the AI driving system undertake a wide range of tasks, beyond simply driving the autonomous vehicle. For example, the AI driving system might be mechanically able to open the car doors. When a human passenger walks up to the self-driving car, it will welcome the person by opening the car door for them. Upon finishing a driving journey, the AI driving system might open the door to let the passenger out of the car.

In that manner of approach, this suggests that a dooring event could still occur and be undertaken or sparked via the driver, though in this use case it is the AI driving system. Oddly, we find ourselves in the same kind of predicament as the onerous case of the human driver. In some respects, maybe worse so because the AI driving system could presumably open any and all car doors.

Envision that the self-driving car has four passengers. Arriving at the designated destination to drop off the passengers, the AI driving system opens all four car doors. All at once. You now have quite a frightening dooring event primed and ready to happen.

The saving grace would be that the AI driving system would assuredly be programmed to look around the self-driving car before opening the doors. Self-driving cars will be outfitted with a sensor suite consisting of video cameras, radar, LIDAR, ultrasonic units, thermal imagining, and other related devices. These can be used to capture data of the surroundings. Via the use of Machine Learning (ML) and Deep Learning (DL), the data can be scanned to try and detect any nearby bike riders.

Unlike a human driver that opts to open the car door, the AI driving system would do this on a more systematic basis. All of the time. Humans are not quite as reliable and consistent at such a task.

Furthermore, the AI driving system would be doing the same for the passengers, in terms of checking to make sure the chances of a dooring event are slim. A human driver might or might not decide to look around and forewarn any passengers. The AI driving system ought to be programmed to do this without any hesitation and provide a green light of sorts to the passengers when they can disembark.

Some argue that self-driving cars should even be able to keep the doors closed, despite any passenger attempt to open a car door. The belief is that if a passenger tries to open a car door, yet imagine that the AI driving system has informed them not to do so, the AI driving system can override the human passenger and refuse to let the door open. This would seem to protect the upcoming cyclist in an instance of a potential dooring event and likewise protect the passenger from potential injury too.

The idea that the AI driving system could utterly refuse to open a car door and countermand a human passenger is crazy talk for some. We ought not to have AI that won't do what a human says to do, they decry. Suppose for example the passenger has a dire reason to get out of the self-driving car and the AI driving system is refusing to allow the urgent exit. Bad stuff.

Conclusion

There are a lot more twists and turns involved.

To what degree will the sensors be able to properly detect a cyclist that is approaching the self-driving car?

You cannot assume that this is a foolproof method of always spotting a cyclist. Obstructions and other factors could reduce the probability that the sensors will catch the quickly moving cyclist.

One hope is that we will eventually have widely adopted electronic devices to have a bike-to-car communication link. Similar to V2V (vehicle-to-vehicle) or V2P (vehicle-to-pedestrian) electronic communications, a cyclist will have a device on their person or perhaps mounted onto the bike that transmits an electronic beacon alerting cars about the presence of the underway cyclist.

Will the AI driving system judiciously park the autonomous vehicle in a suitable place to avoid the chances of a dooring event?

Some would say that the AI developers have enough on their plate right now of getting self-driving cars to go from point A to point B safely. Concerns about where to best stop or halt the vehicle for a disembarking passenger are a lower priority and ranked by some as an edge or corner case (meaning it will be dealt with later on).

Another twist is that the AI driving system ought to warn passersby when the car doors are being opened. Perhaps the flashers of the car are switched on or the horn is honked, occurring automatically by the AI driving system.

Returning to the earlier point that we will still have human drivers, there is even a twist about that otherwise seemingly gloomy element regarding the continuance of dooring events. The odds are that a lot of the high-tech gadgetry used on self-driving cars will be brought over into conventional cars too.

Thus, if there are special features invented for self-driving cars about avoiding dooring, those might be transferred over into human-driven cars too.

The bottom line for bike riders is that you will need to *always* keep your eyes open and your wits about you. As long as cars and bicycles can mingle together on our streets, the specter of dooring will remain a formidable foe. You might be a bit more reassured once there are a lot of self-driving cars roaming around but do not let your guard completely down.

Humans need to be watchful, even when AI is doing the driving.

CHAPTER 15
HEAT WAVE AND SELF-DRIVING CARS

How hot is it?

That's the kind of question that you probably don't want to be asked when you are broiling in the existing heatwave that has engulfed much of the country. This latest mega-heat scorcher is said to be the worst of its kind since this century began.

There is the old familiar line that it is hot enough to fry an egg on the street.

Turns out this is usually a false claim since the required temps need to be about 140 to 158 degrees Fahrenheit to apparently fry an egg (per news reports), and rarely does the pavement or street particularly rise to that esteemed temperature. But in some locales, such as the Las Vegas area, there are current reports that the asphalt is supposedly a sizzling 170 degrees Fahrenheit.

Get those eggs ready if you'd like some street-cooked grub.

When it gets this hot, most people smartly opt to try and remain inside and avoid going outside if at all possible. By staying inside, you presumably have some semblance of shade and hopefully, also have cooling fans or its equivalent to keep you cool.

Stepping outside can be a shock. A blast of hot searing air can confront you. Taking a walk is not only a sweltering activity, it can be dangerous to your health. Hospitals are indicating that there is a rising tide of people suffering from heatstroke. In addition, many go for a walk and find themselves suddenly collapsing from acute dehydration.

Please be careful out there.

There is an added twist that you might not be thinking about, and for which until you live in such hot temperatures you might not intuitively realize is an additional endangering factor.

It is this: *Everyday objects outdoors that we might tend to touch or handle are red hot too.*

There isn't necessarily any signal or sign of this consideration. You just need to keep it in your own mind and be cautious accordingly.

For example, opening a car door can be a surprisingly dangerous task. If the car has been parked outdoors and directly in the blazing sunlight, the door handles can be extremely hot. Really, really hot. So hot that you can burn the skin of your hand when trying to simply open the car door.

Sad to say that there are burn victims that end up in the hospital from the mere act of trying to use their car. Besides the door handles, there are other parts of the car that you might normally touch and that can be equally hazardous when heated up. This might surprise you that even the seatbelt can be a burner, namely if there is a metallic portion that is used to buckle the seat (usually this is the case).

People unknowingly and by normal habit reach up to pull the seatbelt across them and then snap it into the buckle, finding themselves suddenly with a severe palm or hand burn from this innocuous activity. It is at that moment that you become suspicious of everything inside the vehicle as a potential source of bruising heat. Steering wheels are usually coated with a material that is less likely to absorb the heat, so that might be touchable for driving purposes. Knobs and switches are probably tolerable.

Those that live or frequent the hottest areas seem to grow accustomed to these insidious heat-scorching traps. Some try using their foot to pry open the car door or wear gloves or use their shirt to cover their hand as they do so. You can see these contortionist attempts when the temps get searing hot. For those that perchance have a car that provides an automatic door opening feature, they relish the capability during these blistering times.

Using your car in lieu of walking to someplace certainly seems sensible during a heatwave.

That is, as long as your car itself does not serve as some form of heated peril. The interior air that has been trapped inside a parked car can be scorching too. People immediately open all the windows of the vehicle to vent out the hot air. The downside is that if the outside air is quite hot, you are not necessarily gaining that much in terms of somehow transferring cooler air into the vehicle (but still worth trying).

We most likely relish our car at these times for the most wonderful of inventions known to mankind, consisting of air conditioning. You can travel to a destination and bask in the refreshingly cool air that the vehicle provides to you via the air conditioner. Admittedly, some people decidedly go for a ride around town solely to make use of the air conditioning inside their car. Their house or apartment potentially lacks air conditioning and so they opt to use their car for a moment of respite from the heat.

If you use ridesharing or ride-hailing service during these hot days, the odds are that the driver has already cranked up the air conditioning and made sure that the vehicle is cool inside. The driver might also warn you about touching the door handles and the seatbelt buckle. In some cases, the driver could potentially get out of the car to open the car door for you or assist in buckling the seatbelt, perhaps being more adept at avoiding getting burned in the process.

Depending upon where you are going while on a ridesharing journey, there is an additional consideration about where you will be dropped off upon reaching your desired destination.

Here's the deal.

The ridesharing driver notices that there are some delivery vans in front of the office building that you were going to be dropped off at.

This essentially blocks the ridesharing car from being able to park there and let you out. Thus, the driver stops further down the block and tells you that you can get out of the car now.

If this is in a spot without any shade, you can find yourself suddenly baking in the heat. Also, the walking distance from that point to the office building might be onerous. Sure, it could be only a half-block away, yet in this kind of stifling weather, it is like a grueling marathon of walking.

An astute ridesharing driver will try to find the best spot to do a drop-off, including being as close as possible to your desired destination and accommodate any potential shade or similar protection from the heat and the sun.

On a semi-related topic, people sometimes don't realize that they can get a bad sunburn while inside an air-conditioned car. Though the interior of the vehicle might be refreshingly cool, the rays of the sun can be nonetheless beaming into the vehicle. A passenger seated in the front is bound to get more sun rays due to being directly under the windshield and having the side windows as added exposure. Passengers in the backseat can get scorched via sun rays coming into the side windows. Of course, the driver can get sunburned too.

To try and combat this sunburn possibility, some cars have special shades or other materials to cover the windows and try to reduce the power of the sun. This is especially important if you have a baby in a backseat carriage that would otherwise have no direct means of warning you about a sunburn underway. Meanwhile, adults might opt to apply suntan lotion to themselves if they are taking a long driving journey or possibly cover up by wearing sun resilient clothing.

You probably hadn't been thinking about all these facets of using a car while in extremely hot weather.

This is not particularly at top of most minds. Until you find yourself in these mega-heat wave situations, the odds are that you won't be contemplating ways that a car can be both useful to avoid the heat and yet at the same time be a potential threat due to the heat.

Speaking of cars, the future of cars consists of AI-based true self-driving cars.

Allow me a moment to elaborate.

There isn't a human driver involved in a true self-driving car. Keep in mind that true self-driving cars are driven via an AI driving system. There isn't a need for a human driver at the wheel, and nor is there a provision for a human to drive the vehicle.

Here's an intriguing question that is worth pondering: *How might AI-based true self-driving cars be of particular help to us when massive heat waves occur?*

Before jumping into the details, I'd like to further clarify what is meant when I refer to true self-driving cars.

Self-Driving Cars And Coping With Heat Waves

For Level 4 and Level 5 true self-driving vehicles, there won't be a human driver involved in the driving task.

All occupants will be passengers.

The AI is doing the driving.

One aspect to immediately discuss entails the fact that the AI involved in today's AI driving systems is not sentient. In other words, the AI is altogether a collective of computer-based programming and algorithms, and most assuredly not able to reason in the same manner that humans can.

Why this added emphasis about the AI not being sentient?

Because I want to underscore that when discussing the role of the AI driving system, I am not ascribing human qualities to the AI. Please be aware that there is an ongoing and dangerous tendency these days to anthropomorphize AI. In essence, people are assigning human-like sentience to today's AI, despite the undeniable and inarguable fact that no such AI exists as yet.

With that clarification, you can envision that the AI driving system won't natively somehow "know" about the facets of driving. Driving and all that it entails will need to be programmed as part of the hardware and software of the self-driving car.

Let's dive into the myriad of aspects that come to play on this topic.

First, it is believed by many pundits that self-driving cars will be a lot less costly to use than human-driven cars. The notion is that the price per mile that you might be paying to use a human-driven ridesharing vehicle is going to be substantially lower if you use of a self-driving car instead. A key part of this lowered cost is that there is no labor required to drive the autonomous vehicle.

For the sake of society, it is presumed that we might be heading toward a mobility-for-all era. Those that today cannot afford to use a car for transit will now be able to do so. The assumption too is that there will be gobs and gobs of self-driving cars roaming all around, being available at a moment's notice to provide a requested ride.

Here's how this ties to the heatwave topic.

Imagine that someone is in their home and they lack any semblance of cooling capabilities. They don't have air conditioning in their house or apartment. The inside of their home has gotten super-heated due to the overwhelming heat wave taking place. They are becoming anxious at the heat and can feel that they are starting to succumb to it.

One possibility of providing temporary relief would be to send them a self-driving car as a form of refrigerator on wheels, as it were.

The self-driving car is dispatched to the person's home. The autonomous vehicle has automatically engaged the air conditioning inside the vehicle to ensure that the interior is pleasingly cool. Upon reaching the home, the person comes out and gets into the self-driving car.

Self-driving cars will likely be outfitted with Natural Language Processing (NLP), akin to the likes of today's Alexa or Siri. As such, the AI driving system might emit a message to the passenger to forewarn them about the door handles as possibly being hot to handle, and likewise to be mindful of any interior items that might be overly hot.

Designers of self-driving cars are also likely to have a feature enabling the AI driving system to automatically open the doors of the vehicle. This would be handy in the case of a heatwave. A passenger would not need to touch the door handles and instead the AI system would open and close the car doors as needed for the rider.

In conventional cars of today, there is a windshield and numerous car windows, all of which generally are required for purposes of allowing the driver to see the roadway. Self-driving cars will be equipped with video cameras, radar, LIDAR, ultrasonic units, thermal imagining devices, and the like. These will effectively act as the eyes and ears of the AI driving system.

Thus, there isn't any need for a windshield and nor for the windows of the car. They can be replaced with a shell and you would be riding somewhat inside a bubble. Various futuristic car designs showcase this type of structure.

It seems a bit unlikely that people will necessarily be desirous of riding inside a shell. The odds are that at least for some time ahead, passengers will still relish looking out the windows of the vehicle. A counterargument is that this would still be feasible with the shell structure, doing so by using the outside mounted video cameras and having the images streamed onto the interior surface of the shell. In a manner of speaking, you would be "looking" outside, though you are seeing the streaming camera images instead of being able to directly peer out a window.

In any case, the windows of a self-driving car are bound to have the capability to automatically switch from being transparent to suddenly being opaque. You can ask the AI driving system to let you see directly out the windows and the windows will be made visibly clear. You can tell the AI driving system that you want some privacy and the glass will be shifted into an opaque mode. Various efforts are underway to devise windows of this nature. Even if the windows cannot do this directly, there could be shades or similar coverings that would be operable via a human passenger or by the AI driving system.

All of that discussion highlights that the notion of getting sunburned while on a riding journey could potentially be averted via a properly provisioned self-driving car.

The AI driving system would also hopefully be programmed to cope with the drop-off problem that was earlier mentioned. Specifically, upon reaching the desired destination, the AI driving system should try to find the best feasible spot to drop off a passenger. This would include the aspects of being closest to the destination along with the need for shade or another protective cover at the arrival point.

Conclusion

At first glance, it would seem somewhat outlandish to think that people might go for rides in a self-driving car solely for purposes of getting out of the heat. Well, if the cost to use a self-driving car is as low as some believe it will be, this might make the self-driving car an alluring aid in the dire circumstances of a heatwave.

Another angle would simply be that people could more readily get transported to a location that does offer some sustaining cooler conditions.

For example, the government sets up a local site that has plenty of air conditioning and cool water, being available as an emergency center for those that otherwise have housing that is not bearable in the heat. It is handy to have such a place to go, but the question oftentimes arises as to the logistics and cost of getting people to the center (and, later on, providing a lift back home once the heat subsides).

Imagine a fleet of self-driving cars that are sent out to go pick up the people that wish to use the center. Unlike human-driven cars, there is no need to coordinate amongst all the drivers that would be needed for such a large-scale task. You merely schedule online the self-driving cars to go to the designated homes to pick up people and bring them to the center.

In a similar vein, suppose you have a loved one that lives in a heatwave locale. They are suffering from the heat and their home does not have sufficient cooling. You might ask them to drive to you and stay at your place. Perhaps they aren't comfortable at the wheel anymore or lack a driver's license.

You can send them a self-driving car to come to pick them up and bring them to your locale.

In theory, this could be only across town or could be across entire states and even across the whole country.

Here's why.

The expectation is that self-driving cars will allow us to travel greater distances than we customarily do today. With a human-driven car, the driver needs to take breaks, they can get tired and should not be at the wheel while groggy, etc. The AI driving system can drive essentially non-stop, going 24 x 7 as needed (excluding aspects such as refueling, maintenance, and the like).

You can use a self-driving car to take a rather lengthy driving journey. Many proposed designs suggest that the interior seats will be reclinable and allow riders to take a snooze. That long trip from point A to point B can be done while you are sleeping. You get into the self-driving car in the evening, it drives all night long, and in the morning you arrive at your destination, refreshed after traveling possibly many hundreds of miles.

Not all though is quite so rosy about the use of self-driving cars during a heatwave.

Let's consider one potential downside.

A prevailing assumption is that most self-driving cars will be EVs (electrical vehicles). This makes sense for numerous reasons. Where the catch comes in would be that the self-driving cars will need to be charged up and this usually will be done at an electrical charging station. Some locales are at times having electrical blackouts when the heat waves strike. This is partially due to the heightened use of electricity by people running air conditioning units and assorted cooling devices in their homes and offices, consuming boosted levels of electricity when a heatwave strikes.

The point is that if self-driving cars were especially avidly being used as an aid during heat waves, they would be another gobbling source of consuming electricity. This begs the question of whether enough electrical generating capacity would exist to accommodate self-driving cars being used in the fashion described herein.

There might be a need to restrict the use of self-driving cars. Envision that self-driving cars had to be placed onto a priority list as to whether they can fully charge up or not. This would be a thorny choice of potentially idling the self-driving cars versus ensuring that there was sufficient electricity to power people's homes and businesses.

A vexing choice, that's for sure. All of this will need to be worked out as the advent of self-driving cars gradually takes place.

We do have some time available. You should not be expecting self-driving cars will just magically start appearing overnight. The emergence of self-driving cars will take many decades to become pervasive, given that we today have about 275 million conventional cars and those aren't going to be summarily junked or dumped just because self-driving cars become viable.

We can look forward to the day that self-driving cars become widespread, and for which the catchphrase might be that to beat the heat, make sure to use an AI-based true self-driving car.

CHAPTER 16
WHISTLEBLOWERS AND SELF-DRIVING CARS

There is the old saying that you ought to not look in the kitchen when you go to some restaurants or eateries for a bite to eat.

When you see how the food is being prepared it might just make you sick to your stomach. Worse still, eating the food could be detrimental to your health.

There are tons of ways to improperly make a meal. A kitchen that isn't following the right kinds of safety efforts can generate a breakfast, lunch, or dinner that could cause foul problems for the unsuspecting soul that decided to eat the monstrosity. It can be hard to realize that a plate of food placed in front of you might be poorly cooked or contains noxious ingredients that might make you ill.

Most people take for granted that a given eatery is following the proper rules and strictly abiding by the appropriate health codes. You've perhaps seen posted signs at your favorite local diner that showcase what kind of a rating the restaurant has been scored by food preparation inspectors. The rating is supposed to give you a sense of relief and assurance that whatever meal you get there will be well-prepared and unlikely to instill sickness.

Overall, a key point here is that sometimes the things that you can see with your own eyes, such as a plate of seemingly delectable food, might not necessarily be all that it seems to be. There is a chance that the behind-the-scenes efforts have gone awry and the final product hides those ominous lurking flaws that could undercut your health.

Besides the example of food preparation, you can apply this

aforementioned rule to encompass just about any entity that makes any kind of product.

The product might be something as simple as an everyday toaster. Imagine if a toaster was being manufactured in a faulty manner and was likely to catch fire when put into use. We would undoubtedly welcome having an insider that worked in the company making the toaster come forward, beforehand if at all possible.

Complex products are especially instances that we would hope an insider would come forward. Your car for example is a quite complex product. It contains thousands upon thousands of components. The automotive industry has had some notable cases of insiders that aided in revealing serious internal issues regarding car production concerns.

All told, it sure would be nice if someone on the inside were to speak up and try to rectify a behind-the-scenes effort that is producing a bad product, particularly in situations whereby it is hard to otherwise discern that the product is rife with intrinsic and perhaps injurious or deadly problems.

Such an insider that speaks out is typically referred to as a *whistleblower*.

The phrase originated from the notion that it used to be a common practice to blow a whistle to attract attention in certain circumstances. We still somewhat have this whistling-for-attention tradition when it comes to various sports such as football or basketball. A referee blows a whistle to alert the players that something is amiss.

You might vaguely be aware that Ralph Nader in the 1960s and 1970s aided in popularizing the whistleblower catchphrase during his activist efforts. Up until that point in time, the notion of speaking out about an internal issue was oftentimes frowned upon. Employees were generally expected to be fiercely loyal to their employer and dare not to speak out of turn. In fact, to this day, sometimes a whistleblower is ostracized and labeled as a rat or snitch for their efforts.

To clarify, not all whistleblowers are always right about what they report. There are occasions when a whistleblower might be mistaken about what they perceive as a problem. They might misconstrue things. They might overinflate the concern. You cannot blankly assume that a whistleblower is perfect in their aims. At times, a whistleblower might be harboring personal biases and seeking some form of twisted revenge or have other unseemly motives in mind.

But that also doesn't mean that a whistleblower should be axiomatically tainted as a malcontent simply due to acting as a whistleblower. Not at all.

Going the whistleblower route can be arduous and ruinous in many ways. A person can be listed as a kind of traitor and be forever tarnished, wherever they go and whatever else in life they try to do. Deciding to become a whistleblower requires some hefty thinking, trying to balance a personal sense of ethical codes versus the potential for being known as an informer or tattletale.

We can be thankful for those whistleblowers that chose to do the right thing, despite the personal costs, and have exposed substantive problems that would have not otherwise gotten the light of day. And, in many such cases, those types of demonstrative problems were already integral to harming those using the product or potentially could do so in the future. The whistleblower was able to start a chain of events that eventually curtailed or reduced those unsavory or outright deplorable outcomes.

How does a whistleblower come forward and essentially blow the whistle, as it were?

There are usually two avenues for a whistleblower to make known the internal issues that they believe are untoward.

One approach is to be a so-called internal-reporting whistleblower, which generally means that the person doing the whistleblowing does this within the confines of the entity that they are working in. They might bring their concerns to their supervisor or manager. Perhaps the firm has a formalized whistleblower process that entails submitting a safety concern in writing. And so on.

The other approach is the external-disclosing whistleblower. This is when a person that is or was an insider opts to tell externally about the internal aspects that they perceive as disconcerting. The person might tell reporters about what is going on. The person might decide to talk to a third-party consumer protection entity. Etc.

Earlier, I mentioned that cars and the automotive industry have had various whistleblowers.

In the United States, the Vehicle Safety Act (VSA) serves as the overarching guideline about whistleblowing and whistleblowers in the context of vehicular considerations. Here's the formal VSA definition given about what exactly is a whistleblower: "The term "whistleblower" means any employee or contractor of a motor vehicle manufacturer, part supplier, or dealership who voluntarily provides to the Secretary original information relating to any motor vehicle defect, noncompliance, or any violation or alleged violation of any notification or reporting requirement of this chapter, which is likely to cause unreasonable risk of death or serious physical injury" (as a side note, the Secretary being referred to as the Secretary of Transportation).

The normal path for a car-related whistleblower that is going to externally-divulge an issue would be to contact the NHTSA (National Highway Traffic Safety Administration) which is an agency of the U.S. Department of Transportation (US DOT). The stated mission of the NHTSA is to save lives, prevent injuries, and reduce vehicle-related crashes in the United States.

Per the website detailing the NHTSA whistleblower program: "Whistleblowers are an important source of information for NHTSA about potential vehicle safety problems and violations of law. The Vehicle Safety Act protects the confidentiality of whistleblowers and allows NHTSA to pay a monetary award to a whistleblower whose information leads to the successful resolution of an enforcement action for violations of law."

There are a wide variety of nuances to the whistleblower program. If you or someone that you know is potentially considering being a whistleblower related to an automotive issue, make sure to get up-to-speed on the matter. Best to look before you leap. In addition, as stated in the VSA: "A whistleblower may be represented by counsel."

In terms of the scope of what might be considered a whistleblowing warranted submission, here's what the NHTSA website indicates: "NHTSA receives information from whistleblowers on a wide variety of topics, including potential vehicle safety defects, noncompliance with the Federal Motor Vehicle Safety Standards, and violations of the Vehicle Safety Act. NHTSA investigators consider information provided by whistleblowers, which may lead to formal actions like an investigation, recall, or civil penalty enforcement action. NHTSA protects the confidentiality of whistleblowers. NHTSA may pay a monetary award to a whistleblower who provides information that leads to the successful resolution of an enforcement action for violations of law."

You might be thinking that whistleblowing about cars is a somewhat ho-hum topic, namely that though it is certainly important and noteworthy, there doesn't seem to be any cause to make a big deal out of it right now. Whistleblowing about cars has been taking place for years.

Well, there is something new that you need to give due consideration toward.

The future of cars consists of AI-based true self-driving cars.

Allow me a moment to elaborate.

There isn't a human driver involved in a true self-driving car. Keep in mind that true self-driving cars are driven via an AI driving system. There isn't a need for a human driver at the wheel, and nor is there a provision for a human to drive the vehicle.

Here's an intriguing question that is worth pondering: *Are we going to see whistleblowers about the advent of AI-based true self-driving cars, and if so, what impact might we expect?*

Before jumping into the details, I'd like to further clarify what is meant when I refer to true self-driving cars.

Self-Driving Cars And Whistleblowers

For Level 4 and Level 5 true self-driving vehicles, there won't be a human driver involved in the driving task.

All occupants will be passengers.

The AI is doing the driving.

One aspect to immediately discuss entails the fact that the AI involved in today's AI driving systems is not sentient. In other words, the AI is altogether a collective of computer-based programming and algorithms, and most assuredly not able to reason in the same manner that humans can.

Why this added emphasis about the AI not being sentient?

Because I want to underscore that when discussing the role of the AI driving system, I am not ascribing human qualities to the AI. Please be aware that there is an ongoing and dangerous tendency these days to anthropomorphize AI. In essence, people are assigning human-like sentience to today's AI, despite the undeniable and inarguable fact that no such AI exists as yet.

With that clarification, you can envision that the AI driving system won't natively somehow "know" about the facets of driving. Driving and all that it entails will need to be programmed as part of the hardware and software of the self-driving car.

Let's dive into the myriad of aspects that come to play on this topic.

You might be shocked to think that there would be any kind of possible whistleblowing related to self-driving cars.

Most people tend to assume that the internal efforts of developing those state-of-the-art AI driving systems and putting together a self-driving car are being done with the highest and best of intentions. Some liken the effort to landing on the moon, a rather awe-inspiring aspiration.

Surely, everything happening behind the scenes in the act of crafting self-driving cars is completely aboveboard and hunky-dory. No one would seemingly seek to produce a self-driving car that had inherently dangerous overtones. Furthermore, the hope is that self-driving cars will bring forth an era of mobility-for-all, allowing those that today readily do not have access to automotive transit to have seamless access to ubiquitous mobility. And there is also the belief that self-driving cars will dramatically reduce the number of human injuries and fatalities due to human-driven car crashes.

Well, I don't want to unduly shock you, but what is happening in the kitchen has the potential for serving up a meal that has the possibility of harming people.

Some self-driving car efforts are seemingly cutting corners, trying to do the urgent bidding of upper management, and not able to undertake as much double-checking and triple-checking, as they believe, is necessary. Likewise, there are those in upper management that are somewhat unawares or at times clueless about the lack of attention to detail and the omission or skirting of safety quality aspects during the self-driving car development activities in their development groups.

It works both ways.

Keep in mind that there is a race of sorts going on.

Who will attain true self-driving cars first?

Akin to getting to the moon, a lot is riding on the first to make this self-driving car a "giant leap" for mankind. Billions upon billions of dollars are pouring into these vaunted efforts. There is almost no revenue as yet from the self-driving car efforts. Money is going in, and there is an expectation that something miraculous is going to emerge.

Under that kind of pressure, you can imagine that some elements might be given short shrift in a vociferous effort to summarily push ahead. Concerns about safety aspects can at times be placed on the back burner. Features for the AI driving system that seem pivotal can be shoved onto the existing list of edge or corner cases, meaning that those are capabilities that it is assumed can be dealt with later on.

This does not suggest or imply that anything of this nature is somehow rampant or found everywhere.

That would be completely unfair to all of those striving mightily to produce self-driving cars. These are the heroes that are striving mightily, each and every day, aiming to bring to the world self-driving cars, and in so doing reach those earlier cited ideals.

Also, as I have repeatedly mentioned in my columns, in the last several years the automakers and self-driving car makers have fortunately taken a much stronger stance toward safety. This includes having hired high-profile automotive safety experts and launched significant and meaningful internal efforts to boost the understanding of what safety consists of. In addition, many of the self-driving car firms now have internal "whistleblower" programs, usually coined more plainly as safety reporting programs, that are intended to get insiders to come forward when they see something that they perceive as untoward.

The ostensible concern is that there are real chances in such a high-pressure gung-ho atmosphere of a bad apple here or there. To make clear, it isn't necessarily the case that a nefarious person is going to plant something nefarious into an AI driving system (though, that can happen). When AI developers are running around at full speed, there is a chance of missing some important safeguards or not having the right development tools, or being overwhelmed and understaffed.

All in all, the result can be that a hidden bug or problem has gotten into the AI driving system. Not necessarily intentionally so. Just because there are insufficient checks and balances and other complications involved.

When a self-driving car has a backup human driver in the vehicle, the belief is that this is sufficient to catch any untoward actions that the AI driving system might make. In that way of thinking, it is like having a food taster that is sitting at your dining table. The person is supposed to catch anything that can lead things astray.

As mentioned in my columns, not everyone believes this to be a proper way of catching problems and decries that using the public roadways in this manner is wholly improper. If we are using the analogy of a food taster, it is as though the food taster is eating the meal at the same time as a person is dining on the meal. Not a satisfactory form of safety for the person that is simultaneously eating what might be toxic food. In essence, the backup driver might not catch an untoward driving act in time, and the vehicle crashes into a pedestrian or a human-driven car (I've described such instances in my columns).

On the same analogy, I had also earlier stated that the efforts behind the scenes in the kitchen might be generating relatively hidden issues that are not directly obvious via looking at the final product. When you see a self-driving car driving down the street, and doing so without a human backup driver, how can you know that the AI driving system is assuredly going to be a safe driver?

You don't.

The usual retort is that if the autonomous vehicle is making its way down a city street and hasn't hit anyone, this must mean that the AI driving system is doing just fine, thank you very much. Indeed, those that keep taking those rides in self-driving cars and doing those gushing testimonials tend to fall into that same category. They believe that just because the self-driving car safely got them to the grocery store, it is as though this provides ample and unquestionable proof that the self-driving car can go anywhere safely.

They are falling into a classic mental trap. It is a common statistics-oriented mistake. They assume that their one particular instance makes for outstretched generalizations.

It could be that the AI driving system will come upon a situation such as a pedestrian that suddenly darts into the street, and the self-driving car won't stop in time (let's assume it could have). The person that had taken the trip to the grocery store had not encountered an interloping pedestrian, and thus they have no idea what the self-driving car will do in such a setting. Out of sight, out of mind.

Let's get back to what the NHTSA says about cars overall and the scope of possible whistleblowing that might be applicable: "NHTSA receives information from whistleblowers on a wide variety of topics, including potential vehicle safety defects, noncompliance with the Federal Motor Vehicle Safety Standards, and violations of the Vehicle Safety Act."

Traditionally, this kind of scope tends to focus on the mechanical parts of a car.

Nowadays, cars have become essentially computers on wheels. The software is increasingly veering into the scope of topics that entail vehicle safety defects, noncompliance, and violations of the VSA.

In what areas of the AI driving systems might we anticipate potential issues?

First, sensors are used to collect data about the driving scene. Self-driving cars usually make use of video cameras, radar, LIDAR, ultrasonic units, thermal imaging devices, and the like. These are the eyes and ears of the AI driving system.

Suppose an insider knows that the sensors chosen for the self-driving car model they are working on have safety concerns that are not being dealt with. Once the self-driving car is fielded, it could be that under certain conditions a particular sensor is going to provide faulty data. From this, the AI driving system might not have been programmed to calculate properly what to do.

A serious and somber bad result can happen while on our public roadways.

Another possible avenue consists of the fusion of the data across multiple sensors. Known as MSDF (multi-sensor data fusion), perhaps the fusion technique being used is based on the video cameras being considered "right" even if the radar input says otherwise (the discrepancy is simply discarded rather than raising a flag or requiring some added steps to try and resolve). How are safety concerns being incorporated into this form of programming?

The list goes on and on.

There is the virtual model that is maintained by the AI driving system and internally depicts the existing and predicted surroundings. There could certainly be safety concerns about how that code is working. There is the action-planner portion of the AI driving system that tries to compute what next actions of the autonomous vehicle are most prudent to take. Again, safety concerns could reside in there. Etc.

Conclusion

Here's the bottom line.

As self-driving cars begin to increasingly emerge from labs and R&D efforts, they will be seemingly used on public roadways. The number of such self-driving cars on the roadways will start to increase. The increased number of such autonomous vehicles will tend to somewhat increase the odds that something adverse is going to arise.

These usually make big headlines in the news.

Did the self-driving car incident that gets the headlines have an internal issue that might have been known by an insider, and yet they decided not to tell about what they knew or seriously suspected?

I would wager that we are likely to see an emergence of whistleblowers that come forth about self-driving cars.

Not all such instances will be valid whistleblowing instances.

Some will.

The impact is likely that this will cause some of the automakers and self-driving car tech makers to revisit what they are doing. You can certainly expect that those types of whistleblower reports will stoke further regulatory interest.

Whatever way you ponder the matter, it will seemingly be a surprise to some, and not at all a surprise to others. Those that have worked in such "kitchens" before, and already sense that some of the self-driving cars that are coming onto the roadways are a scarily and inadequately cooked meal.

We'll find out once the whistles start to blow..

CHAPTER 17
FALSE UNCRASHABLE AND SELF-DRIVING CARS

Please cover your ears since I am about to tender some rather harsh language.

Are you ready?

For those vendors and pundits claiming that AI-based self-driving cars are going to be *uncrashable*, I say hogwash.

The absurdist claim isn't just your normal kind of hogwash, it is some of that amazingly potent unadulterated hogwash.

Claptrap. Nonsense. Rubbish. Preposterous.

Sorry about the use of such unsavory terms.

Maybe it would be simpler for me to make this bold and unequivocal assertion: *Self-driving cars are not going to be uncrashable, ergo, they absolutely can in fact get into a car crash or similar form of automotive collision.*

If you've not been following the latest news about self-driving cars, you might not have seen or heard the recent claims that self-driving cars are going to be uncrashable. To be clear, this type of talk actually (sadly) goes back numerous years. The baloney about having uncrashable self-driving cars has a lengthy history and seems to be revitalized from time to time.

Today, in this discussion, I'd like to help put a "destroy the zombie" steel pole directly through the heart of such tripe.

One supposes that the proper and balanced place to start the discussion would be to provide the alleged basis for why self-driving cars will be uncrashable. In essence, let's see if we can surface the rationale for those that make such a claim. It is usually best in these types of arguments or debates to ensure that each side has a chance to share its posture on outsized controversial and contested matters.

After seeing what the uncrashable camp has been proffering, I'd like to then take a step-by-step dismantling of their argument and showcase the tomfoolery involved. You will abundantly then be aware of why the position of the uncrashables is entirely untenable.

I realize that you might be tempted to think that this is nothing more than an insider's bruhaha and doesn't seem to be of concern to anyone other than those that are in the midst of crafting AI self-driving cars.

You know how these things sometimes go. There are internal heated debates amongst experts in a given field. Eventually, things get worked out, presumably, and the ruckus falls by the wayside.

I'd like to suggest that this is altogether a strident matter that has an outstretched current impact and extends far beyond the usual inner sanctum of talking heads heated discourse.

If vendors and others go around touting to everyone that self-driving cars are going to be uncrashable, it sets some wholly unsettling and unrealistic expectations. With all of the potentially positive aspects that self-driving cars are going to produce (I'll list those aspects momentarily herein), having the uncrashable allegation on the list is the bad apple in the bunch.

The thing is, since the uncrashable mantra won't be achievable, it mars the other realistically feasible positive aspects in the barrel of societal gains from self-driving cars.

The public will be wondering what the heck ever happened with the uncrashable nature of self-driving cars. Where did it disappear into? And, if that element wasn't achievable, perhaps others on the list are also tainted (the bad apple spoils the rest of the barrel).

There are enough false impressions and exaggerations about self-driving cars and we assuredly don't need more to be piled onto the already stacked up pile.

I'll add something else to the factor about why referring to self-driving cars as presumably able to be uncrashable creates a series of problems.

First, regulators might be so enamored of this possibility that they would be willing to take undue chances at how self-driving cars are to be regulated. Anyone that genuinely believed that self-driving cars will never crash would certainly be doing a service to society by trying to get self-driving cars on our public roadways at the soonest possible moment.

It just stands to reason.

Ponder some crucial statistics.

In the United States alone, there are a reported 6.3 million car crashes per year.

Now, those are just the reported car crashes, thus, there are likely more. Another way to construe the count is to consider that there are about 700 or so car crashes every hour of every day, somewhere in the United States. International stats that account for global car crashes across all countries is a daunting set of figures and will make you feel queasy and dampen your heart.

For the U.S., those reported car crashes generate about 2.5 million injuries per year. I'm talking about serious injuries, life-altering injuries. And the number of deaths or annual fatalities in the U.S. due to car crashes is about 40,000 souls. Take a moment to let that sorrowful number sink in.

Anyway, the hope certainly is that self-driving cars will incur a much lower number of car crashes, and therefore the number of car crash-related fatalities will drop tremendously, as will the number of associated injuries. You can also expect that this would mean that the societal costs associated with car crashes would also be reduced immensely, such as the costs devoted to car crash cleanups, court cases, car repairs, and the like.

You can sensibly assume that the number of car crashes ought to go down because of the differences between how humans drive and how AI driving systems are being devised. Human drivers are rife with human foibles, such as drinking while driving, being distracted while driving (such as watching cat videos or texting), and so on. The AI driving systems should not incur those car crashes that otherwise would have happened if a human being was at the wheel and exhibited those types of human foibles.

If we can create AI driving systems that are at least on par with human drivers in terms of undertaking the driving task, we could logically opt to deduct the sour instances involving car crashes that were due principally to human foibles while at the wheel. The AI driving systems ought to not be making those kinds of driving mistakes or incurring those kinds of driving risks, all else being equal.

That's all part of the anticipated benefit of having self-driving cars.

Furthermore, the hope is that self-driving cars will bring forth a semblance of mobility-for-all.

Those in our society that today are mobility constrained and do not have ready access to a car will potentially readily have such access in the future. This is partially due to the ease of making use of self-driving cars because there is no human driver needed. In addition, the expectation is that the per-mile price associated with riding in a self-driving car will be a lot less than the comparable driving journey in a human-driven car.

I think you can already discern that there are lots of big reasons to be trumpeting the eventual attainment of self-driving cars.

We don't need to include falsehoods.

Such as self-driving cars being uncrashable.

Before I dive into the uncrashable viewpoint to highlight what their underlying assertions are, it might be handy to provide a bit of background about the emergence of self-driving cars.

Allow me a moment to elaborate.

There isn't a human driver involved in a true self-driving car. Keep in mind that true self-driving cars are driven via an AI driving system. There isn't a need for a human driver at the wheel, and nor is there a provision for a human to drive the vehicle.

Here's an intriguing question that is worth pondering: *What is the basis for claiming that self-driving cars will allegedly be uncrashable, and how is this a nonsensical assertion?*

I'd like to further clarify what is meant when I refer to true self-driving cars.

Self-Driving Cars And Uncrashable Nonsense

For Level 4 and Level 5 true self-driving vehicles, there won't be a human driver involved in the driving task.

All occupants will be passengers.

The AI is doing the driving.

One aspect to immediately discuss entails the fact that the AI involved in today's AI driving systems is not sentient. In other words, the AI is altogether a collective of computer-based programming and algorithms, and most assuredly not able to reason in the same manner that humans can.

Why this added emphasis about the AI not being sentient?

Because I want to underscore that when discussing the role of the

AI driving system, I am not ascribing human qualities to the AI. Please be aware that there is an ongoing and dangerous tendency these days to anthropomorphize AI. In essence, people are assigning human-like sentience to today's AI, despite the undeniable and inarguable fact that no such AI exists as yet.

With that clarification, you can envision that the AI driving system won't natively somehow "know" about the facets of driving. Driving and all that it entails will need to be programmed as part of the hardware and software of the self-driving car.

Let's dive into the myriad of aspects that come to play on this topic.

One quick aside on the uncrashable notion all told. You'll quickly see that is a useful tangent for strictly clarification purposes.

Some people interpret the word "uncrashable" to mean that the autonomous vehicle is made up of or composed of some kind of material that is perfectly impervious to car crashes or automotive collisions of any sort.

Think of an armored truck. Armored trucks are made of specially strengthened materials and can take quite a beating. If you were to inadvertently ram into an armored truck with a conventional car, the car would likely be the loser and the armored truck would be the winner, at least regarding the amount of respective damage suffered.

I think we might all agree that this is decidedly not any semblance of being *truly* uncrashable.

It is instead a version of crashing that just so happens to seemingly lessen the adverse outcomes of an instance or crash-related encounter. Crashes are still going to occur in this scenario. They might be less bruising but are going to happen and we will still have damages, injuries, and fatalities.

In the context of self-driving cars, perhaps one might envision a special wrapping of protective armor that would encompass the autonomous vehicle. Or maybe the autonomous vehicle would be made from the strongest materials known to humanity.

Nobody but nobody that is seriously in the uncrashable camp would genuinely try to use the armoring angle as the basis for why self-driving cars are going to be uncrashable. They know this is a laughable proposition because it still entails the act of crashing.

So, we can dispense with the armoring consideration and instead focus on why the uncrashable camp usually touts the uncrashable banner.

An additional supplemental point to the impervious material concept is an alternative that employs a forcefield akin to something you might see in those wonderous and exceedingly imaginative sci-fi movies. The self-driving car could be made out of balsawood or even flimsy cardboard since it is miraculously protected by an all-encompassing forcefield. Anything that strikes the forcefield is summarily pushed away. If the self-driving car perchance hits something, no damage at all occurs to the self-driving car.

I'd like to right now place an order for that forcefield device and I am vociferously eager to have it arrive, hopefully via next-day overnight shipping service. Wait for a second, darn, turns out that there is no sense in hanging out at my front door tomorrow for such a delivery. There isn't that kind of a device yet available, despite what the sci-fi movies showcase.

I will acknowledge this, it might be possible to someday have devices that can produce this kind of forcefield. It might further be possible to mount such a device onto a car or vehicle, conventional or autonomous. I guess in that case you could argue that the result is an uncrashable vehicle. Sure, go ahead and place this forcefield-fueled uncrashable concept into the futures file.

Not wishing to be finicky, but doesn't this still imply that a crash occurs?

Imagine that two objects collide with each other. The forcefields keep them from getting smushed. They did though indeed crash into each other if you count their forcefields as part of them, correspondingly. Fortunately, no damage resulted from the collision. It was seemingly a crash in the strictest dictionary sense of two or more objects that violently collide.

Ponder that quirky conundrum for a brief instant.

Moving on, here's the key everyday logic for the customary uncrashable exhortations.

Self-driving cars will be making use of an extensive sensor suite, including video cameras, radar, LIDAR, ultrasonic units, thermal imagining, etc. These sensors collect data during a driving journey and the onboard AI driving system computationally analyses the data in real-time. This oftentimes makes use of contemporary Machine Learning (ML) and Deep Learning (DL), which is simply the use of computational pattern matching techniques. There isn't anything magical about the ML/DL.

In any case, a cornerstone assertion is that the AI driving system will utilize these sensors so ably that any and all potential car crash scenarios will be indubitably and fully anticipated before the point of potentially getting into a car crash.

Plus, because the AI driving system will be always forewarned about an imminent crash, the AI driving system will take evasive action, and the self-driving car will never ever get entangled in a crash.

Thus, self-driving cars will be uncrashable.

This meaning of the word "uncrashable" is bona fide if indeed the aforementioned could really take place. There would never be any crashes involving self-driving cars. The AI driving systems would ensure this. Since there wouldn't be any crashes, you can gamely say that those autonomous vehicles are uncrashable.

Sounds wonderful!

We would all welcome a means of transit that never involves any crashes or collisions. Imagine that we had zero crashes. This means zero fatalities as a result of crashes (because there aren't any crashes). This means zero injuries as a result of crashes (because there aren't any crashes). I would dare to suggest that this is Nobel Prize-worthy.

How do you feel about the uncrashable self-driving car?

Gives you a heartfelt feeling.

More like heartburn.

Zero crashes have a zero chance of happening.

Here's why.

The logic proffers that the sensors of a self-driving car will always and unfailingly detect any and all objects that might be within the feasible realm of invoking a car crash. These are perfect sensors that do this, along with idealized or absolutely perfect computational analyses of the sensory data that identify and are able to mathematically detect all such objects. Always. Every time.

The logic proffers too that the AI driving system will utilize these perfectly detecting sensors and perfectly in turn always avoid any potential car crashes by maneuvering the self-driving car, perfectly so.

A whole lot of perfects are in there.

That's not the real world that we happen to live in.

The sensors are not perfect. They cannot detect everything totally within a driving environment such that all objects of any potential crash-related demeanor will be detected. In addition, sensors are electronic and mechanical devices that have various inherent limitations. They also can break, falter, or have other anomalies.

Even if the first part of this could exist in some fantasy land, the second part is the other crucial and added weakness to the whole shenanigans. Namely, the AI driving system has to be so perfectly devised that it can always and without fail to find a means to avert a crash.

Plus, if you don't mind my saying this perhaps obvious point, another hefty constraint that belies the uncrashable pipe dream is the laws of physics. Sorry, those have to be observed too.

Consider the following example.

A self-driving car is going down a neighborhood street at 25 miles per hour. This is approximately a movement of about 37 feet of distance for every one second of time.

There are cars parked on the street, legally so. It is an ordinary residential area. Nothing unusual or out of the ordinary.

A small child is hiding between two of the parked cars. The toddler cannot be seen due to the higher stature of the parked cars.

Just as the self-driving car rolls alongside the parked cars where the child is hiding, the toddler regrettably decides to dart into the street. No prior notification is given. In case you are thinking this would never happen, I believe you might want to visit some residential areas that have children residing and playing in these communities. This can happen. It does happen.

The self-driving car is now within about 15 feet of the child, for which the toddler has emerged directly into the oncoming path of the self-driving car.

Let's go ahead and assume that at this juncture the sensors detect the object in the roadway, and using the ML/DL pattern matching identify the object as a child. This is passed along to the AI driving system. The AI driving system is now faced with a situation involving a child that is within a distance of 15 feet of the autonomous vehicle that is going at 37 feet per second.

You might say that the AI driving system will summarily and

without hesitation hit the brakes. That's the hope.

The braking distance at this stated speed on a good set of tires with a good set of brakes on a dry road that is sealed and level would be about 40 feet or so. You would usually need to include the human driver reaction time and as such the stopping distance is a lot more, but we are going to be generous and assume that the AI driving system can instantaneously apply the brakes.

A multi-ton self-driving car that instantaneously hits the brakes and that has fully detected the toddler in the roadway is going to crash into that wayward child.

This is a crash.

I don't believe you can argue about that. I suppose you might try claiming that the self-driving car could attempt to steer away from the child. I assure you, that doesn't work out either. The amount of time available to avoid the crash is insufficient to indeed avoid the crash.

Note that the sensors did their best, but they were unable to detect the hiding child. Note that the AI driving system did its best, doing so by immediately applying the brakes. In the end, the child was embroiled in a car crash.

Unless you change the law of physics, this would be undeniably a car crash.

During this example, we have given the benefit of the doubt that the sensors were working flawlessly and the AI driving system was working flawlessly. If we were to add into this example the probabilities that the sensors might be faltering, or that the AI driving system might be faltering, we would have an even more pronounced basis for the crash. In that case, the crash might be worse in terms of severity.

There are many, many, many examples of how self-driving cars will not be able to assuredly detect objects that are potentially going to invoke or involve a car crash. Likewise, we cannot expect that AI driving systems will run perfectly and that they will be programmed to handle all possible permutations and combinations of all possible car crash scenarios.

Nor can we pretend that there will always be adequate time available to have the AI driving system divert from a car crash.

In addition, as I've repeatedly stated, we need to deal with the Trolley Problem.

This is a notion that there are going to be circumstances of two undesirable choices and having to make a tough decision as to which ought to be selected. Some industry pundits refuse to acknowledge that the Trolley Problem is applicable to AI self-driving cars.

Conclusion

There won't be uncrashable self-driving cars.

At least not in any reasonably foreseeable future of what cars conventionally consist of. We might eventually have flying self-driving cars, in which case you could reconsider the toddler in the street instance and try to determine whether the autonomous vehicle would have sufficient time to fly over the child.

Fine.

But for the real world as we know it today, do not put your money down on any uncrashable cars because it is hogwash.

Meanwhile, you should gird yourself for the oft-used kneejerk standard retort about there not being any uncrashable self-driving cars. Here's what the riposte is.

Hold on, brace yourself.

Those spouting the uncrashable self-driving car, and when backed into a corner about their claim, will say that they meant to emphasize that self-driving cars will be *veritably* uncrashable. Nonsense.

CHAPTER 18
ROADSIDE DISPLAYS AND SELF-DRIVING CARS

Right lane closed ahead.

Or sometimes it is stated as RIGHT LANE CLOSED AHEAD.

That's what you often see displayed on those official roadside electronic displays. According to official guidebooks, the messages are supposed to be clear and concise. This seems necessary since a harried motorist driving along does not have a lot of time to focus on those signs. Getting immediately to the point at hand is a sensible and altogether essential precept.

The displays are supposed to show messages that are timely, accurate, and up-to-date. You've undoubtedly seen some instances whereby the sign has warned about a wreck in the roadway ahead, yet when you get to the ahead portion there isn't any wreckage to be seen. The odds are that a clean-up took place prior but the workers responsible for the display sign have not returned to update the message board.

Here's a good rule of thumb that is worth pondering: *Convey only a single thought per panel.*

I like that.

If a display is flashing a message and then proffers a second message, this is probably better than trying to cram too much into just a single message. Our minds can readily grasp a message that has a definitive instruction or warning. When the message is muddied by having a conglomeration of thoughts, you can easily get confounded. You might even not realize that there is a twofer in the single message, thus completely fail to glean that there are two things you need to be aware of.

For example, the message that the right lane is closed ahead would seem a reasonably standalone thought. You've got the portion that tells you where things are awry, namely in the right lane. Upon that indication, you surely would wonder what about the right lane is worthy of attention. As a nice touch, the message tells you that the right lane is closed ahead.

Sweet and simple.

Imagine that two things were happening at once. The right lane is closed ahead, plus the upcoming next exit is closed. It might be tempting to jam this together into one message. Maybe saying something like the right lane is closed and so is the next exit. Of course, there are only so many characters available to be displayed at one time, akin to how Twitter allows a maximum number per tweet.

Perhaps the message might say "Right Lane Closed Ahead, Next Exit Closed Too" which might squeak in at the allowed number of characters. A shortened version could be "Right Lane + Next Exit, Closed" though this could be a bit ambiguous and open to interpretation. Meanwhile, those hectic drivers seeing the sign are bound to find themselves devoting undue mental exertion to the signage.

Probably safer and more useful if you display one message about the right lane, and then after the usual interval of a second or two, go ahead and display the second message about the next exit aspects. You can debate this approach, though the overall point is that sometimes a single message might not be viable and you genuinely are better off displaying two or more instead.

The messages that seem to extraordinarily get the goat of many drivers usually entail platitudes or seemingly vague exhortations. The classic being to drive safely ("DRIVE SAFELY") or the urging to use caution ("USE CAUTION").

Why do those messages cause a ruckus among some drivers?

Because the feeling is that these are not conveying any conclusive instructions or specific down-to-earth useful statements. Knowing that the right lane ahead is closed would be quite useful and provides a driver with a heads-up for making early lane changes or slowing down. Knowing that you should drive safely is, well, seemingly already a known commodity. Sure, we should always be driving safely, one might retort at the sign.

In fact, the concern arises that maybe there is some reason that you are being cautioned to drive safely at this moment in time on this specific highway or street. Could a gaping hole exist in the roadway up ahead and that's why you are being implored to drive safely? When being informed to use caution, your mind wanders to the possibility that mighty sea monsters are beyond the bend and will swallow whole your vehicle as it passes.

Couldn't the display have warned specifically about the sea monsters?

Anyway, you get the notion that some drivers are irked by general proclamations.

We want specifics.

We want to know something that is directly crucial to driving while in the throes of driving. I'm sure that some others would argue that reminding all drivers to drive safely and use caution is indubitably helpful. It wakes up those drivers that are in a zombie-like mental fog as they drive a moving car at over 60 miles per hour.

Thank goodness that the display kicks those dolts into mental gear, some exclaim.

The irony is that a sign that asserts for you to drive safely might trigger some idiots into suddenly deciding to do just the opposite. These might be people that eschew any kind of authority. They detest being told what to do. The advisory that the right lane is closed provides merely advice, and it is up to the driver to decide what to do with that vaunted piece of information. In contrast, the drive safely message is a strict order, an authoritative command, an iron fist edict from those that control our lives.

You can't win on these matters.

Another rub is that there is a notable chunk of time and attention consumed by a driver to look at and make sense of the messages.

First, the driver has to look away from the traffic ahead of them to see and read the display. Second, the frenzied driver has to put on their thinking cap to decide what the message has stated. One potential argument is that the messages are a distractor from concentrating on the roadway. You certainly don't want drivers to end up in car crashes because they were busy deciphering a traffic display and become wholly preoccupied doing so.

That is yet an additional irony, whereby a message that said to drive safely was considered as distracting and drivers got into car collisions precisely as a result of the presumed helpful flashing display.

You really cannot win on these matters.

From time to time, the news provides reporting that an electronic roadway display had been temporarily "hacked" and someone posted an untoward message.

To clarify, these are rarely bona fide hacks per se. The most frequent way that these message boards get reprogrammed with an oddball message is that the display panels usually have a default password that the roadway crew never changed. It is akin to having a password such as 12345 and any dullard that knows about the default can try and see if it gets them into the display controls.

I don't especially consider that to be any semblance of hacking. A real hack would involve having to crack through some form of computer security and do so by employing genuine programming finesse. That is a rarity when it comes to the traffic display boards.

Though I've been describing these as display boards, the proper nomenclature is that they are Variable Message Signs (VMS). Furthermore, if the display board or VMS is readily movable and not fixed permanently in place, it is considered a Portable Variable Message Sign (PVMS). You see the PVMS displays that are temporarily placed at the scene of a bad car crash or used in a construction zone that will only be there for a few days or weeks.

The mainstay purpose of the PVMS is to allow for aiding drivers whenever there is an incident underway. The display boards are equally useful for activities including construction zones, special events, environmental conditions such as heavy smoke or when forest fires occur, congestion management, law enforcement, and at times for public service campaigns.

Again, the messages need to have a demonstrative and notable basis for existing. There is a vital trade-off between not displaying anything at all and allowing drivers to figure out whatever is taking place versus the act of displaying something and possibly distracting or confounding drivers inadvertently.

This takes us to an interesting instance of a PVMS "hack" that occurred recently (as reported initially on Twitter, of all places).

It happened in Brooklyn.

In case you've been living under a rock, Brooklyn is a well-known borough of New York City. For those that know about Brooklyn, they either would be upset that a PVMS was hacked or they might be proud, perhaps prideful that everything happens in Brooklyn and so why not include display boards that get reprogrammed by malcontents or rowdy roadway warriors (or whomever).

Just to mention, it is against the law to reprogram those officially programmed displays.

And, it goes without mentioning that a reprogrammed display could be a distractor to drivers, conveying info that has nothing to do with the existent traffic conditions and roadway safety. This then becomes an unquestionable distraction and could produce car crashes that lead to injuries or deaths. Thus, it isn't a laughing matter and we should condemn any such practices.

In the recently reported instance, the reprogramming went whole hog, as it were.

There is usually one particular thing that the person wants to display. The most common message seems to be something replete with curse words or a single thought about the world at large. At times, the pirated message is whimsical, though this does not excuse the lawlessness of the hacking act.

In this specific case, the message display was reprogrammed to display eight successive messages, quite seemingly serious and somber remarks, each one separated from the other by the usual few seconds allotted per message seen on a conventional display panel.

Here it is:

- Honking Won't Help
- Cars Are Death Machines
- Use Bus Subway Or Bike!
- Cars Kill Kids
- Car Melt Glaciers
- Cars Ruin Cities
- Stop Driving!
- Get Rid of Your Car

None of these contain profanity, which provides some solace. That being said, they have certainly emboldened statements that raise controversy and not everyone would find the messages to be appropriate. All told, regardless of whether you agree or disagree with the content of the messages, using an official roadway PVMS for this purpose is illegal.

Let's shift away from the matter of improperly making use of a PVMS and consider that those same or notably similar remarks can be found on the Internet. You see, there are plenty of social media postings that contain the same sentiments.

As suggested by the messages, the overall tone and expression are that cars are bad and we ought not to be using them.

Mull that over.

Meanwhile, consider that the future of cars consists of AI-based true self-driving cars.

There isn't a human driver involved in a true self-driving car. Keep in mind that true self-driving cars are driven via an AI driving system. There isn't a need for a human driver at the wheel, and nor is there a provision for a human to drive the vehicle.

Here's an intriguing question that is worth pondering: *Should we even be seeking to produce AI-based self-driving cars or is the very notion of cars of any kind something that we ought to be averting?*

Before jumping into the details, I'd like to further clarify what is meant when I refer to true self-driving cars.

Self-Driving Cars And Whether Cars Are Bad To The Bone

For Level 4 and Level 5 true self-driving vehicles, there won't be a human driver involved in the driving task.

All occupants will be passengers.

The AI is doing the driving.

One aspect to immediately discuss entails the fact that the AI involved in today's AI driving systems is not sentient. In other words, the AI is altogether a collective of computer-based programming and algorithms, and most assuredly not able to reason in the same manner that humans can.

Why this added emphasis about the AI not being sentient?

Because I want to underscore that when discussing the role of the AI driving system, I am not ascribing human qualities to the AI. Please be aware that there is an ongoing and dangerous tendency these days to anthropomorphize AI. In essence, people are assigning human-like sentience to today's AI, despite the undeniable and inarguable fact that no such AI exists as yet.

With that clarification, you can envision that the AI driving system won't natively somehow "know" about the facets of driving. Driving and all that it entails will need to be programmed as part of the hardware and software of the self-driving car.

Let's dive into the myriad of aspects that come to play on this topic.

There is a tremendous amount of effort and billions of dollars going toward devising AI self-driving cars.

The hope is that self-driving cars will ultimately bring forth an era of mobility-for-all. This is a catchphrase suggesting that the use of these newer kinds of cars will be much more widely available and utilized than conventional cars are today. Presumably, conventional human-driven cars will gradually fade out of use, and meanwhile, self-driving cars will readily become predominant.

A basis for believing that this will arise is due to the expected low cost or lowered per mile price for the use of self-driving cars, predominantly as a result of no longer requiring a human driver at the wheel.

In addition, a further hope is that there will be a lot fewer car crashes whence we have an abundance of self-driving cars. Currently, in the United States, there are about 6.7 million car crashes annually, producing approximately 2.5 million injuries and around 40,000 fatalities.

Many of those car crashes are attributed to human driving foibles such as drunk driving, distracted, driving, etc. Since self-driving cars will be using an AI driving system, there should not be any of those human foibles occurring as a prompter for a car crash. As an aside, this does not ergo imply that self-driving cars will be "uncrashable" (and oft claimed aspect), see my analysis at **this link here**. Self-driving cars will still at times get into car crashes, though this is anticipated to occur infrequently in comparison to comparable human driving occurrences.

We now ready to tackle those pointed remarks that had been posted on the Brooklyn roadside display panel.

First, consider two of the most straight away haymaker accusations, namely that cars are death machines and that cars kill kids.

What are we to make of that claim?

Those strident contentions take us into the classic realm about the nature of humanity and the tools that humans devise for use. I think we can reasonably agree that a car by itself is not particularly a death machine and nor does it seek to kill children. A car is a car. A non-running parked car is a highly unlikely producer of deaths.

When a human drives a car, there is a risk that the human driver will somehow fail or falter while driving a car and ergo get into a car crash. A car crash can decidedly involve injuries and also fatalities. Furthermore, it is the case that a human driver might inadvertently ram into children crossing a street. This happens, of course sadly so. In other instances, there might be children inside a car as passengers, and an adult human driver is at the wheel, for which the driver perchance loses control of the car, and all inside the vehicle are regrettably lost.

The point is that we might need to elongate the assertions and more clearly state that human drivers can make use of cars and in the act of doing so can potentially produce fatalities. By and large, this occurs not by direct intent and instead by some form of failing on the part of the human driver (let's for sake of discussion excise out the rare instances of someone that opts to use a car for the intentional purpose of harming others).

This brings us around to the hoped-for advantages of AI self-driving cars. The belief is that the AI driving systems will be programmed to drive in a manner that averts the human foibles of driving. If that occurs, the claim about cars being death machines and killing kids will change quite radically.

Here's how.

As I've repeatedly indicated in my columns, the number of car crashes should come down tremendously, along with a corresponding reduction in the number of injuries and fatalities. That being said, self-driving cars won't be "uncrashable" and there will still be some instances of car crashes that involve self-driving cars (reemphasizing my earlier point).

All told, it is anticipated that the number of deaths via the acts of self-driving cars will eventually be extremely low. Any deaths at all are naturally abhorrent, but the emphasis at least is that there will be many fewer by far. This would also suggest that the number of children killed by a car, specifically self-driving cars, will also be substantially reduced.

What makes things a bit of an added twist is that you could be on more grounded turf by then claiming that it was indeed the car that did the unfortunate deed. The finger is normatively pointed at the human driver, though in the case of self-driving cars it will be the AI driving system.

Before you get into a conniption about whether the AI driving system is a "being" and therefore bears the responsibility for the driving act, I am not one of those that buys into that theory. Per my earlier comments, today's AI is not sentient, and not even close to being sentient. It is my view that the AI driving system is not a responsible party and that it is instead those that devised and fielded the AI driving system that ought to be held responsible. Usually, this would be the automaker or self-driving tech firm that crafted the self-driving car, along with whatever entity is operating the autonomous vehicle for use on public roadways such as a fleet operator.

So, we are going to gradually switch from the notion that human drivers at times go awry or falter and inadvertently turn cars into so-called death machines, and shift toward the possibility that AI driving systems might do likewise, but with greater rarity, and that the humans behind-the-scenes that actually developed and subsequently operate the autonomous vehicles are to be held responsible for what the car does. As a society, we will need to grapple with the tradeoff of having self-driving cars versus the paucity of still existent fatalities from car crashes, which significantly changes the usual equation of balancing modern-day risks versus modern-day accessibilities.

That's probably enough for now on those two in-your-face incendiary remarks about cars.

The next conveyed thoughts seem to cover the bold declaration that we ought to avoid using cars. We are told that we should use the bus, subways, or bikes, rather than using cars.

No particular beef on that recommendation. Cars tend to be relatively inefficient when it comes to transporting people. The amount of space and energy consumed for the transport of one person in a car is not nearly as efficient as when using a bus or subway that contains lots of people all at once.

The rub is that a car provides a point-to-point form of transit, while a bus or subway typically does not.

If you want to get from your home to an office building on the far side of a city, a car can usually take you from the door of your domicile directly to the door of the office structure. In comparison, to use a bus, you need to somehow get from your home to the bus stop. Once the bus transports you, there is a need to somehow get from that drop-off to the desired final destination.

It is hard to compete with a mechanism that is essentially seamless and provides one-stop shopping of sorts. A car is pretty handy since it goes from point A to point B, and there isn't a need to change across modes of transport. It would seem that human nature is likely to gravitate toward the convenience of the point-to-point option.

It would further seem that AI self-driving cars will make that seamlessness even more abundantly apparent. The assumption is that self-driving cars will be readily available 24x7. Making use of a self-driving car is going to be easier than having to arrange for finding a suitable human driver that is available to give you a lift. Overall, the allure of using self-driving cars will further exacerbate the challenges of encouraging people to use other forms of transport such as busses, subways, and even bicycles.

Moving on, one of the remarks on the display panel was about the aspect that cars melt glaciers.

This is a somewhat complex commentary and would take a lot of ink herein to fully unpack.

In short, the likely idea is that conventional combustion engines are a notable contributor to adverse climate impacts. For self-driving cars, the likelihood is that EVs (electrical vehicles) will be used, partially due to the aspect that the onboard processors for the AI driving system require gobs of electrical power and that EVs are especially well-devised for that requirement. To some extent, an argument could be made that this will demonstrably undercut the melting glaciers decree when it comes to the advent of self-driving cars, all else being equal (it's a complicated matter).

Another allegation was that cars ruin cities.

This is an oft-repeated exhortation and certainly has some sound considerations. The basis partially has to do with the need to accommodate a tremendous amount of surface space toward simply having roads and also set aside space for parking. In many ways, this leads to a design of cities that is off-putting and disruptive to how people live.

Whether self-driving cars will significantly change the design of cities is still an open question. Some for example strongly argue that we will be able to remove the parking aspects and merely instruct self-driving cars to go outside of the city whenever they might need to be in a parked posture. This alone would radically reduce various space constraints in cities. And so on.

The roadside electronic display told us to stop driving, and that we ought to get rid of our cars.

Via self-driving cars, you indeed will stop driving. The AI driving system will be doing the driving. Seems like that appeal is satisfied.

Well, that admittedly is a bit smarmy as an answer, since the conveyed remark is ostensibly about not using cars, and thus for the case of self-driving cars might be reworded to something like "Stop Being A Car Passenger" or the equivalent heralding.

In terms of getting rid of your car, one viewpoint about the emergence of self-driving cars is that we will become predominantly a ridesharing or ride-hailing society, whereby very few people will own a car. When you need to use a car, you will request a lift via an app and a self-driving car will come to undertake your driving journey. The cost and convenience of doing so will eclipse any interest in owning your car (there is more to this, so see my columns for added explanation).

Conclusion

This brings us to the last remark to be covered.

It was this advice: *Honking won't help.*

Now that seems to be the most uncontested quip and one that we can all generally accept as a truism.

As you certainly know, the moment you honk your horn, you don't know what the reaction will be. Even though you might be honking as a considered kind gesture to alert a fellow human about some pending danger, the odds are that most of the time the honking will backfire. Many road rage incidents began with the use of a honking horn.

Will AI self-driving cars undertake the act of honking?

Probably so.

Please don't get mad. No need to go into a road rage outburst against an AI driving system. Besides, it won't be able to put up its dukes and defend itself. Seems like it wouldn't be a fair fight.

Who knows, we might need to put up electronic displays that alert those self-driving cars to not do anymore honking, and this might be officially posted on a formal PVMS by the proper authorities, obviating the hacker messages that decry the same sentiment.

CHAPTER 19
HOTTEST VEHICLES AND SELF-DRIVING CARS

Fast cars.

Furious cars.

A potent and volatile mixture is seemingly created by combining the two into being both fast and furious. Maybe a movie ought to be made with that as a predominant theme. Just a wild idea.

Whoa, someone already thought of that.

Yes, indeed, the Fast and Furious film franchise certainly seems to know about cars and especially what people want. The movies, TV series, video games, and even theme park rides are ostensibly jam-packed with out-of-this-world action, including outlandish heists, ingenuous spies, over-the-top villains, and of course cars.

Not just any cars, mind you.

Fast and furious cars.

What does that mean, exactly?

Let's take a quick glance at the cars being used in the infamous series and see if we can tease out a semblance of what gets the glorified title of being fast and furious.

First, the cars are usually real cars, rather than imaginary cars that were devised simply for purposes of making a movie. By and large, the notion is to take existing cars and do just a tad of upgrades to make them into super-powered cars. Probably a bit more than merely a tad of souping up. More like concocting a dream car by injecting the strongest automotive steroids known to humanity.

The initial source has to be a car that already has an aura of being suitable for getting into the rarified air of being anointed as truly fast and furious. You can't start with a dud car. The initial lump of clay, as it were, must be something that people already generally acknowledge is pretty much a nifty vehicle, to begin with (though not everyone will necessarily agree).

Such a car has to already be fast or can be made into being fast. This means that under-the-hood there should be lots of horsepowers. Turbocharging the engine will get it further into the rocketship shape that needs to be had.

Odds are that the source car is already known for its street appeal. Many look with envy at those that own and showcase that kind of car. The vehicle is considered stylish. The culture has potentially made songs about that type of car or featured the vaunted car in other fashionable movies. Cool people drive that car. Cool people relish the car.

You can expect too that some street racing has taken place with the model of cars that serve as the cornerstone of what gets into the fast and furious category. These are mean machines and at times have been used in illegal races on our public highways and byways. They are so-called bad boys to the bone in terms of the luminosity of what the car represents.

Turns out, they do have to be drivable.

That seems perhaps obvious, but the point is that a human is expected to sit behind the steering wheel and drive the wonderous automotive wonder. In fact, the line goes that some people are just not suited to drive these kinds of cars. You've got to be the right kind of driver. If you aren't a hot street metal handler, you ought to not be in the kitchen, the assertion goes.

A recent analysis by a car industry aficionado came up with a proclaimed list of the Top Ten best cars in the Fast and Furious series. This is entirely an opinion-based ranking and can readily be argued until the cows come home.

Get yourself ready if you are a gearhead and already in your heart have racked and stacked the hottest cars in the Fast and Furious franchise. I warn you that you might blow a gasket that some of your favorites didn't make the cut.

Anyway, here's the proffered list:

- 1997 Mazda RX-7 Veilside (*The Fast and the Furious: Tokyo Drift*)
- 2000 Honda S2000 (*2 Fast 2 Furious*)
- 1971 Chevrolet Monte Carlo (*The Fast and the Furious: Tokyo Drift*)
- The Flip Car (*Fast & Furious 6*)
- 1995 Mitsubishi Eclipse (*The Fast and the Furious*)
- Land Rover Defender (*The Fate of the Furious*)
- W Motors Lykan HyperSport (*Furious 7*)
- 1999 Ford F-150 SVT Lightning (*The Fast and the Furious*)
- 1971 Jensen Interceptor (*Fast & Furious 6*)
- 1970 Dodge Charger R/T (*Furious 7*)

How do you feel about the listing?

It might be a list that you believe sincerely hits the mark. Kudos goes to the listmaker. On the other hand, the list might be infuriating. How could they include such and such? Why in the heck did they not include the other such and such? And on it goes.

For those of you that aren't particularly into cars, the list is perhaps mildly interesting, yet doesn't provoke any concern either way. Sure, you might be saying to yourself, those seem like a reasonable set of choices. Not my cup of tea per se, you are thinking.

We can move on then and add a twist to the whole shenanigans.

Remember that I just a moment ago emphasized that these are all cars that require a human driver. I dare say we would not expect anything other than human-driven cars since that's what today's cars generally require, namely a human at the wheel.

Consider that the future of cars consists of AI-based true self-driving cars.

There isn't a human driver involved in a true self-driving car. Keep in mind that true self-driving cars are driven via an AI driving system. There isn't a need for a human driver at the wheel, and nor is there a provision for a human to drive the vehicle.

Here's an intriguing question that is worth pondering: *What will the future of fast and furious be whence we have a prevalence of AI-based true self-driving cars on our public roadways?*

Before jumping into the details, I'd like to further clarify what is meant when I refer to true self-driving cars.

Self-Driving Cars And Fast Plus Furious

For Level 4 and Level 5 true self-driving vehicles, there won't be a human driver involved in the driving task.

All occupants will be passengers.

The AI is doing the driving.

One aspect to immediately discuss entails the fact that the AI involved in today's AI driving systems is not sentient. In other words, the AI is altogether a collective of computer-based programming and algorithms, and most assuredly not able to reason in the same manner that humans can.

Why this added emphasis about the AI not being sentient?

Because I want to underscore that when discussing the role of the AI driving system, I am not ascribing human qualities to the AI. Please be aware that there is an ongoing and dangerous tendency these days to anthropomorphize AI. In essence, people are assigning human-like sentience to today's AI, despite the undeniable and inarguable fact that no such AI exists as yet.

With that clarification, you can envision that the AI driving system won't natively somehow "know" about the facets of driving. Driving and all that it entails will need to be programmed as part of the hardware and software of the self-driving car.

Let's dive into the myriad of aspects that come to play on this topic.

First, keep in mind that there are over 250 million conventional cars in the United States alone, which is a whole lot of cars. The reason that I point out this salient fact is that we are not going to overnight suddenly ditch all conventional cars and miraculously adopt entirely and only self-driving cars. There is going to be a mixture of conventional cars and self-driving cars on our public roadways for many years to come.

Indeed, some insist that you will never take away the steering wheel from them, other than via prying their cold dead hands from the wheel.

We don't know whether society might insist that all conventional cars be ultimately set aside and no longer made available. The logic for such a decree would be that self-driving cars aren't going to be subject to the normal human foibles exhibited by human drivers, such as drunk driving, distracted driving, drowsy driving, etc. The belief is that self-driving cars will dramatically lessen the number of car crashes, along with correspondingly reducing the number of fatalities and injuries associated with car crashes.

As such, there is bound to be societal pressure to aim toward using self-driving cars and avert using human-driven cars.

From a fast and furious perspective, the odds though are pretty high that human-driven cars will continue for a long period ahead and might continue indefinitely. Perhaps special restrictions will be placed around the use of human-driven cars. This might include only allowing such vehicles in certain locales at particular times of the day. It could be that those human-driven cars won't be permitted on the public roadways, other than an occasional parade or similar activity that showcases those "old and outdated" human-driven vehicles (yikes!).

Imagine how exciting it will be to watch a movie about those now antiquated human-driven cars (pretend you are in the future) and see how they can *still* be used to save the world and catch the dastardly villains.

All around you in everyday society and including outside of the movie theatre there are self-driving cars in abundance. That is in fact how you got to the movie theatre. Very few human-driven cars are seen on the roadways, if ever. Thus, going to see an exciting movie about fast and furious *human-driven* cars that are heroically utilized is, undoubtedly, bound to be quite invigorating and a riveting plot.

Some youngsters in the audience might question how those human-driven cars in the movie are being driven. Where's the AI driving system, the inquisitive young movie-goer might ask. Do you mean to say that there isn't an AI driving system in those cars? Unbelievable. When did that take place? Why didn't they use AI driving systems instead of muscling the car via their own brute strength, the youth might ask incredulously?

You might have noticed that the aforementioned Top Ten list of the Fast and Furious franchise contains cars that are over fifty years old (even in today's terms). As such, there would certainly be a reasonable likelihood that future movies will feature human-driven cars of long ago, even if the rest of society has moved on and opted to gradually switch over to self-driving cars.

Other perspectives can be envisioned by those always creative Hollywood writers of the future.

If people are relishing AI self-driving cars at that future point in time, it could be that the portrayal of the old fast and furious cars is made out to seem like a beleaguered pastime that no longer is worthy of rapt attention. Envision that the plot of such a movie consists of humans driving some stylish human-driven cars but they mess up and make things worse by doing so. The villain gets more powerful or the world sits on the edge of disaster because those fast and furious human-driven cars are somehow inadvertently fueling the demise of humanity.

Sad face.

Of course, you know how it is, movies can quickly turn heroes into louts. Anything to get butts in seats and make a buck or two.

Meanwhile, perhaps that kind of plot then has self-driving cars that come to the lucky rescue. Thank goodness, the viewers exclaim, some self-driving cars are entering into the story, finally so. Those magnificent self-driving cars are going to summarily dispatch the evildoer and ensure that the globe is safe again.

Yay, kudos go to the AI driving systems and the AI developers that programmed them.

More twists and turns are conceivable.

One supposes that on the path toward adopting self-driving cars, there are bound to be many people that are upset that self-driving cars are increasingly being used on public roadways. These are diehards that believe only human-driven cars are the proper kind of cars. Anything else is something that should be used only at theme parks and carnivals.

In that case, perhaps the movie plot would be that self-driving cars are incapable of dispatching the villain. After a valiant try by the AI driving systems, they are unable to drive as adroitly as human drivers. In that case, the human drivers appear and drive conventional cars that are rigged to be fast and furious.

An alternative might be that those gallant human drivers yank out the AI driving systems and take over the self-driving cars. They also happen to turbocharge the self-driving cars, converting them into becoming fast and furious.

Smiley face.

Humanity proves once again that automation is not as good as the human hand and human mind.

One aspect that you might be wondering is whether a self-driving car can be considered as potentially being a fast and furious car. Maybe you cannot use that catchphrase in association with self-driving cars.

Here's why.

In one sense, AI driving systems are presumably going to be devised to drive calmly and lawfully, thus they will not be driving like a maniac. If that is the case, you would probably have a hard time being enthused about watching a self-driving car trying to save the day. No fast starts. No furious driving. Just driving like things are meant to be easygoing, staying within the lanes of traffic, and coming to a complete stop at all Stop signs and red lights.

Would you really pay to go see a movie like that?

The thing is, there isn't any hard and fast requirement that self-driving cars cannot go beyond the bounds of calm and legal driving.

This is an assumption about how AI driving systems are going to be devised. It does make sense since we would all be likely upset to see a self-driving car peeling down the street and laying out a bunch of tire rubber. Not something we would be expecting to see.

That being said, get ready for a bit of a surprise. You can likely expect that there will be AI driving systems devised to drive like an all-out speed demon. I've predicted that we will have AI-based self-driving cars used in automobile races and do the kinds of driving tricks that right now only humans do

Conclusion

In theory, we will potentially someday be rating the makes and models of self-driving cars and assessing which are topmost in stylishness and capabilities.

Not all self-driving cars are necessarily going to look alike (they won't).

Some industry analysts assert that there will be a bit of a sordid competition among self-driving car makers to try and have their autonomous vehicles stand out in comparison to others on the roadways. It could be that the way for an automaker or self-driving tech firm to make their driverless cars seem alluring would be to deck them out and make sure the vehicles are considered hip and worthy of taking a ride in.

Those might then, later on, become the source vehicles for a future plot entailing that revered fast and furious driving.

The storyline might be that a hacker turns that model of a self-driving car into some malevolent AI driving system, wreaking destruction all over the place. Meanwhile, our human hero is also a hacker (the good kind) and converts a different model of a self-driving car into a hot street metal lifesaving AI driving system.

The two AI driving systems and their souped-up self-driving cars go head-to-head in a battle of the century.

Which one will prevail?

I realize that you are on the edge of your seat.

Looks like you'll need to purchase a ticket to go see the movie. If I told you the ending, you wouldn't likely buy a ticket and the whole franchise might fall by the wayside.

That's something that the movie theatres and the filmmakers would not find desirable, and nor would the avid fans that need a turbocharged dollop of fast and furious in their ongoing automotive diet).

CHAPTER 20
HORN HONKING AND SELF-DRIVING CARS

Horn honking.

We've all done it.

Some more so than others.

It used to be that honking a car horn was quite customary and an expected element in the act of driving.

Indeed, when I first learned to drive, the driver training class included a brief segment devoted to the use of the car horn (yes, that used to be a normal part of learning to drive). We were mindfully instructed on the use of a car horn. For example, we began by employing the horn in a delicate fashion such as lightly tapping the horn to generate some casual and modestly alerting toots. We also were later taught to lean on the horn and generate an ear-shattering blast, just in case an outstretched use of the car horn was warranted.

All told, the notion was that you needed to know how to use your car horn for a wide variety of circumstances. The horn was integral to driving a car. Akin to knowing how to steer, speed up, slow down, and the rest, you likewise should be versed in the use of the car horn. This was a seemingly obvious fact and nobody thought that the matter was somehow unusual, superfluous, or extraordinary in any manner of thinking.

The logic was quite direct, namely that if cars are equipped with car horns, there is assuredly a reason for having them, and ergo any newbie driver should be proficient in using such equipment.

You might go so far as claiming that the use of a car horn was fine art if you will. The person using a horn was considered responsible for doing so. They had to sparingly use a horn. This was not a trifling of a feature on a car. It was a potentially lifesaving device.

The situations that warranted the use of a car horn were supposed to be relatively serious and not for simply playing around. If another car was dangerously veering into traffic and it seemed that the driver was not aware of what they were doing, a hefty dose of the horn was considered appropriate. Better to alert the driver and perhaps overstate the case via the sharpness of the horn versus allowing a bad predicament to turn into an injurious car crash.

Besides the occasions when a horn was able to be used to aid and protect yourself, and other cars, and even pedestrians, there was leniency to sometimes use the horn for fun. You might be driving along and see your best friend nonchalantly walking on the sidewalk, so you would do a light tap of the horn to get their attention. The friend would smile and wave at you. You would wave back. All in all, an innocent and everyday occurrence.

Of course, like most things, car horns eventually became used in rather abrasive ways. As they say, that's what happens sometimes with nifty toys. They get extended into untoward uses that go far beyond what was initially expected.

One of the most common uses of a horn that is decidedly over-the-top consists of honking a horn at the very instant that a traffic signal goes from red to green, doing so when a car is sitting directly ahead of you and that hasn't gotten underway just yet. It is one thing to wait a solid handful of seconds and then consider doing a courteous short burst as a reminder that the light is green, while it is something entirely different to use the horn like a massive claxon and browbeat the other driver by stunning them with a bone-breaking blast of sound at the instant a light goes green.

That's not cool.

The thing is, a person using their horn in this aggressive manner is seemingly saying that the other driver is a complete dolt. Wake up, you idiot! Get your car in gear and get the heck going! That's what it conveys to the person that might have been ready to get underway and merely needed a moment to start doing so. They might consciously be waiting momentarily for the intersection to clear or have some other bona fide safety basis for slowly proceeding ahead.

Meanwhile, the horn blasting person is boiling mad that the driver has not pushed the pedal to the metal. Maybe this feverish horn blaster is late for work or has been caught behind slowpoke drivers throughout the entire day. For whatever reason, the person armed with a horn decides that it is the best way to motivate others around them.

Regrettably, this way of thinking often means that they use their horn repeatedly, almost constantly, for any perceived "infraction" by other drivers or pedestrians.

Of course, the response to getting bleated with a harsh horn blast is not necessarily going to be what the horn user expected.

Some drivers that get an anxious horn smacking are apt to go into a form of road rage. They might decide to purposely not proceed at all, staying still, doing so to further frustrate the person that has used a horn. Take that, is the thinking of the horn respondent. In turn, the horn user will likely try using the horn again, perhaps more so than the first blast.

The whole matter cascades out of control.

Another possibility is that the horn blast causes the driver to look around in anticipation of seeing something that causes them purposely to remain still. In other words, their interpretation of the horn blast was that the driver behind them was helpfully warning them about a danger brewing. Perhaps this horn user saw that a pedestrian had wandered into the street and was trying to make sure that the car getting honked does not mow down the innocent person on foot.

You might roll your eyes on that one.

The odds that someone would use their horn as a means to aid others and not due to a semblance of self-greed would seem like a stretch in today's world. To be clear, I'm not saying that it never happens, only that the chances of that occurring are relatively slim. A hornblower is usually telling others to pretty much get the heck out of their way, rather than seeking to keep the peace and altruistically aiding others. I realize that seems a bit pessimistic, sorry to say.

That's part of the whole problem with using a horn. Like a box of chocolates, you never know what you are going to get (well, more directly, you don't know why the car horn was utilized).

The insurmountable problem is that a horn blast has no particular meaning associated with it. The horn does not tell what the horn has been used for. Nobody knows, other than the horn blaster. What might be in their minds is at times an utter mystery. There could be a good reason for the horn being used, or there could be a wild and completely nutty reason for using the horn.

In addition, you don't know who the horn is being aimed at. Is it the car immediately in front of the horn honker? Is it somebody standing on the sidewalk? Is it a vehicle barely visible and already down at the end of the block?

Consider what reactions can occur to the use of this non-specific form of communication.

I've seen some drivers that were blasted with a horn that decided to allow the horn blasting car to proceed ahead of them. The driver then sneakily positions themselves directly behind that car. Once they are in the needed position, they start honking their horn at the other driver. Incessantly. The idea is that presumably, it makes sense to give that horn user a taste of their own medicine.

It could be that the original blast of the horn had nothing to do with them. Unfortunately, given that the horn is a scatter-style communique, everybody within earshot might think the horn was intended for them.

The resulting road rage incidents can turn deadly and drag an entire slew of participants into the melee. None of them necessarily know why the horn was used. None of them necessarily know who the intended target was. All they know is that somebody used their car horn and it was irksome that they did so.

People go to fisticuffs or worse sometimes.

All because of the use of a car horn.

In California, the DMV (Department of Motor Vehicles) has this official Vehicle Code verbiage about car horns (see Section 27001): "The driver of a motor vehicle when reasonably necessary to insure safe operation shall give audible warning with his horn," and furthermore "The horn shall not otherwise be used, except as a theft alarm system."

The formal rules emphasize that a car horn is only to be used when reasonably necessary and otherwise isn't supposed to be used.

There is a bit of a loophole in that the interpretation of what is reasonable versus unreasonable is open-ended. Thus, a malcontent might in their noggin believe that using their car horn was *reasonably* necessary, even though to any independent third party the usage was egregious and utterly unnecessary in the circumstances. This is something that judges and courts often have to decide when such horn squawking cases arrive at the courthouse.

Within the California DMV Driver's Handbook, the recommendations are that you should only use the horn when necessary, doing so to avoid collisions. You can also use the horn to get eye contact with other drivers, though presumably once again as a means to avert a collision. And there are allowed special cases such as using a horn on a narrow mountain road (providing a verbal alert for cars that are also using the road but might be hidden from view).

For those of you that have ever visited New York City, you might remember that the jarring sounds of car horns used to be a well-known part-and-parcel element of being in the city that never sleeps. During the day, you would witness and unwittingly hear the constant din of honking horns. On top of that, all night long there would be the blaring sounds of car horns too. Cabbies used them extensively. Everyday drivers used them. Truck drivers used their horns. It was an orchestra of grand proportions, though playing essentially one note, over and over again.

The joke used to be that assuredly this must be the city that never sleeps, due to the fact that the yapping horns kept you up all night. You had no choice but to remain awake. Anyone trying to sleep in their hotel room or apartment had to cope with the never-ending sounds of those ubiquitous and sleep wakening horns.

Eventually, enough was enough, and the authorities decided to try and curtail the incessant horn honking. Official traffic signs were posted that warned drivers to be aware that no honking was allowed in the realm of the posted sign. Laws were passed that stated the use of a horn was only allowed for emergency circumstances. A hefty fine was assigned to any tickets that involved the unnecessary use of a horn. Etc.

Some would say that discouraging the use of car horns is fundamentally wrong.

If that catches your attention, allow me a moment to explain.

They would argue that horns can be a vital tool for driving. Imagine all the lives saved or injuries averted by having used a horn as a keystone to achieving safety. If you suppress the desirability of using a car horn, you are going to lose out by making drivers second guess the use of the horn. In turn, when situations arise that somebody would have been saved by the chance of a horn bleating, the driver probably won't use their horn and the otherwise in-danger person will suffer whatever calamity was awaiting them.

It is akin to the old expression about tossing the baby out with the bathwater (a piece of wisdom that by today's standards is a bit rusty). The point being overall that the horn can be used for good, and by making the use of a horn into a bad thing, you are swinging too far and going to fall prey to situations that a horn use would have been crucial.

That's one position or perspective about the intrinsic value of using a car horn.

Here's another one that might raise your eyebrows.

Ready?

Some have argued that honking your car horn is a First Amendment right.

You see, a horn could be construed as a form of expression. Perhaps you opt to honk your horn in protest of some matter that concerns you. The car horn is not being used at that moment for traffic or driving purposes. Instead, it is the use of sound as an expression of your angst or declarative statement that you are trying to convey.

Generally, the courts have not especially given the green light to such a legal posture. You've probably heard about the famous notion that your freedom of expression does not necessarily allow you to yell "Fire!" in a crowded theatre. To some degree, the use of a horn when in traffic has a similar connotation. This is a complicated legal aspect and something still being bandied about in the courts.

Whew, that's a lot about car horns.

Based on this overall discussion, I would guess that you've likely come to the conclusion that car horns have many useful and yet also nebulous facets.

The horn itself is not especially the issue. It is those that choose to use the horn. Sure, we could remove all horns from all vehicles, dispensing with the topic entirely, but this would undeniably excise the chances of using a horn for the revered reasonable and contributory purpose it is intended.

It is relatively safe to say that car horns will remain a standard feature of cars.

Meanwhile, consider that the future of cars consists of AI-based true self-driving cars.

There isn't a human driver involved in a true self-driving car. Keep in mind that true self-driving cars are driven via an AI driving system. There isn't a need for a human driver at the wheel, and nor is there a provision for a human to drive the vehicle.

Here's an intriguing question that is worth pondering: *What will happen if you opt to use your horn toward an AI-based true self-driving car that might be nearby you while underway via your conventional human-driven car?*

Before jumping into the details, I'd like to further clarify what is meant when I refer to true self-driving cars.

Self-Driving Cars And Some Honking Going On

For Level 4 and Level 5 true self-driving vehicles, there won't be a human driver involved in the driving task.

All occupants will be passengers.

The AI is doing the driving.

One aspect to immediately discuss entails the fact that the AI involved in today's AI driving systems is not sentient. In other words, the AI is altogether a collective of computer-based programming and algorithms, and most assuredly not able to reason in the same manner that humans can.

Why this added emphasis about the AI not being sentient?

Because I want to underscore that when discussing the role of the AI driving system, I am not ascribing human qualities to the AI. Please be aware that there is an ongoing and dangerous tendency these days to anthropomorphize AI. In essence, people are assigning human-like sentience to today's AI, despite the undeniable and inarguable fact that no such AI exists as yet.

With that clarification, you can envision that the AI driving system won't natively somehow "know" about the facets of driving. Driving and all that it entails will need to be programmed as part of the hardware and software of the self-driving car.

Let's dive into the myriad of aspects that come to play on this topic.

The question to be pondered here is what will happen if you honk a horn at an AI self-driving car.

Turns out, I am around self-driving cars quite a bit and witness people that do indeed honk their horn at a self-driving car. But before I delve into those details, we can consider a somewhat allied question.

If a tree falls in a forest, will it make a sound?

You've certainly heard that question before. Seems like an age-old conundrum.

The answer to that question is relatively straightforward, plus it provides insights into what will happen when someone honks at a self-driving car. Those two topics seem to be completely disconnected, but you'll see in a moment that they are similar in key respects.

When a tree falls in a forest, there will undoubtedly be vibrations or waves that carry through the air. Anyone or presumably anything that can sense the vibrations and has apparatus known generally as the act of hearing will ostensibly hear the crashing sounds. If you define the word "sound" as referring solely to the vibrations and ergo omit the need for a hearing mechanism, you could claim that the fallen tree did make a sound, regardless of whether anyone or anything was nearby to hear it.

Meanwhile, if you insist that "sound" must encompass a hearing mechanism, and suppose there aren't any hearing mechanisms within earshot, you could contend that the falling tree did not make a sound.

In that case, when there aren't for example any people or animals around that have the sense of hearing, it is feasible to argue that there wasn't any sound associated with the crashing tree.

Hope that straightens things out.

This is directly related to a self-driving car via the notion of whether or not a self-driving car has any provision for detecting sounds that emanate from outside of the autonomous vehicle. Some self-driving cars are not yet equipped with externally facing microphones. Thus, the self-driving car is unable to detect sounds coming from the streets such as the engine noises of other cars, the chatter of nearby pedestrians, and nor the sound of a honking horn.

Without some sensory device intended for detecting sounds, the AI driving system is not going to have any tangible input that a horn is being honked by someone. Note that there might be microphones within the interior of the self-driving car, often established to allow for interaction with passengers, though these microphones would only tangentially pick up external sounds, if at all.

In short, for the case of self-driving cars that are not set up with externally-oriented microphones, the honking of a horn at a self-driving car is futile and will not be detected. I suppose you might conceive of this as akin to having a human driver at the wheel that is unable to hear anything that originates outside of the vehicle, perhaps because of their lack of hearing or due to the vehicle being so airtight that no sounds can penetrate the interior.

One concern about self-driving cars not being equipped with external-facing microphones entails the lack of being able to detect that an emergency vehicle might be nearby. Human drivers are expected to listen for ambulances, fire trucks, police cars, and other emergency vehicles that use their sirens to forewarn other drivers of their presence. An AI driving system would not viably be able to do this type of detection without an audio input capacity, other than scanning visually via the video cameras or using radar, LIDAR, etc.

Another qualm is that AI driving systems are potentially unable to detect any spoken commands or shouting that might occur by people around or near a self-driving car. A pedestrian might seek to yell loudly at a self-driving car to watch out for a child up ahead, yet the AI driving system might not detect such a warning due to a lack of outward-mounted microphones.

In the case of self-driving cars that have a human serving as a backup safety driver, there is a chance that this human might hear a honking horn (and other external sounds too, naturally). You see, many of the existing self-driving car tryouts on our public roadways have a person employed and sitting at the steering wheel as a monitor of the AI driving system. The human is supposed to disengage the AI and take over the driving controls when needed (see my discussion at **this link here**).

We, therefore, have two variations about the hearing of a honking horn. One is that the self-driving car won't detect the horn since there aren't any audio devices provided for that use. The other is that a human backup driver might be in the vehicle and potentially hear the honking horn, for which the driver might then take over the driving.

Those are the most likely aspects currently.

The third variant is a self-driving car that is equipped with externally facing microphones. This suggests that the AI driving system will possibly detect the honking horn. The key will be whether the AI developers have programmed the AI driving system to take as input the audio detections, along with having some form of pattern detection to ascertain that the sound is in fact a honking horn (there obviously can be a lot of street-related sounds detected during a driving journey).

Imagine that you are an AI developer and you need to program the AI driving system to contend with what appears to be the sound of a honking horn. What would you have the AI driving system do upon its detection of a horn sound?

That's a tough one.

Recall that we've already covered the vacuous nature of a honking horn. A human that is honking a horn might be doing so for innumerable reasons. Furthermore, the horn honking might have nothing whatsoever to do with the self-driving car. A person might be honking at other cars, or pedestrians, or at a duck that was waddling next to a pond that is adjacent to the roadway.

Human drivers oftentimes have no semblance of why someone honked their horn. Figuring out whether there was a bona fide roadway safety concern requires looking around extensively and trying to ferret out what might be the basis for the honked horn. This analysis of the driving scene might turn up empty as a revealing indicator for the horn being used.

Conclusion

There are a lot more twists and turns on this seemingly simple topic.

Via observation, I've ascertained that some human drivers honk their horns at self-driving cars because they are trying to declare that hey, this is neat, it's a self-driving car. This is akin to seeing something unusual on the roadway and honking just to point out the extraordinary appearance of the object or thing. Of course, this is generally an improper and illegal use of a car horn, assuming that the circumstance does not involve the pending possibility of a collision or equivalent.

In addition, some smarmy human drivers believe they are being clever by honking at a self-driving car, as though this is a means of testing the capabilities of the AI driving system. Please don't do this. Once again, it would be usually considered an illegal use of a car horn.

Then there are the sincere cases. A human driver might genuinely be using their car horn upon noticing that the self-driving car appears to be heading toward a collision. The hope presumably is that the AI driving system will detect the sound and take evasive action, or that a human backup driver is present and will take over the driving controls.

CHAPTER 21
AFTER COLLIDING AND SELF-DRIVING CARS

We all dread getting into a car crash.

I'm hoping that you've never had such an occurrence.

You might find of interest that there are about 6.7 million car crashes in the United States each year. Sadly, this produces about 2.3 million injuries and approximately 40,000 fatalities. All told, a car crash or collision is something we anxiously hope to avoid.

Even if you have nerves of steel, the moment that you realize that a car collision is imminent, you are emotionally bracing for the worst. The physical jarring is one aspect of a car crash, while the mental and emotional toll is another substantive factor. It is hard to keep your mind focused on what to do once the collision has happened.

The odds are that you have been taught or been told about the types of things you should do when a car crash occurs. Perhaps your car insurance company has provided you with a handy list of steps that you keep inside your vehicle at all times. Rather than trying to remember off the top of your head what to do, it can be crucial to have a written list. Your mind isn't going to be as clear as a bell in the aftermath of a collision and so any notes or prompts could be essential.

Some people use an app to provide guidance during the post-crash effort. That can be helpful, though the crux is that your smartphone needs to still be in working order. If the phone got cracked or damaged, you might be out of luck in terms of trying to use any salient apps. For that reason, oftentimes people keep a paper-printed version in their cars or their wallets or purse. Yes, something could happen adversely to those lists too, so the idea is to have a multitude of sources that one or another will still be viable for access.

Probably the most important first step entails making sure that everyone is safe.

Let's assume that you are driving your car and get into a collision with another vehicle.

You would want to see how you are doing and whether you are hurt from the collision. If you have any passengers in your car, you would want to check on them too. In terms of the vehicle you collided with, the question arises about whether the driver is okay and also whether the passengers of that vehicle are okay.

Safety might encompass getting out of your now collided vehicles. Heaven forbid that the fuel tanks are leaking or a fire has started. The bashed-up cars are prone to potential hazards that can further instill harm, beyond the initial impact of the collision.

Another consideration is whether the vehicles are potentially in an active roadway and might imperial additional vehicles to crash into you all. Traffic zipping past the scene could inadvertently get carried into the mess. This endangers those drivers and their passengers. It obviously further endangers you, your passengers, the other driver of the collision, and the passengers in that vehicle.

After trying to achieve some appropriate level of safety, the next step usually involves reporting the incident, such as by calling 911, if applicable. There might also be a need to request that medical assistance arrive. If the vehicles are in bad shape after the collision, perhaps a towing service will be required.

Finally, after all that, you are likely to begin exchanging pertinent info with the other parties involved.

This usually consists of exchanging data such as driver's licensing info, car registrations, and car insurance particulars. You would be wise to try and document the accident while still at the scene, assuming you are able to safely do so. In some instances, you might use your smartphone to take pictures, or possibly utilize an app provided by your car insurance company to document what happened.

That covers some of the top points, though there are certainly lots of additional steps that can be taken.

It is easy beforehand to think that you will calmly be able to perform those steps. In the midst of experiencing a car crash, those seemingly simple and obvious steps do not necessarily fill your mind. You are probably in a partial state of shock and not able to think clearly. This is especially the case if the collision is the first time you've ever been in such an incident. For those people that have experienced car crashes previously, they have formed a type of mental muscle memory, as it were, recalling what took place and what they need to do this time around.

Note that the foregoing description about what to do in a car crash or collision is predicated on the notion that the other car had a driver at the wheel. That seems absurdly obvious, perhaps. We would certainly expect that the other car had a human driving the vehicle, else it would not seemingly be in traffic and on an active roadway (I'm for the moment excluding parked cars from this discussion, and likewise a car that maybe was left in neutral and is rolling down a hill on its own, those kinds of special cases are a different matter).

Why do I bring up the blatantly obvious point that there is a human driver in the car that you've collided with?

Because you might soon enough collide with a moving car that has no human driver at the wheel.

Say what?

Consider that the future of cars consists of AI-based true self-driving cars.

There isn't a human driver involved in a true self-driving car. Keep in mind that true self-driving cars are driven via an AI driving system.

There isn't a need for a human driver at the wheel, and nor is there a provision for a human to drive the vehicle.

Here's an intriguing question that is worth pondering: *What should you do if you collide with an AI self-driving car?*

Before jumping into the details, I'd like to further clarify what is meant when I refer to true self-driving cars.

Self-Driving Cars And Collisions

For Level 4 and Level 5 true self-driving vehicles, there won't be a human driver involved in the driving task.

All occupants will be passengers.

The AI is doing the driving.

One aspect to immediately discuss entails the fact that the AI involved in today's AI driving systems is not sentient. In other words, the AI is altogether a collective of computer-based programming and algorithms, and most assuredly not able to reason in the same manner that humans can.

Why this added emphasis about the AI not being sentient?

Because I want to underscore that when discussing the role of the AI driving system, I am not ascribing human qualities to the AI. Please be aware that there is an ongoing and dangerous tendency these days to anthropomorphize AI. In essence, people are assigning human-like sentience to today's AI, despite the undeniable and inarguable fact that no such AI exists as yet.

With that clarification, you can envision that the AI driving system won't natively somehow "know" about the facets of driving. Driving and all that it entails will need to be programmed as part of the hardware and software of the self-driving car.

Let's dive into the myriad of aspects that come to play on this topic.

First, consider whether you would even realize that the car you've collided with *is* a self-driving car.

That might be harder to discern than you would otherwise assume.

Most self-driving cars will be equipped with externally mounted sensors such as video cameras, radar, LIDAR, ultrasonic units, thermal imagining, and the like. This does tend to make self-driving cars stand out in a crowd. You can usually see that these various contraptions are protruding and are not normally seen on a conventional human-driven car.

Well, it could be that it is a self-driving car but that it is being overseen by an onboard human driver that is serving as the backup or safety monitor for the AI driving system. This is being done on many of the existing public roadway tryouts of self-driving cars. The idea is that a trained and versed human driver is sitting at the wheel and ready to take over the controls if needed.

I bring this up because the self-driving car might have been in the self-driving mode or it might have been disengaged by the human driver and thus the human driver was directly controlling the autonomous vehicle at the time of the collision. In that sense, the self-driving car really isn't any longer a self-driving car and merely another variant of a human-driven car.

If that perchance is the case, namely a human driver was driving the presumed self-driving car, everything that you would do as a result of having crashed with a human-driven car is still entirely applicable. Essentially, there is no notable difference at that juncture.

For sake of discussion, let's assume that the self-driving car does not have a backup or safety driver present and therefore the AI driving system is considered the driver of the vehicle.

You have genuinely collided with a true self-driving car.

Some of the more outrageous vendors and even some of the pundits would insist that this could never ever happen. In other words, they claim that self-driving cars going to be uncrashable. Sorry to say, that is unmitigated balderdash and completely misleading.

Okay, so I am readily and unreservedly asserting that you could indeed have collided with a self-driving car.

Note that we aren't at this juncture of this discussion caring about the responsible cause or party of the car crash incident and instead focused on what steps to take while at the scene of the collision. It could be that you made a booboo and rammed into the self-driving car, which I've reported previously about people that have rear-ended self-driving cars (see my column coverage). It could be that the self-driving car rammed into your vehicle.

The key is that a collision has occurred and in the aftermath what you should be doing. Eventually, yes, there will be a need to discover who was at fault. This is part-and-parcel of any car crash, including crashes that involve self-driving cars.

As an aside, you might have heard some pundits exclaiming that we are going to be in some nebulous mushy area of the law about the fault since it will be the question of whether the human driver (you, in this case) or the AI driving system was responsible for the collision. This kind of logic goes overboard and tries to suggest that the AI driving system is sentient and will need to be held accountable as though it is a thinking being of an equivalent to a human driver.

I emphasized earlier herein that today's AI is not sentient. Not even close. You can't even try to contend that the AI is somehow in the same ballpark. It is not.

The key that I am driving toward (a pun!) is that the responsible party for the self-driving car is the automaker or self-driving tech firm that crafted and fielded the AI driving system amidst the self-driving car, plus the fleet operator that is running and overseeing the self-driving whilst on our roadways. Those are humans that opted to put the self-driving car onto our public streets and byways. They bear the responsibility for what the self-driving car does.

You cannot try to let them skip out of this and point their fingers at the AI. It might be a clever way to *attempt* to dodge a big financial fine or try to skirt out of their legal responsibilities, but it doesn't cut the mustard. The self-driving car and the AI driving system are human-made products that will legally be held to the same repercussions as other products that we use or interact with daily (see my columns for further elaboration).

Now, let's get back to the scene of the crash.

You have just collided with a self-driving car. There isn't a human driver in the self-driving car. That is our starting point of figuring out what to do next.

The same rule-of-thumb about achieving safety is still a tried-and-true mantra in this use case.

Are you injured? Are any of your passengers injured? You want to right away assess the status of the people involved.

This includes the aspect that the self-driving car might contain passengers. Though there wasn't a human driver at the wheel, there might have been people riding in the self-driving car. They could be injured and require immediate medical attention.

Again, similar to the earlier look at what should happen in the case of a human driver that collides with another human-driven car, consider whether anyone is in imminent danger. The danger might be from the vehicles themselves. For example, the expectation is that self-driving cars are likely going to be EVs (electrical vehicles), which makes sense partially to glean the needed electrical power to run the onboard processors for the AI driving system. As we've all seen in the news, sometimes the EV batteries can be especially endangering when a car crash occurs.

I'm not suggesting that only self-driving cars will be EVs, don't take things that way. There will be lots of human-driven cars that are going to be EVs. Regardless of whether the vehicle is a human-driven vehicle that is an EV, or it is a self-driving car that is an EV, the qualm is that the batteries could entail special risks as a result of a car crash.

Continuing our steps, a bit of a twist arises about the aspect of possibly being in the way of other ongoing traffic. If you have conventional cars involved in a collision, you can sometimes safely move the cars out of the way of the active setting. This has to be assessed cautiously. Do you try to physically handle the cars and push them out of the way? Do you attempt to start the cars and drive them out of the way? This depends on a plethora of factors. The vehicles might not be drivable. They might not be safe to be moved. Etc.

To some degree, this also arises with a self-driving car.

Suppose the self-driving car is considered in a viable drivable state and could be driven out of the way of traffic. The problem is that there is typically no provision for a human to get into the autonomous vehicle and drive it. You need to somehow convince the AI driving system to make this driving effort. This is problematic because most of the existing AI driving systems are not programmed to handle this kind of extraordinary driving situation.

By and large, the AI driving systems are being programmed to drive from point A to point B, such as from someone's house to the grocery store. You indicate the starting point of the driving journey and the ending point, and the AI driving system attempts to safely navigate there, using digital maps and other means of devising the path.

Imagine that your collision has occurred in the slow lane of the freeway. Both vehicles are now straddling the emergency lane and the slow lane. You want to try and move both vehicles out of the slow lane and entirely into the emergency lane, or perhaps onto some flat space that is adjacent to the roadway and looks safe to be parked in.

The odds of your being able to merely tell any of today's AI driving systems to move over like this is ostensibly close to nil. In practical terms, you would more likely need to confer with a fleet-approved remote agent that could either direct the AI driving system as to what to do or possibly have that remote agent directly take over the driving controls remotely (the latter is something that I have argued vehemently is going to be highly suspect, see my columns).

This does bring up a related aspect.

When a self-driving car gets into a car crash, most of the automakers and self-driving tech firms have the autonomous vehicle send an alert to the fleet operator. At that juncture, presumably, the fleet operator is aware that the self-driving car is in trouble and assistance will be needed. Usually, the fleet operator will dispatch a prearranged team to quickly get to the scene of the incident.

All of that is a bit iffy. The self-driving car might not have been able to send an alert or might be so damaged that it cannot send an alert. The fleet operator might or might not receive an alert. The fleet operator might or might not have a team readied to head to the location. The location might be far away from the nearest team and therefore it will take time to have them arrive. And so on.

I mention this because some self-driving car companies would have you believe that a top-notch crew will be at the scene instantaneously. That's just not realistic in all cases. Unless the self-driving car is being closely trailed by such a team, which some self-driving tryouts are in fact doing, there is going to be some semblance of delay between when the crash occurred and when humans pertinent to the self-driving car arrive.

If the self-driving car is still in viable shape, you might be able to talk with the fleet operator via the self-driving car in-car telephonic system. That's one means to discuss the situation with a remote human. I have also urged that the self-driving car companies ought to be posting a glaringly obvious phone number on the outside of the autonomous vehicle, kind of like those bumper stickers that urge you to call a number about the driving of a vehicle.

In states that are allowing self-driving cars to operate, they usually have a provision that the autonomous vehicle must have readily inside somewhere an indication of the car registration and the car insurance. In theory, you would be able to find that, though this could be difficult in terms of having to try and rummage around inside the self-driving car, something that could be a danger due to the effects of the collision and what the autonomous vehicle status is.

This brings up another consideration, namely that the self-driving car could attempt to continue driving, despite having gotten into a collision.

In theory, the AI driving system should pull over and come to a proper stop, entering into what is known as an MRC (minimal risk condition). You have no guarantee that this will happen, nor that it will happen flawlessly.

When a human driver is at the wheel, you can usually plainly see if they are trying to drive the vehicle and perhaps seeking to drive away or maneuver for some reason. With a self-driving car, it will be quite hard to know what is going on.

The inner workings of the AI driving system are not readily apparent to outside observers.

Overall, you ought to approach the self-driving car is an extremely cautious manner. The AI driving system might be confounded and make other potential driving moves that are dangerous. Another possibility is that the AI driving system has been damaged and therefore is of little use for the moment. I've discussed in my postings that this also presents challenges to first responders.

Conclusion

I trust that you can see that coping with a collision involving a self-driving car has its own quirky elements that are a variation of what happens when crashing with another human-driven car.

The overarching steps are still pretty much the same.

It can be unnerving though to be standing outside of a self-driving car and not immediately have at hand the other driver that you can discuss the situation with. Some lawyers might suggest this is handy because people tend to say things that perhaps they ought not to be saying while still in the shock of the collision.

The possibility of course exists that you will have encountered a collision for which there isn't any other human immediately involved. That is actually somewhat reassuring. You would presumably be always worried about the other driver and whether they are okay. If the self-driving car doesn't have any passengers, it also means that there aren't any other humans inside of it.

In a manner of thinking, it is as though you collided with a light pole or any kind of object that one might ram into. There is going to be damage done to the vehicles, but other than you, no other human damages (assuming no passengers in the self-driving car, and none in your car).

Meanwhile, imagine the outsized story that you'll have to tell your friends and even strangers. Hey, I got into a minor fender bender the other day, you might indicate. I'm okay, wasn't hurt at all.

An attentive listener might quickly ask, was the other driver okay?

Sure, it was just an AI system. Replace a few circuit boards and it will be ready to hit the road again. No emotional toll. No broken bones.

At least until the day that we have those walking and talking robots, for which when they are driving cars, you might want to be careful approaching the "driver" since they might be really irked and have those vaunted *The Terminator* glaring look in their menacing robotic eyes.

AI can be one tough android to deal with after a car crash.

CHAPTER 22
LINES PARKING AND SELF-DRIVING CARS

Are you a middle parker or a sideline-hugging parker?

This is going to be a vital question for you, which you'll grasp more unambiguously in a moment.

Here's the deal. A recent TikTok video went viral about how we all should be parking our cars when doing so in those parking lots that have clearly marked lined spaces. A brouhaha has now arisen. I'll share the sordid tale with you and bring you into the fold, as it were.

You know how it goes. As you drive down a row of parked cars, you are spying for any next open space. Upon spotting one, you quickly drive up to the prized piece of turf and maneuver your car into the allotted space. There are painted lines on the asphalt that denote what amount of floor space you are considered entitled to consume.

The question posed to you is whether you tend to park directly midway between those lines, or whether you aim to be closer to one side or the other of your teensy bit of earth. Take a moment to think this over. Your answer is very, very, very important.

Most of the time, your primary concern is probably that you don't want to scrape against any other cars as you manage to get into the parking spot.

Trying to somehow line up perfectly in your now grabbed up parking spot is secondary in priority. They say that possession is nine-tenths of the law, so your crucial first step is to satisfactorily occupy the space. Dive in there, however, you can squeeze into it. This keeps other interlopers from trying to claim they saw it first (which, they might have, but you now "own" that space and have presumably won an intergalactic battle in doing so).

Okay, after making sure that the landing has happened and you've secured the vaunted spot, now you look around to see how much room there is between your car and the adjacently parked vehicles. Sometimes those other vehicles are rudely protruding into your now conquered space.

Outrageous!

If you could summarily have those intruders' vehicles towed, you would do so, and gleefully relish seeing it happen. What kind of a nitwit sticks out and enters into other adjacent parking spots, you are thinking. Those that obnoxiously park in this manner are likely to believe they are somehow entitled to extra space. They presumably don't have a care in the world that it might inconvenience someone else. Sometimes people do this to try and sneakily take up two parking spaces, which they hope will discourage anyone from parking next to their cherished vehicle.

Anyway, let's assume for sake of discussion that you've found a parking spot that is not being encroached upon.

The adjacent vehicles are within their lines and not transgressing into your space. I would guess that most of the time that's how things are. It seems relatively rare that people blatantly bloat over into an adjacent parking space, though it, unfortunately, does indeed occur. We'll set aside that consideration for now.

You have the full extent of width available in your captured parking spot.

How much space do you have width-wise?

It all depends, but the traditional width for conventional parking spots is about eight to nine feet or so. A car is typically about six feet to perhaps six and a half feet in width. For ease of discussion, let's agree to use six feet for the width of a normal car and use eight feet for the width of a typical parking space. I realize we can easily quibble about those sizes, so just please go with the flow for now since it will make the discussion a bit more straightforward. If you like, after you've entirely read the rest of this discourse, you can readjust the presumed dimensions and reread it again, for which things will still make sense, I assure you.

Based on the presumption that a car is six feet wide and the parking spot is eight feet wide, we can use our heads to calculate that the difference is a matter of two feet. You have about two feet to play with inside *your* parking space. I suppose you could set up a lemonade stand and make some added dough with your "extra" space, though it would have to be a quite thin stand.

Anyway, the two feet are likely to be needed for purposes of getting out of your car. Likewise, once you return to your parked car, you'll need some of that space to get into your car. The two feet are your means of making egress and ingress related to your parked vehicle.

Consider how these two feet of space can be allocated.

By parking perfectly in the middle of the parking spot, you would in theory have one foot of open space to your left and one foot of open space to your right. To the inch. Well, that's in our theory land, but you get the gist.

What we also need to include in our calculus is whether the vehicles adjacent to you have managed to include any available space in their respective parking spots. It could be that the vehicle to your immediate left is hugging the line that borders upon your two cars. In that case, you have no added room by trying to temporarily make use of the space to your left, perhaps wanting to momentarily intrude as you open your driver's side car door.

Similarly, if the vehicle to your immediate right is hugging the line that borders upon your parking spot, this means that trying to use any space beyond your "internal" one foot of available space is going to be rebuffed. There isn't any more space available because that other vehicle is hugging the line.

In a squeeze play of a parking situation, whereby the adjacent vehicles are each hugging the line, you only have your own two feet of available space to exploit. There is no immediately available temporary space to leverage. This is nearly as bad as when adjacent cars encroach, though not quite so since you did at least get into the parking spot successfully.

The thing is, now you might not have any means to get out of your car.

Darn!

Sure, you found a parking spot and ought to be darned happy that you did. Set off some fireworks and party like you won the lottery. Nonetheless, you might be stuck inside your vehicle and unable to get out. That's not what you probably had in mind when you were searching for a parking spot. The usual assumption is that you can park your car, you can get out of it, you can go do whatever you had in mind, and when you return to your parked car that you will be able to get into it.

Seems simple enough, but that doesn't always happen readily.

Getting into and out of your vehicle can at times be a contortionist's job. You tentatively open the driver's side door, trying desperately not to have your door touch the side of the adjacent car. The odds are that it will bump against the other car in this squeeze play scenario. You look around to see if anyone noticed. Assuming the coast is clear, you steady the door and ooze your body out of your driver's seat, along with thinking extremely thin thoughts in hopes that your body can become one-dimensional and slide out without any further problems.

Let's though use a smiley face version of the parking situation and pretend that the adjacent cars have parked perfectly in the middle of their parking spots. We will continue using the assumed sizes of six feet for the car width and eight feet for the width of the parking space.

This is a blessing.

It means that you have one foot of temporary space from the car that is to your left, and you have an additional foot of temporary space to your right. All told, you now have available two feet to the left of your car, and two feet to the right of your car. Mathematically, this is your one foot of space to your left inside your space, plus the one foot of space that is to the right of the space to your left. And then there is the one foot of space to your right, combined with the one foot of space that is to the left of the car that is to your right. Say that quickly, ten times, as it is quite the tongue twister.

I emphasize that this is a calculation of the temporary space. You are not parked into their spaces, and only borrowing momentarily their available space when you need to get into and out of your vehicle.

You have the enviable and luxurious scenario of being able to use an entire two feet to get out of your car on your side, and if you perchance have a passenger in the seat next to you, they have two feet to use on their side too. The world has suddenly become a joyous place. Birds are singing, flowers are blooming. It is fortuitous that those adjacent cars were able to perfectly park in the middle of their spaces.

Ponder that notion.

We pretty much assume that most people will try to park their cars in the center of their parking spot. Doing so seems prudent. It gives the maximum allowable space on either side of your car, within the constraints of your limit lines. It makes plain sense to do so.

Envision a nirvana in which everyone always impeccably parked their cars in the exact center of the parking spots that they opted to occupy. In the case of six-foot-wide cars and eight-foot-wide parking spaces, there would be two feet to either side of each car. Every time. Guaranteed.

Side note, a smarmy know-it-all might argue that we don't know what portends for the cars parked at the very edges of the entire row. I think we can safely argue that they would likely have even more than two feet available. The assumption is that there isn't anything blocking the ends of the row. Of course, this might not be the case and possibly a concrete wall or some barrier is there. Those that park at the end of such rows will decidedly be shortchanged, a sad fact of life.

Do today's drivers achieve the purity of parking in the center or middle of their captured parking spot?

Nope.

Any casual glance at cars parked in a contemporary mall or movie theatre parking lot will showcase abundantly that people do not park that way with any semblance of consistency.

On top of this, it is easy to justify not parking in the center of your parking spot if there is a vehicle in the adjacent spot that is not abiding with the park-in-the-middle mantra.

For example, you drive up to a parking spot and only you are in your car. Only you will need to get out of and later back into the car. You don't need to worry about having any available space to the right of your car since you don't have any passengers on board. You notice that the car to your left is hugging the borderline.

What do you do?

Indubitably, you would mentally deduce that you ought to park as much to the right in your parking space, providing maximum distance between your driver's side door and the border to your left. In essence, this creates two feet of space, entirely confined within your available parking spot. The dolt to your right has essentially forced you into doing this, due to their careless parking and not having obeyed the rule to always park in the center of a parking spot.

You had no choice. The other driver made the choice for you. The moment they hugged the line on their right, it meant that any driver pulling into that parking space to their right is going to inevitably shift over to the right too, seeking to maintain a reasonable distance to get out of their car.

A close observation of cars parked in a parking lot will oftentimes reveal this cascading effect. Once a vehicle opts to park to the edge of their parking spot, the car adjacent will necessarily opt to do the same. And the next vehicle will do likewise. On and on this goes, causing an entire row to end up being lopsided in parking close to the line.

It just takes one weak link (instigator) in the chain to get all the other drivers to do the same thing.

I'm not suggesting this is entirely undertaken. It all depends upon where the lopsided parking effort originates. It also depends obviously on the actual widths of the cars, and so on. The point overall is that this can happen generally and does in fact occur.

A difficulty for many drivers is that they are not good at gauging where the center of the parking spot is, and nor how to align their particular vehicle accordingly. It seems that a lot of drivers have no visceral comprehension of the width of their car. They do things by wild estimation. Even if their lives depended upon precisely pulling into a tight parking spot and had to be in middle (else, say a menacing gorilla will leap onto the hood of their car), one doubts they could do so.

In short, parking in the middle of a parking spot is just too much to handle for most drivers.

Kind of a heartbreaking commentary about how we drive. Sad face.

This brings us to the viral video.

As though the video maker had just discovered the source of the Nile or the secret to those alien spaceships and UFOs, the video asserts that we should all park toward the left line of any parking spot and this would solve the world's problems. At least with respect to parking.

The notion is straightforward.

By everyone parking as close as possible to the left line, we would always be leaving open that roughly two feet to our right. Guaranteed (under the assumptions herein about the widths involved). Now, I realize you are thinking that you could do the exact same thing by everyone agreeing to park immediately next to the right sideline. Yes, that's true.

The basis for adopting the left line is that in a society wherein the cars are designed with the driver in the left side seat, presumably, drivers can easily align with the left line. Going back to how badly drivers seem to gauge the width of their cars, asking them to saddle up to the right line would seemingly be a disastrous proposition. Cannot be done, they would exhort.

You would hope that most drivers could at least align their vehicles with the left line. Naturally, any country that has the driver's side to the right side of the vehicle would probably want to use the right side line, leveraging the same logic already mentioned.

That is then what got a viral spin going.

Apparently, some people on this planet think that this is the best idea since the invention of sliced bread. Others scratch their heads and wonder why in the heck this simple idea should be so bandied about and get a buzz in the social media realm. One supposes that this does have a bit more complexity and weightiness than videos that show a cat meowing or a baby that spits up milk (please don't harp on me about that, I love cats, and babies are certainly adorable too).

Speaking of cars, the future of cars consists of AI-based true self-driving cars.

There isn't a human driver involved in a true self-driving car. Keep in mind that true self-driving cars are driven via an AI driving system. There isn't a need for a human driver at the wheel, and nor is there a provision for a human to drive the vehicle.

Here's an intriguing question that is worth pondering: *Would the left side hugging of a parking spot be more feasible due to the advent of AI self-driving cars, and if so, should this be implemented?*

Before jumping into the details, I'd like to further clarify what is meant when I refer to true self-driving cars.

Self-Driving Cars And Parking In Parking Spots

For Level 4 and Level 5 true self-driving vehicles, there won't be a human driver involved in the driving task.

All occupants will be passengers.

The AI is doing the driving.

One aspect to immediately discuss entails the fact that the AI involved in today's AI driving systems is not sentient. In other words, the AI is altogether a collective of computer-based programming and algorithms, and most assuredly not able to reason in the same manner that humans can.

Why this added emphasis about the AI not being sentient?

Because I want to underscore that when discussing the role of the AI driving system, I am not ascribing human qualities to the AI. Please be aware that there is an ongoing and dangerous tendency these days to anthropomorphize AI. In essence, people are assigning human-like sentience to today's AI, despite the undeniable and inarguable fact that no such AI exists as yet.

With that clarification, you can envision that the AI driving system won't natively somehow "know" about the facets of driving. Driving and all that it entails will need to be programmed as part of the hardware and software of the self-driving car.

Let's dive into the myriad of aspects that come to play on this topic.

Programming of self-driving cars to always park at the leftmost edge of a parking spot would be relatively straightforward.

You see, self-driving cars make use of various sensors such as video cameras, radar, LIDAR, ultrasonic units, thermal imagining, and similar devices to derive the nature of the driving scene. You could construe the sensor suite as somewhat akin to the eyes and ears of the AI driving system.

In the case of parking in a lined parking spot, the AI driving system would receive data via the vehicle-mounted sensors that are scanning the surroundings, and then utilize computationally pattern matching techniques such as Machine Learning (ML) or Deep Learning (DL) to identify the specific parameters associated with a parking spot. Via the video being real-time streamed from the onboard video cameras, the painted lines would be hopefully detectable. The AI driving system would then issue commands to the autonomous vehicle driving controls to maneuver into the parking space accordingly.

Generally, you could reasonably expect that this would be done with extremely high reliability.

The odds are that the self-driving car would nearly always park in the leftmost portion of a parking space if that's what it had been programmed to attain. Occasional exceptions might arise, such as if the adjacent parked cars prevented positioning in the leftmost portion or possibly due to obstructions or other oddities about a particular parking spot.

I might add that in the case of human drivers trying to always park toward the leftmost edge of a parking spot, there is a lingering doubt about the reliability of humans being able to do so. Though the earlier point was made that human drivers would presumably find it easier to park toward the left line and do so more consistently than parking in the center of a parking space, that omits the notion that humans innately have human foibles and therefore are not especially robot-like in their behaviors.

You can imagine how things might go in the case of human drivers trying to adopt a left-line parking rule.

Some people would flatly refuse to do so. They would potentially feel it is their constitutional right to park within a parking spot wherever they darned wish to do so. We would undoubtedly end up with some parking lots that had the left line rule, while others proclaimed you can park anywhere within the lines. This would draw some drivers to one of those parking lots and other drivers to the other ones. Of course, at some point, a left-line person would get irked that an anywhere person opted to park in the left-line parking lot, and fisticuffs would possibly fly.

On top of this, it would seem overly optimistic to believe that human drivers would properly align to the left line, even if that was their desired intent. I'm sure that many would cross over the line while attempting to kiss the line. As a result, there would probably be some sizable percentage of parked cars that edged over into the left adjacent parking spot.

Anyway, all of those complications would fall by the wayside with the AI driving systems at the wheel. No-fuss, no muss. Parking to the left line would be easy-peasy.

Case closed.

Wait for a second, maybe there is more.

Yes, there sure is.

We are going to have both self-driving cars and human-driven cars for many decades to come. There are about 250 million conventional cars in the United States alone, and those regular cars are not going to disappear overnight. In short, we can expect that our public roadways will be replete with a mixture of self-driving cars and human-driven cars.

This includes being in parking lots too.

Though the self-driving cars could readily and consistently park to the left line, there would certainly be human drivers that violated this principle. It would then toss asunder the precept that all of the cars would need to park in the same manner. We are back to square one.

You could have parking lots that are devoted exclusively to self-driving cars. In that case, the left line rule would be viable. Will human drivers possibly get upset that they are being kept out of the parking lots being used by self-driving cars?

Possibly so, depending upon where those parking lots are located, such as near a convenient place to be able to park your car.

Conclusion

Lots more twists and turns arise.

A self-driving car could essentially park anywhere within the lines, consistently, regardless of whether we wanted this to happen on the left or the right. As such, it might not make sense to enforce the left-line rule. You could instead program the AI driving systems to center the car in the parking spot. This would have the same general effect as parking to the left. It would be done consistently and ostensibly smackdab in the middle.

Some pundits insist there would never be a need to park a self-driving car in a parking lot, or anyplace else. They claim that self-driving cars will always be on the go, other than when getting fueled or undergoing maintenance. Self-driving cars will seemingly always drop off passengers at some suitable drop-off point, and likewise, pick up passengers at some appropriate pick-up spot.

Thus, it is conceivable that mass parking of self-driving cars is not needed. Furthermore, when self-driving cars are parked, humans will not get into or out of the self-driving car while it is in a parked position. Instead, the AI driving system will bring the autonomous vehicle to the passengers. You could then pack self-driving cars together like sardines, assuming you did want them to park someplace.

CHAPTER 23
LOYALTY PROGRAMS AND SELF-DRIVING CARS

The elephant is entering the room.

Yes, in terms of customer loyalty programs, McDonald's is on the cusp of rolling out a nationwide rewards point's effort called MyMcDonald's Rewards. I boldly assert that this is the elephant marching into the room because you are probably shocked that McDonald's doesn't already have such a vaunted program in place.

It seems that every company on the planet has already rolled out a comprehensive loyalty program at one time or another. For those of you that are coffee drinkers, I'm betting that you are either a member of or certainly know about the Starbucks loyalty program. Grocery stores have loyalty programs. Big businesses and small businesses have them. There was a time in the past when establishing a loyalty program was a novel idea and required crafting something out of thin air.

Not anymore, since loyalty programs are now a dime a dozen.

Of course, that's going to be an exception in the particular case of McDonald's, given the gargantuan super-sized motif of this acclaimed QSR (quick-service restaurant) chain.

Being touted as taking some sixty-five years in the making, the posted tagline that "loyalty never tasted so good" is bound to strike a chord with fast food diners. Various online stats posted by researchers suggests that perhaps 25 million people visit a McDonald's per day. That's per day, mind you. A whole lot of Big Macs, Happy Meals, Filet-O-Fish, Chicken McNuggets, and other such delicacies are ringing up the cash registers every hour.

The loyalty emboldening tactic of the MyMcDonald's Rewards is straightforward. You buy some McDonald's food and you'll earn points (subject to various conditions and fine print). Generally, it is a garnered 100 points for each dollar spent toward qualifying purchases. Four tiers underlie the consequent rewards that you can get. For example, consider that Tier 1 includes a free hash brown, while Tier 2 gets you a freebie Medium Fries. Moving onward and upward, Tier 3 gets you the revered Filet-O-Fish, but that's peanuts in comparison to scoring a Big Mac at Tier 4.

It seems hard to imagine that this loyalty program will be anything other than a mighty blockbuster and become one of the most popular customer loyalty efforts in history. That being said, this all presumes that customers and prospective customers will become aware that it exists, which is a hurdle to yet be attained. In addition, the odds are that a continual reminder will be required to get beyond an initial uplift based on media coverage and the usual word-of-mouth on these rollouts.

Time will tell.

Speaking of time, the use of loyalty programs as initiated by the airlines some many years ago was what really seemed to put the notion of loyalty efforts on the map, as it were. Customers taking a flight were wooed into joining an airline's customer loyalty program. You could earn points and then turn those into quite nifty benefits. The range of rewards included drinks or food during the flight, and encompassed perhaps the most sought-after advantage, being able to upgrade your seating. Getting free or significantly discounted flights was attractive too.

I recall a story told to me by Max Hopper, considered one of the greatest all-time Chief Information Officers (CIOs) and a pioneer in the strategic use of Information Technology in business. He had been the head of IT at American Airlines for many years, along with being the Chairman of The Sabre Group of AMR Corporation.

During a casual lunch that Max and I had together one day (we served on several boards together), he related to me an engaging indication about the formulation of the now famous and altogether pioneering loyalty program at American Airlines. Max related that the CEO of American Airlines, the notable Bob Crandall, had approached him while they were having a buffet-style meal in-house and wanted to discuss the creation of a loyalty program for American Airlines customers.

Throughout that meal, they discussed the overall parameters or general design of the loyalty program.

One thought was to focus on the number of trips that a flyer took. This seemed logical. After a bit of bandying, they realized that someone that took a lot of very short hops, perhaps getting from one locale within a state to another locale, would relish the use of this metric. On the other hand, someone that flew across the globe on essentially one flight would end up shortchanged. It didn't seem equitable to base the loyalty metric on the number of trips taken.

They then considered basing the loyalty measure on the number of dollars spent. This seemed like a unifying metric. The problem though was that they already offered various discounts and special arrangements for how much someone would be charged for a flight. This meant that things could be uneven by using money as the common ingredient.

Toward the end of that dialogue, they decided that the number of miles flown was the best all-around metric. This smoothed out the number of trips and the amount of money that someone was spending on their flights. It was pretty easy to keep track of. It was easy to explain how someone was accumulating their loyalty points. And, it ostensibly would allure people to flying greater and greater distances, which was a handy means of subtly getting people to fly further and more so.

Bob apparently then put Max on the spot by asking how long it would take to put together such a loyalty program, including all of the computer programming and other processes needed to get it underway. Knowing that he would be held to the letter on whatever he said, and also knowing that if the timeframe was seemingly too long that Bob would be distraught, Max was in quite a bind. Darned if you do, darned if you don't.

Max provided a suitable answer and the next thing that happened was that a skunkworks development team was rapidly put together to get the project going. All eyes were now focused on getting this speedily done and rolled out. Plus, they sought to keep things secretive and not let their competitors know about it. The AAdvantage frequent flyer program was ostensibly ultimately borne from that effort.

An exciting story of how something small can become bigger than life, along with the need to have a vision and work that vision into reality. I'd like to add, Max was a memorable figure and forever to be remembered.

Airlines used to get all the brouhaha about loyalty programs.

Nowadays, besides airlines having frequent flyer programs, there are loyalty programs associated with using cruise ships, using passenger trains, using cars, using scooters, and all manner of transportation.

The automotive-oriented frequent rider programs are especially popular. In particular, ridesharing or ride-hailing services tend to provide loyalty programs and the frictionless ease of signing up for those has made them quite widespread. For example, Uber has its Uber Rewards, containing four status levels labeled as Blue, Gold, Platinum, and Diamond. By signing up for their frequent rider program, you get points for using their ridesharing service. Benefits include flexible cancelations, priority support, priority pick-up at airports, faster response to ride requests, and so on (as usual, there are various restrictions and limitations, naturally so).

Is there anything that doesn't yet have a loyalty program?

Maybe nothing else is left.

Wait for a second, there is something.

Self-driving cars.

Loyalty programs associated with self-driving cars are still a gleam in the eye. That makes sense because, well, self-driving cars are still pretty much a gleam in the eye. But we might be remiss by not anticipating that self-driving cars will eventually and inevitably become prevalent.

Brazenly though assuredly, the future of cars consists of AI-based true self-driving cars.

To clarify, there isn't a human driver involved in a true self-driving car. Keep in mind that true self-driving cars are driven via an AI driving system. There isn't a need for a human driver at the wheel, and nor is there a provision for a human to drive the vehicle.

Here's an intriguing question that is worth pondering: *What will self-driving car loyalty programs consist of for the vaunted day that AI-based true driverless cars or robo-taxis are universally crisscrossing our streets, highways, and byways?*

Before jumping into the details, I'd like to further clarify what is meant when I refer to true self-driving cars.

Self-Driving Cars And Loyalty Programs

For Level 4 and Level 5 true self-driving vehicles, there won't be a human driver involved in the driving task.

All occupants will be passengers.

The AI is doing the driving.

One aspect to immediately discuss entails the fact that the AI involved in today's AI driving systems is not sentient. In other words, the AI is altogether a collective of computer-based programming and algorithms, and most assuredly not able to reason in the same manner that humans can.

Why this added emphasis about the AI not being sentient?

Because I want to underscore that when discussing the role of the AI driving system, I am not ascribing human qualities to the AI. Please be aware that there is an ongoing and dangerous tendency these days to anthropomorphize AI. In essence, people are assigning human-like sentience to today's AI, despite the undeniable and inarguable fact that no such AI exists as yet.

With that clarification, you can envision that the AI driving system won't natively somehow "know" about the facets of driving. Driving and all that it entails will need to be programmed as part of the hardware and software of the self-driving car.

Let's dive into the myriad of aspects that come to play on this topic.

Your first thought might be that there will not be any need for self-driving cars to make use of customer loyalty programs since everyone will relish using self-driving cars. In essence, if the marketplace already abundantly wants to use your product or service, perhaps the numerous costs associated with establishing and maintaining a loyalty program are unworthy from a strictly ROI (return on investment) perspective.

Keep in mind that many pundits predict that the price per mile for using self-driving cars is going to be much lower than the comparable human-driven usage. This significantly reduced cost is principally due to the removal of human drivers from the driving service equation. Human drivers cannot drive non-stop as can an AI driving system. Human drivers exhibit human foibles including driving drunk, driving distracted, driving drowsy, etc. That won't be the case for self-driving cars.

As such, the expectation is that we will enter into an era of mobility-for-all.

Those today that cannot afford to use a car will be able to make use of self-driving cars. The populace that is currently mobility disadvantaged will finally get an opportunity to utilize cars. And they won't need to know how to drive, nor have a driver's license or otherwise have any concerns related to driving. The AI driving system will entirely take care of the driving chore.

We can add further to this hoped-for aspiration by emphasizing that self-driving cars will not presumably incur as many cars crash as do human-driven cars. Today, in the United States, there are about 6.7 million car crashes, consisting of approximately 2.7 million injuries and around 40,000 fatalities. The expectation is that those numbers will shrink considerably. Some outspoken proponents claim the counts will drop to zero because self-driving cars will be allegedly "uncrashable" which I've debunked and pointed out that this has a non-zero chance of happening.

In short, why in the heck would self-driving car loyalty programs even be provided?

The answer is relatively simple, namely that competition is going to necessitate it.

There will be competition between those that provide self-driving cars as a ridesharing option and those that provide human-driven cars for such purposes. You can be assured that for quite a long time to come, likely decades, there will still be those that prefer using a human driven car over using a self-driving car.

Some people will eschew the notion of relying upon a seemingly invisible AI driving system that they cannot readily see, whereas a human driver is evidently there in the driver's seat. Some people will prefer the human banter and flexibility of having a human driver that will readily adjust to their needs on the fly.

For example, it is said that self-driving cars will likely be programmed to always stridently drive legally.

Suppose you want to be dropped off at a busy office building and want the driver to do a quick double-park to let you out. That's not going to presumably be allowed by an AI driving system, while a human driver might do so. Somewhat ominously, this leaves open the ongoing debate about how far might human drivers go to seem "better" than the restrictive AI driving systems.

Even if you are willing to discount the idea of competition between selecting self-driving cars versus choosing human-driven cars, there is the head-to-head competition entailing self-driving cars themselves.

Each automaker or self-driving tech firm is going to be angling to have their self-driving cars become the predominant autonomous vehicle in the marketplace. You can absolutely anticipate that the competition of ridesharing services that offer self-driving cars will be fierce, trying to outdo the other.

All told, as a means to try and attract customers to one fleet over another of driverless cars or robo-taxis, you can bet your bottom dollar that there will be customer loyalty programs related to self-driving cars. Assuming that we can agree that this is a realistic potentiality, the next consideration involves the shape and scope of customer loyalty programs when it comes to the revered self-driving car as a mode of transit.

There is a multitude of ways to lure riders into using self-driving cars and subsequently seek to keep those passengers coming back for more.

The most obvious aspect involves awarding points based on the number of rides taken via a self-driving car (as per within a given fleet being proffered for ridesharing or ride-hailing). Each time that you opt to be a paying passenger in a self-driving car, you get reward points. Those points would likely be tallied and there would be some form of multi-tiered rewards benefits that you could use, similar to existing and customary loyalty programs.

Note that I mentioned this would apply to paying passengers. I bring this up because there are likely going to be lots of opportunities for people to be riders and not have to pay a dime. In those instances, the question is whether the points get included would have to be ascertained depending upon the circumstance.

Why would passengers potentially ride free in a self-driving car?

It is envisioned that there will be a ton of deals struck between those that have self-driving car fleets and a slew of potential companies and entities that want access to the riders that use those autonomous vehicles.

When a rider gets into a self-driving car, you have achieved the classic butts-in-seats leverage. The question arises as to what you might do once that person is sitting there. The obvious viewpoint is to get them safely from point A to point B. The thing is, a lot more money-making activities can happen during that self-driving trek.

You have the proverbial eyes on screens that can be exploited.

The interior of a self-driving car will likely have large screen LED displays. These displays could show advertisements. Advertisers would pay the fleet operator to have their ads shown. The passenger is more than merely an object to be transported, they are a human that can be targeted for all kinds of other products and services. Meanwhile, the riders are pretty much trapped, being inside the self-driving car for the time involved in the transit operation.

Of course, passengers might balk at being bombarded by ads while simply trying to get a lift to the grocery store. Perhaps then the use of customer loyalty points could help entice passengers into a greater willingness to watch the ads.

If you aren't paying for the ride, it could be that the ads are covering the cost of the driving journey. On the other hand, if you are paying for the ride, and yet ads are being displayed, this might be made easier to accept as long as you were getting say bonus points. Depending upon how fierce the competition becomes, you might get points even when you aren't paying a cent for the ride itself.

Another consideration is the often-used catchphrase about capturing the so-called share of stomach.

This relates to enticing riders to have a bite to eat on the way to their destination. Perhaps a popular hamburger chain might be willing to cut a deal with a fleet operator to make things especially easy for riders to drive-thru their particular QSRs. The self-driving car will smoothly take you to a nearby drive-thru and you can dine inside the autonomous vehicle while enjoying the rest of the ride.

You can earn points for each trip taken in a self-driving car, and for how much you paid for the trip, along with points achieved by being willing to watch ads and possibly getting a bite to eat.

There is also the apparent aspect of getting points for the number of miles of your journeys too (akin to the story earlier about airlines and how to best assign those vaunted reward points).

There is also a share-of-mind.

This might involve your taking an online course while inside a self-driving car. Each day, during your daily commute, you might be taking a remotely instructed course on some topic that you hope will upgrade your skills. This will be easy to do.

You aren't driving. You have plenty of time on your hands while undergoing the commute. Might as well learn something new. And, earn points doing so, for which the fleet operator would presumably do a charge-back to the online course provider to compensate accordingly.

Yet another angle involves your destination. You see, a retail store might entice the fleet operator to route you to be dropped off in front of their retail establishment, being close to your indicated destination. The hope is to glean more awareness about the store and garner additional foot traffic. The same can be said for malls and essentially any destination that wants to attract potential customers.

Conclusion

Per the famous inspirational line in *The Princess Bride*, I'm only getting started on the innumerable ways to earn points via using self-driving cars.

Realize that you can be using a self-driving car and not even be a passenger in it.

Yes, you can use a self-driving car to go pick up something for you or to deliver something for you.

That is easy-peasy.

Suppose a friend that lives a few miles away wants to loan you their backpacking equipment for an upcoming desert hike. The friend summons a self-driving car, tosses the backpacking items into the autonomous vehicle, and the self-driving car comes straight to your home. Voila, delivery effected.

Seems like you ought to get points for being a loyal customer, regardless of whether you were inside the self-driving car or not.

The same can be said about having your children ride in a self-driving car, doing so without you and without any direct adult supervision at all.

When you send your kids off to school in the morning, you might be too busy to drive them, so you use a self-driving car to take them there. Now, some have a lot of angst about this notion of children riding without adults in self-driving cars, but it is likely going to happen.

I trust that you can see the big picture that a customer loyalty program for self-driving cars makes indubitable sense.

We have waited a long time for McDonald's to bring forth a nationwide loyalty program. In the use case of self-driving cars, I'd suggest that we ought not wait quite so long. You will assuredly start to see loyalty programs to entice riders to use self-driving cars, a lot sooner than you might think.

A quite rewarding thought.

CHAPTER 24
HIGHWAY DOLLARS AND SELF-DRIVING CARS

Highway dollars.

The news is replete with discussions about our national roadway infrastructure.

In case you didn't already know, there are a lot of concerns and complaints about the status of our highway system. Experts indicate that a lot of work needs to be done. The effort involves not only fixing those maddening potholes but also making sure that our roadways are properly navigable and won't fall apart upon us.

Our coast-to-coast highway system was initially devised back in the 1950s through the 1970s. An estimated 47,000 miles of multilane byways and highways were laid out, solidified, and put into use. Most economists would assuredly agree that this provided a notable boost in our economic growth and was a wise investment (well, economists rarely entirely agree on anything, so I suppose there are contentious viewpoints on this matter, along with thorny debates about what those economists are planning to eat for lunch tomorrow).

Anyway, we made ourselves a new toy that was gosh-darned useful. But then we let the toy degrade and seemingly deteriorate before our very eyes.

This is pretty much a commonplace form of behavior. I'm betting that you've bought products that forewarned you to undertake proper maintenance, and yet you neglected to do the recommended upkeep. Over time, the product began to falter and decay. If you allowed this state of woe to continue, eventually the product became difficult to use. Potentially veering into a danger zone.

Some pundits assert that our highways are in that sphere of getting towards endangerment.

I think we can all reasonably accept the premise that we need to have a functioning highway system. Our use of the network of highways throughout the land is essential. It would make no sense at all to abandon the highways and decide they can be junked like an old jalopy.

Okay, so we do need our highway system, and we want it to be useable. Cars and trucks ought to be able to traverse the highways. This includes not having to encounter gaping holes or drive across bridges that seem ready to collapse. This includes a relatively smooth ride that won't bust your axel or pop your tires. This includes a clear indication of where the lanes are and indications about how to safely navigate the roadways.

Does that seem too much to ask?

Some want us to go further and undertake a futuristic upgrade of our highways. I'll discuss this ambition more so in a moment. Right now, let's merely focus on ensuring that the highways are sensibly fixed up and made safe enough that we can drive them without undue worries. In other words, putting to the side for a brief moment the advanced stuff, we ought to make sure that the basic blocking and tackling is being undertaken, if you get my drift.

There is a cost to getting the highways system back into shape, along with potentially furthering its readiness for the future.

And that's where those highway dollars come into play.

How much do we need to spend on our highways?

Hold your breath, it is estimated to be into the billions and possibly trillions of dollars.

You could say that any prudent discussion about this kind of big dollars spending ought to also include a discussion about what we will get from those expenditures. Essentially, what is the ROI (return on investment) for the infrastructure bucks that are to be spent?

This brings us to the latest twist that is buzzing around.

In brief, our initial investment back in the 1950s through the 1970s was a first-time shot in the arm to our economic prowess. We gained a lot (most would reasonably agree, as mentioned earlier). This second booster shot is said to be less amorous in that it is not going to produce similar and pronounced long-term economic results.

Sure, there will be a lot of economic activity in the near term due to hiring taking place for roadway construction and while the infrastructure supply chain ramps up to revel in the spending. The qualm is that this is only a momentary boost and will not have a long-term effect per se. The crux to this argument is that we already derived the long-term bonuses by that initial investment of some many decades ago (a half-century, one might suggest).

Let's ponder this.

Suppose you bought a product that helped you get into shape and would build your muscles and tone your body. You used the product for quite a while. Your body got into tremendous shape. Good for you.

The product though was wearing out over time. This meant that it was not doing quite as good a job at keeping you in a muscle-bound condition. The product still worked, fortunately, just not as best that it could. Worse still, the product might reach a point of injuring you, unintentionally so. The various mechanical parts and internal belts could snap at any time.

Each time that you use the product, you are now taking an increasingly heightened risk. On the one hand, the product was generally able to keep your body in shape. At the same time, there is a scary and mounting chance that the product might suddenly go haywire and you become harmed, doing so while simply trying to do what you've normally been doing with the product.

For various reasons, your only choice is to fix up the product, rather than replacing it outright.

The money that you spend to fix it is now going to aid in keeping your already toned body in ongoing shape for a while ahead. When you originally bought the product, it took you from being a weakling to the muscular specimen you are today. That was already accomplished. As such, this new investment is just going to keep things as they are.

That could be a disappointment if you were thinking that somehow the new investment was going to entirely remake your body. Nope, it is an investment that will keep you going, but not provide outsized or outstretched results.

The genie was already let out of the bottle. Those grand results are now under the bridge, in the sense that they were already incurred.

Are you going to be happy with this new investment?

It depends. If you expect that the investment is going to pretty much keep things at status quo, you presumably are satisfied with what the result is going to likely be. On the other hand, if you believe that the investment is going to have massive and heretofore unrealized gains, you are heading toward some quite sour disappointment.

This is the same sentiment generally being expressed by some about the new proposed investments in our highway system. The highway dollars are going to produce some temporary and near-term economic benefits, plus keep things going. This will also avert the dangers of injurious conditions that otherwise the highways were decaying into. Those are all dandy.

Anyone expecting that we will then see an economic boost to productivity or other societal factors are going to find themselves staring at a barren cupboard, some pundits proclaim. In a nutshell, we have presumably already reaped the mainstay of the benefits associated with a highway system. Seems like we are saddled with having to make the new investments for the sake of keeping things going. The icing on the cake is that short-term economic spike from highway construction activity.

Sad face.

We should always though be cautious about predicting the future.

I say this because many famous predictions have been made that were based on the prevailing conditions at the time of the prediction being fostered. You might recall various infamous predictions that the worldwide market for computers would only necessitate having to provide a handful of computers (in the days of those bulky and multi-ton hefty mainframes), or that there wasn't any reason for someone to have a computer in their home (during the minicomputers era), or that 640KB should be enough for anyone to have in their computer (early days of microcomputers).

Those were seemingly sensible at the time they were stated. The prevailing mindset at the time of those predictions was ostensibly calibrated and guided by what was generally known and understood at that particular point in time.

Similarly, you might know that there is a fascinating debate about the use of horses in the early days of the automobile. Horses as a form of transport were the norm. Cars were just beginning to emerge. Some historical accounts indicate some people insisted that the horse was there to stay and the automobile was nothing more than a passing fad or quirky novelty. Supposedly, if you asked people what they wanted, they would have clamored for faster horses rather than seeking to have cars further embellished and made widely useable.

Again, this makes indubitable sense if you put yourself into the shoes of those living at that time. You see what you see, and make your predictions accordingly. It is easy to therefore not see what you cannot yet see. That's a bit of a tongue twister. The point is that you tend to make assumptions shaped on whatever you have in hand.

Speaking of cars, the future of cars consists of AI-based true self-driving cars.

There isn't a human driver involved in a true self-driving car. Keep in mind that true self-driving cars are driven via an AI driving system. There isn't a need for a human driver at the wheel, and nor is there a provision for a human to drive the vehicle.

Here's an intriguing question that is worth pondering: *Could the advent of AI-based true self-driving cars be a heretofore missing and vital ingredient toward predicting the future benefits of having a viably maintained highway system?*

Before jumping into the details, I'd like to further clarify what is meant when I refer to true self-driving cars.

Self-Driving Cars And Our Highway System

For Level 4 and Level 5 true self-driving vehicles, there won't be a human driver involved in the driving task.

All occupants will be passengers.

The AI is doing the driving.

One aspect to immediately discuss entails the fact that the AI involved in today's AI driving systems is not sentient. In other words, the AI is altogether a collective of computer-based programming and algorithms, and most assuredly not able to reason in the same manner that humans can.

Why this added emphasis about the AI not being sentient?

Because I want to underscore that when discussing the role of the AI driving system, I am not ascribing human qualities to the AI. Please be aware that there is an ongoing and dangerous tendency these days to anthropomorphize AI. In essence, people are assigning human-like sentience to today's AI, despite the undeniable and inarguable fact that no such AI exists as yet.

With that clarification, you can envision that the AI driving system won't natively somehow "know" about the facets of driving. Driving and all that it entails will need to be programmed as part of the hardware and software of the self-driving car.

Let's dive into the myriad of aspects that come to play on this topic.

The question to be considered is somewhat straightforward.

Could the advent of AI-based true self-driving cars alter our prevailing viewpoint about predicting the benefits that will be accrued from investing in our highway system?

The answer is somewhat complicated, though decidedly worthwhile to give due consideration.

My short answer is that yes, I believe there is a basis and substantive value in incorporating the emergence of AI driving systems and self-driving autonomous vehicles into the calculations and equations used to make predictions about the payback from investments in an ongoing functional national highway system.

If you look at many of the economic models used to predict the impacts of new investments in our highways, they usually assume that cars are cars and that trucks are trucks. This means that cars are being driven by humans and that trucks are also being driven by humans.

Boldly, reconsider those fundamental and altogether crucial assumptions. Suppose there were AI driving systems that could sufficiently drive cars and do so without any human driver at the wheel. Assume the same about trucks.

Human drivers are relatively expensive. They are human labor and we have seen repeatedly that automation can typically perform the equivalent tasks at a much-lowered cost. Of course, let's make clear, there are numerous exceptions to this rule. Especially if the task required employs human judgment or human skills that are not readily automatable.

In a manner of thinking, you could certainly question whether AI driving systems will rise to the level of human driving that is sufficient to replace the human labor used for driving purposes. We don't yet know.

The existing tryouts are very narrow in their scope. It could be that we can make no further progress and end up with self-driving that only works in extremely constrained circumstances, such as at slow speeds in areas set aside for self-driving vehicles. Though that alone is beneficial, it isn't the wide-scope hoped-for autonomous vehicle world that some enthusiastically envision.

Go with me for the moment and assume that we will achieve self-driving cars and self-driving trucks, doing so to the degree that the AI driving systems are able to drive (at least) on par with that of human drivers.

This ought to change how predictions are being made on the related economic benefits of a functioning highway system. Word to the wise: Remove from the traditional models those integral portions that are based on human-driven cars and human-driven trucks, and redo the modeling with autonomous vehicles such as self-driving cars and self-driving trucks.

This might require a significant overhaul of those prior models.

I say this because when I mention the notion of replacing one for the other, this has to be done sensibly. Those that merely plug in self-driving vehicles as though there is nothing different about them, other than lacking a human driver, are woefully under gauging the impacts of having self-driving among us.

There will be a sizable impact in many ways, including the legendary amplification of induced demand.

Induced demand consists of essentially unleashing hidden demand that comes out of the woodwork once something is more easily available or accessible. We've all undoubtedly experienced what happens when a new lane is added to a highway. Pretty soon, the new highway starts to get as swamped as did the other lanes of traffic. In the case of self-driving cars, many pundits predict that we will find ourselves entering into an era of mobility-for-all. People that until now have been mobility disadvantaged or impinged will start making use of cars.

Overall, you can expect:

- More people will be using cars (i.e., self-driving cars spur demand)
- Many more trips will be undertaken (easier to get around)
- Trips will become longer and longer in distances traveled (easier to travel afar)

Long-distance travel will especially blossom.

Much of the focus on the benefits of self-driving cars tend to concentrate on driving around town or within the confines of a city. That's the mindset that goes along with labeling self-driving cars as robo-taxis. We only consider taxis to be an around-town kind of contrivance. You might recall those humorous scenes in movies and TV shows that used to make a joke about someone taking a taxi to get from one city to the next, or utterly ridiculing the notion of using a taxi to get from one state to another state in the US.

Heaven forbid, nobody would do such a thing.

Time to toss out that mislabeling.

People are likely to utilize self-driving cars for all types of long-distance travel.

For example, you get up in the morning at your rural home and use a self-driving car to drive you downtown as part of your daily work commute. Whereas you used to have to be the driver, contending with all the usual driving frustrations, and be fully alert and awake as you do so, the self-driving car allows you to catch some extra sleep on the way to the office. Assume that's about a one-to-two-hour daily commute, each way.

You have friends that live in a city that is many miles away from where you live. Driving to go see them is always a pain since you had to make that exhausting drive. Via a self-driving car, you can joyfully make the journey. While inside the self-driving car, you can bring up some online videos or movies on the interior LED displays and leisurely count the time it takes to get to your friend's place. Assume that's a two-to-three-hour drive, each way.

As a keystone heads-up, I've explained in prior columns that the widespread advent of self-driving cars will likely alter our cultural perception of distance and time. In case that seems rather inflated, consider what happened when we transitioned from horses to the use of automobiles. The perception of long distances tended to shrink in the sense that you could go much longer distances in a relatively shorter period of time. This same reorientation will occur due to the prevalence of self-driving cars.

Follow me on this with some quick examples.

Suppose you are living in Los Angeles. Pretend the weekend is coming up and you want to drive to Las Vegas, Nevada. That is about a 270-mile drive and can be quite boring since it is primarily a traversal through desert highways. Via a self-driving car, and still going at the legal speed limits, the otherwise four or maybe five-hour drive can whisk you to Vegas while you are snoozing or watching films (maybe about gambling and how to win at the poker table).

Okay, we've now gotten ourselves readily taking a five-hour driving journey, but without having to do any driving since the AI driving system is handling it all for you.

There's more.

Some relatives of yours are living in Phoenix, Arizona, and are those proverbial snowbirds (people that come to Phoenix during the winter from other colder climates as a means of escaping the freezing snow and ice). You would relish going to see them but the drive from Los Angeles is about six or seven hours long.

No problem with a self-driving car.

After work on a Friday night, you get into a self-driving car and by the time morning arises, you've arrived in Phoenix. Unlike trying to fly there, you didn't have to go to a packed airport, you didn't have to sit in an airplane with a bunch of impatient and irritating fellow flyers, etc. You enjoyed the personal comforts of a private and quiet car ride.

Think about all the changes that will occur regarding the expanded view about:

- Visiting of friends
- Visiting of relatives
- Leisure or vacation trips
- Commuting to work
- Attending conferences
- Business trips
- Etc.

That's why you cannot simply take a model that has conventional cars as the mode of transit and in any perfunctory way swap out those cars for instead the use of self-driving cars.

A paradigm shift is required.

The impact will occur for trips:

- Within and across a town or city
- Within and across a region
- Within and across a state (intrastate travel)
- Amongst and across states (interstate travel)
- Among and across countries (e.g., USA, Mexico, Canada)

The national highway system is the interconnecting piece to all of this.

Without the nationwide highway system up to par and being in decent shape, you would only end up with localized benefits of self-driving cars. Essentially, the self-driving car usage would be confined to primarily local kinds of travel and not readily be able to make those fuller long-distance trips.

There is a well-known computational model that covers long-distance travel and was devised via the support of the U.S. Department of Transportation and the Federal Highway Administration (FHWA). Known commonly as the rJourney model, it has no official provision as yet for the inclusion of self-driving cars and nor self-driving trucks. Researchers have been leveraging the model to see if it can be retrofitted or potentially revamped accordingly.

Here's what the DOT had originally indicated about the model (which was initially based on travel data from 2010):

> "The US Department of Transportation (US DOT) recognizes that long-distance travel represents a significant portion of all travel and that this type of travel is economically important. In 1995, the date of the last long-distance passenger travel survey in the United States, 25% of all person-miles traveled in the United States were classified as long-distance travel. Long-distance travel includes both Business and Leisure travel, both of which are major contributors to the United States economy. As a result, the US DOT desires to support continued high levels of personal mobility for both economic and social purposes."

This clearly showcases the logical and altogether sensible assertion that our travel has substantive impacts economically.

Therefore, if our travel habits and tendencies are going to dramatically be reshaped due to the use of self-driving cars, it stands to reason that we are bound to experience notable economic differences.

It's time to figure those out.

Conclusion

There are a lot more twists and turns on this topic.

For example, as earlier intimated, some argue we need to ensure that the highway dollars go toward adding all sorts of high-tech to our roadway infrastructure.

In short, the question arises as to how much of the money should go toward fixing the highway system so that it is passable by human driver standards versus doing presumed upgrades or advancements that will further enable the use of autonomous vehicles.

One fervent posture is that the funds ought to be used to make things easier for self-driving cars and self-driving trucks to traverse our highways. Not everyone concurs about that perspective, especially if this implies that there is somehow less done toward ensuring that human drivers are able to sufficiently traverse our national highways.

At least that recognizes the importance of thinking about autonomous vehicles.

The main gripe surfaced in this discussion is that numerous modelers and pontificators about the highway system are seemingly ignoring the potential emergence of self-driving vehicles all told. They aren't even downplaying the impact, and instead are omitting it mindlessly (out of sight, out of mind).

I realize it is hard right now to envision a nation that is being continually traversed by self-driving cars. Notice too that I didn't even bring up the notion of empty self-driving cars, ones that are making a road trip and there isn't any human inside the autonomous vehicle. This is another use of self-driving cars that we have to encompass into our models.

If we look back at history and recalibrate those early predictions associated with computers, we know now that the world did indeed need more than just a handful of computers, and that we do have computers generally in every home, and that we surely needed more than just 640K bytes of memory for our computers.

Do this: Turn the clock forward toward the near future.

Let's please not be chagrined and upon belated reflection have a dismal sinking feeling or abject realization that we blatantly forgot to consider the role of self-driving vehicles. That's a "missing factor" that will leave us ill-prepared and decidedly ridiculed by an endless stream of stinging and satirical memes, or worse.

That will be gosh-darned hard to stomach and a pitiful shame.

CHAPTER 25
EYESORE GRAFFITTI AND SELF-DRIVING CARS

Graffiti can invoke quite heated debates.

Some assert that graffiti is a blight, a blemish, altogether offensive, and ought to be condemned as a practice. Many municipalities have laws on the books that make it illegal to produce graffiti. It is considered a form of vandalism. Besides creating an eyesore, there are lots of other qualms about allowing graffiti to exist and potentially flourish.

For example, arguments are made that graffiti is oftentimes a precursor to worse crimes. If you allow graffiti to be marked here and there, you are presumably saying that lawlessness is being tolerated and potentially even encouraged. This is the contention behind the slippery slope theories about graffiti. Once you start falling down the graffiti abyss, it can end up badly and generate a soul-crushing crime spree of shocking proportions.

A contrarian view is that graffiti is art. If you try to censor or prevent graffiti, this is tantamount to suppressing freedom of expression.

Furthermore, the argument sometimes goes, the display of graffiti is nothing more than letting off a bit of harmless steam. When you try to keep the steam bottled up, it will merely boil and eventually explode, perhaps transforming into wanton crime. Thus, the claim is that attempts to stop graffiti are what leads to crime, rather than the acceptance of graffiti upon our public facades.

Dizzying.

One thing to keep in mind is that graffiti is apparently about as old as the capability of humanity to mark on walls, perhaps including primitive cave walls. There is certainly substantial evidence that graffiti seemed to exist in ancient Greece and during the Roman Empire. Of course, just because graffiti has been around for a long time does not necessarily make it right.

Again, you can posit postures both for and against graffiti.

Law enforcement tends to point out that graffiti can be a type of territorial marking by street gangs (frequently accompanied by tagging or including specific markings connoting the particular gang). In that case, the notion is that the otherwise "innocuous" graffiti has shifted out of the artsy framework and become a crime-inducing tool. A street gang that marks with graffiti is likely to be willing to defend their turf by armed means. A rival gang is bound to take offense at markings that are displayed in their territory. The inevitable clashes can produce deaths and injuries, not only among the gang members but extend into the innocent public at large.

On the other hand, in some stifling political settings, the use of graffiti might be the only viable means for a suppressed populous to express their beliefs in any publicly seen way. The spray painting or marking that is undertaken to produce graffiti is usually done in a secretive manner, doing so at nighttime in darkness or when others are asleep or not watching. This provides a semblance of anonymity, which could be vital if there are powerful political forces that would harshly stifle those wishing to voice alternative beliefs.

Back and forth we can go on the merits and demerits of graffiti.

Where does graffiti usually appear?

I'm sure that you've seen graffiti in a wide variety of places. We almost seem to shrug our shoulders somewhat and accept the idea that there will be graffiti on the walls of subways or inside pubic bathrooms. That just seems to happen as though by some mystical force.

When driving your car, I'd bet that you come across graffiti if you are driving with any regularity and especially when driving in busy cities or anyplace of a sizeable population. There is graffiti written or splayed onto the walls of office buildings. There is graffiti on bus benches. There is graffiti at times on traffic signs such as Stop signs that are marked with graffiti.

You might think that being on a freeway would somehow avoid any chance of seeing graffiti. Not so. There is likely graffiti on the walls that serve to guard the freeway and protect from pedestrians or others meandering out onto an active byway. There is graffiti on the overpasses. There is graffiti on the underside of overpasses. And so on.

In fact, while driving, you are bound to see graffiti in every which way. Upon driving along, you might see graffiti on the walls of the freeway. In addition, you can clearly see buildings that are built adjacent to the freeway, and perhaps the walls that front the roadway are coated with graffiti. The traffic directional signs that tell you what the next exit will be can have graffiti on them. Etc.

You almost have no choice but to see such graffiti.

Why so?

As a driver, you are obligated to keep your eyes on the road. This includes the entirety of the driving scene. Even though you might be concentrating on the cars and trucks ahead of you, nonetheless you are cognizant of the other roadway objects too. Your eyes are gazing all around, looking to make sure that there aren't any surprises that might suddenly alter your driving efforts.

I've known drivers that mentally blotted out the graffiti after seeing it day after day. In other words, when driving in a new area that you've not previously encountered, you are likely to be hyper-aware and be looking at everything around you. Once you've made the same commute dozens of times, you begin to only notice something new and unusual. If there has been graffiti there the entire time, this tends to go into your mind as not pertinent to the driving task and it mentally gets disregarded.

That doesn't mean that out of mind also means out of sight.

You still can see the graffiti.

If someone were riding with you and they had never gone that route, they are bound to point out to you that there are numerous graffiti markings. At that juncture, you might be jarred out of your complacency and suddenly see anew that which had begun totally familiar and humdrum. The other person might comment on the question of how you can tolerate all that graffiti, and the verbalization of the qualm is enough to knock you out of the fog that blanketed the graffiti in your noggin.

There is a whole lot more to the matter of graffiti and we ought to cover herein some additional insights worth noodling on.

Some stridently point out that graffiti can produce negative environmental effects. There is the visual blight involved, assuming that the graffiti is seen as an eyesore. The graffiti might be produced via the use of toxic chemicals and therefore produce adverse environmental consequences. Consider too the effort to later remove the graffiti which can also consume and generate toxic mixtures and cause disposal nightmares.

A local municipality might not be able to afford the cost to get rid of graffiti in the sense of bearing the burdensome costs to find and remove the graffiti. Someone making graffiti can do so relatively cheaply. The labor and effort to remove the graffiti can be very costly. There is a decided cat and mouse game that often occurs in the graffiti-producing and graffiti-removing gambits. The problem for those removing the graffiti is that the price tag to do so is woefully out of proportion to those that are generating the graffiti (cheap to make, costly to excise).

To try and cope with graffiti, some administrations will create a database that catalogs the graffiti in their township. This provides a means to track where the graffiti is appearing, along with noting when it will be removed and tracing the costs and labor consumed to do so.

Patterns can be potentially uncovered by analyzing the database info.

For example, perhaps a database analysis reveals that graffiti in a particular city tends to be applied to buildings that abut the freeway and for which there is no fence around the building and little or no lighting at nighttime. If that is the case, there is a chance that some modest preventative efforts might aid in curtailing the graffiti. By getting the building owners to put up fences and add lighting, it might shut down those surfaces from being so readily exploited by the graffiti makers.

Lamentedly, in the ongoing cat and mouse ploy, the graffiti makers might perceive that those erected blockages are merely a challenge to be merrily overcome. As such, they might cut through the fences and attempt to knock out the lighting.

Or the graffiti makers might decide to find places that are less difficult to mark, and ergo opt to do their graffiti elsewhere and you've not reduced the graffiti impulse per se. Some pundits worry that various "defensive" efforts to curtail graffiti that only focus on ways to make graffiti harder to apply simply push the graffiti makers around town, spurring those makers into finding new spots. Thus, they are not being discouraged from continuing to proffer their graffiti. It is for that reason that some argue you need to get at the root causes that are stoking the graffiti, and presumably, rein in the graffiti by lessening those factors.

The databases that are used to track graffiti can be utilized in a multitude of ways.

Police might analyze the data to gauge where various gangs are setting up the turf. In addition, when the markings of one gang start appearing into the presumed sphere of another gang, the police might be able to anticipate that gang-related shootings and stabbings are going to arise. This can give a heads-up for those community programs that are trying to solve local gang confrontations. Plus, law enforcement can beef up efforts to try and stop the skirmishes before they erupt.

When you are driving your car in an area that has graffiti, it can be surprising to see the graffiti and act as a wake-up call about where you are. In some instances, this might be a safety-oriented wake-up call. In other cases, perhaps the wake-up is that there needs to be more done to cope with the underlying causes that are spurring the graffiti efforts. One supposes that at times, the graffiti can also be seen as a work of art and admired for what it portrays.

There is one thing about graffiti that we can nearly all definitively agree with.

For drivers, graffiti is a potential distractor from the driving task.

Despite whatever else you might believe about graffiti and whether it is a rightful practice or a wrongful practice, it can be a distractor to drivers. A person at the wheel of a car should be paying attention to the roadway and all of the objects in the driving scene that is directly pertinent to the driving chore at hand.

The graffiti is not adding value as an indicator of the roadway status. You could argue that it is doing much worse. If the graffiti is marked on traffic signs, this might make it harder to discern what the traffic sign is meant to convey. Any delay in being able to properly read a traffic sign can produce driver errors. Driver errors can lead to getting into fender benders or all-out car crashes.

On top of this, a driver that tries to look upward at graffiti painted on the underside of an overpass is tempting fate in a very terrible way. While looking up at the graffiti, the car or truck immediately ahead of them might be applying their brakes and this distracted driver is unaware of that impending action. Wham and the distracted driver smashes into those other vehicles ahead.

I'm sure that some smarmy retorts would be that only drivers that are dolts would be distracted by graffiti. The argument would be that any driver that is worth their salt ought to be able to drive fully and unencumbered despite whatever graffiti might exist around them.

The problem with that retort is that anyone making such a claim does not seem to be driving in the same real-world as the rest of us. Drivers are distracted by all kinds of things and you cannot make a blanket claim that only bad drivers do so. Added to this distraction is that even a careful driver might be fooled into thinking that the graffiti is some form of roadway indication, or in the case of marking on roadway signs the graffiti is purposefully preventing the driver from being fully attentive.

My point is that you would be hard-pressed to contend that graffiti is not distracting to drivers. And you would be further hard-pressed to argue that drivers should miraculously ignore the graffiti as though it isn't there at all. Pardon my French, but face up to reality, please.

Graffiti that is visible to drivers is adding risk to the driving task.

You can try to debate what level of risk is being derived, and you can assuredly point out that there are lots of other distractors in the everyday driving arena, but the bottom line is that graffiti is a distractor. Whatever other value you might place on graffiti, it has to also accept the unfavorable burden of being a driving distractor. That is rather cut and dried, I'd say.

Speaking of cars, the future of cars consists of AI-based true self-driving cars.

There isn't a human driver involved in a true self-driving car. Keep in mind that true self-driving cars are driven via an AI driving system. There isn't a need for a human driver at the wheel, and nor is there a provision for a human to drive the vehicle.

Here's an intriguing question that is worth pondering: *How will AI-based true self-driving cars handle graffiti that is visible in the roadway scene, and how might we leverage the advent of self-driving cars toward society contending with graffiti?*

Before jumping into the details, I'd like to further clarify what is meant when I refer to true self-driving cars.

Self-Driving Cars And Graffiti Around Us All

For Level 4 and Level 5 true self-driving vehicles, there won't be a human driver involved in the driving task.

All occupants will be passengers.

The AI is doing the driving.

One aspect to immediately discuss entails the fact that the AI involved in today's AI driving systems is not sentient. In other words, the AI is altogether a collective of computer-based programming and algorithms, and most assuredly not able to reason in the same manner that humans can.

Why this added emphasis about the AI not being sentient?

Because I want to underscore that when discussing the role of the AI driving system, I am not ascribing human qualities to the AI. Please be aware that there is an ongoing and dangerous tendency these days to anthropomorphize AI. In essence, people are assigning human-like sentience to today's AI, despite the undeniable and inarguable fact that no such AI exists as yet.

With that clarification, you can envision that the AI driving system won't natively somehow "know" about the facets of driving. Driving and all that it entails will need to be programmed as part of the hardware and software of the self-driving car.

Let's dive into the myriad of aspects that come to play on this topic.

The first aspect to cover encompasses the detection of graffiti by self-driving cars. If self-driving cars aren't able to detect graffiti then the case is summarily closed and we can move on. Thus, detection is vital.

Self-driving cars will be outfitted with a sensor suite that is used to detect the driving scene. Devices include video cameras, radar,

LIDAR, ultrasonic units, and the like. These sensors are active while the self-driving car is underway and feed data into the onboard AI driving system. The AI driving them uses the data as though the sensors are essentially acting as the eyes and ears of the autonomous vehicle.

Many people seem to falsely think that self-driving cars will only be sensing whatever is immediately necessary for purposes of driving the vehicle.

That kind of narrow sensing is not especially in the cards, as it were.

In reality, the sensors are capturing a wide array of data that is far beyond just sensing a driving scene. When a self-driving car goes down your neighborhood block, keep in mind that the sensors are likely collecting video that showcases the children playing in front yards and people tending to their own efforts while meandering outside their homes. I have been referring to this vastness of data collecting as the roving eye.

The data being collected by a self-driving car is customarily used to guide the driving actions of the autonomous vehicle. That is what the stated purpose of the sensors seems to be. Nonetheless, the data collected can be used for a myriad of other purposes. I've emphasized that this data can be monetized by the fleet operators of self-driving cars and that we have yet to firmly establish who owns this data.

Undoubtedly there will be privacy intrusion claims raised.

The good news about the data collection of self-driving cars is that they can potentially be used for crimefighting purposes. Imagine that the data from zillions of roaming self-driving cars gets uploaded into cloud databases. Those cloud databases are then assessed to ascertain what happened at crime scenes, in the same way, that law enforcement today might try to find nearby security videos that perchance captured something of relevance. Once we have self-driving cars aplenty, it is going to be a massive and readily used means of figuring out where a criminal committed a crime, along with where they went afterward.

What does this have to do with the detection of graffiti?

That's easily answered.

You could piece together the video camera recorded imagery from self-driving cars and do computational pattern matching to try and identify graffiti. All those self-driving cars driving down an everyday freeway would have a video showing the freeway walls, the buildings adjoining the freeway, the overpasses, and so on. Algorithms could be readily applied to the collected video data and indicate where graffiti is visibly present.

The difficult part of this is figuring out what constitutes graffiti.

A billboard that has a funky-looking display could be misconstrued as graffiti. Graffiti that is put on top of a billboard that has some other advertising imagery might blend in and not be easily asserted as graffiti. In short, graffiti can at times be ambiguous, even when completely visible to the naked eye.

On the other hand, humans pretty much can discern graffiti when they see it. In that semblance, we could anticipate that crafting computer-based algorithms to detect graffiti will be somewhat straightforward to do. The detection would most likely include a set of probabilities to denote the likelihood that images labeled as graffiti were in fact graffiti.

You can expect that there will be some amount of false assignments. Something that appears to be graffiti might get marked with a high probability of being graffiti, even though it turns out to not be graffiti. That's a false positive. There is also a chance that something not rated as graffiti is indeed graffiti. That's a false negative.

On the whole, though there will be those mismatches or misinterpretations by the algorithms, you can expect that those will gradually become less so once the Machine Learning (ML) and Deep Learning (DL) approaches further improve. In addition, humans would likely be used to aid in guiding the algorithms and be able to catch the false positives and false negatives.

Let's go ahead and agree that detection of graffiti by self-driving cars will be relatively possible.

Now what?

Well, similar to today's simpler databases, graffiti detection could be maintained in an online database. Those that are seeking to cope with graffiti could use the database to explore where the graffiti is being placed. Crimefighting such as the earlier depiction of police trying to identify gang activity could take place.

One perhaps not so obvious advantage of self-driving cars being used to detect graffiti is that it is almost a no-cost added-value proposition.

Self-driving cars are already going to be collecting the visual video scenery, doing so for purposes of driving the autonomous vehicle. The data can be stored locally onboard the self-driving car and then uploaded when it is possible to undertake an OTA (Over-the-Air) electronic communication. This is pretty much going to be happening anyway.

From an added cost perspective, the main aspect will be devising algorithms to detect the graffiti in the visual imagery captured and uploaded. This won't be particularly costly. There is the cost of storing the data, but that's also relatively straightforward in today's large-scale cloud environments.

Presumably, the fleet operators could charge fees for those that want to access the data that has been collected from their self-driving cars. A city that wants to analyze the data for graffiti would pay a fee or possibly subscribe to the database. Same for a law enforcement agency. There might be third-party companies that formulate such systems to provide this capability for those that want to tap into a graffiti tracking online system.

Perhaps nonprofits would get a special break on pricing for

making use of the graffiti databases, assuming that the entity was striving to help reduce graffiti and was working with the local community in doing so.

Conclusion

Recall that earlier there was an important point raised that graffiti can be distracting to human drivers.

You cannot generally say the same for AI driving systems. In short, the computational processing of the driving scene is already trying to pinpoint what is important and what is not important when seeking to drive a self-driving car. The graffiti is not especially distracting, unlike for a human that might linger mentally on the graffiti and ponder all sorts of deep thoughts about the significance and meaning of the graffiti.

Let's be clear, I am not giving a free pass to graffiti. The AI driving system and the onboard hardware processors are going to have to ferret out what the flaunted graffiti is perhaps hiding or what it might portend related to the driving task. There is that kind of cost involved. Nonetheless, it isn't anything on par with the type of distraction that would be exhibited by human drivers.

If it is the case that self-driving cars are relatively unaffected by graffiti, maybe this would spark those graffiti makers into becoming wilder and bolder, some might worry.

Maybe so, maybe not.

Via the use of automation to track graffiti, the odds are that various other societal forces would have a much easier time trying to find ways to discourage or excise the graffiti. The cat and mouse game slightly begins to tilt towards those cats trying to stop or catch the mice.

And there's something else to realize too.

Self-driving cars might end up being built as though they are bubbles. You get into a self-driving car and it has no discernable windows. There isn't a need for windshields and nor windows, since there isn't a human driver at the wheel. Passengers might prefer the privacy of being inside a bubble. If they want to look outside, all they need to do is display whatever the video cameras are seeing, and this can be shown onto the interior LED displays.

This subtle but poignant point is significant to the nature of graffiti. Will makers of graffiti make their graffiti if no one is looking at it? This is almost akin to the infamous question about a tree falling in the forest and whether it will be heard if no one is around (I've discussed this matter and answered this in my columns).

Pedestrians can still see the graffiti. But anyone riding inside an autonomous vehicle on the freeways or highways might not be watching it. Without that audience, presumably, a sizable chunk of graffiti would no longer be created. Or, as discussed earlier, the marking of graffiti would gravitate to places that primarily cater to foot traffic and thus where pedestrians would see it, rather than where roadway vehicles necessarily are principally found.

I realize that some might try to argue somewhat to the contrary on this emphasis about graffiti perhaps not being particularly paid attention to by humans inside self-driving cars.

Here's the logic.

Since people won't need to drive anymore, they can leisurely look at the passing scenery while idly riding as a passenger in self-driving cars. This might mean that there are eyeballs that today would be so preoccupied with the driving scene that they would give short shrift to looking at graffiti. But now that those eyeballs are unshackled from driving, they can gape in amazement at graffiti.

If that were to be the case, the graffiti makers would see this as an opportunity to make their marks known. The audience for graffiti will gradually become massive and attentive due to the emergence of self-driving vehicles. Time to get out the spray paint and start doodling on the walls and surroundings of our cities and towns.

Oopsie.

As I said, we don't know which way things are going to bend. You'll have to decide for yourself whether the advent of self-driving cars is going to be principally a graffiti inhibitor or a graffiti promoter. In my book, tensions would seem to sway toward the graffiti disruption side of the equation. Time will tell.

Anyway, a future conversation about graffiti might go like this.

Hey, did you see that graffiti on the south side bridge?

The answer: No I didn't, but I can check in with my self-driving car and find out what that's all about.

Case closed.

CHAPTER 26
CULTURE RULES AND SELF-DRIVING CARS

As many headlines will ostensibly tell you, culture is apparently quite hungry and always eating someone's breakfast, lunch, or dinner.

That's a bit of a tongue-in-cheek commentary, but the expression that culture is eating something comes up quite a bit. The general emphasis is that culture will tend to intercede in whatever the matter consists of. Furthermore, culture will rule the day when it comes to whether the matter of focus will succeed or falter.

I'd dare say that this is a kind of viral saying that rolls off the tongue and enchants the imagination.

We are dutifully fascinated when told that one thing can overtake another. This can either be surprising and therefore startlingly informative, or perhaps be construed as mundane though well worth pointing out for those that hadn't given much thought to the issue.

Dog bites man is an example. This line is bound to be notable, depending upon the circumstance. Switch it around and indicate that man bites dog, which then can be particularly eyebrow-raising. Nearly in any direction, the line is going to be sufficiently intriguing to draw your attention. One thing is overtaking another.

Note that the overtaking posture proffered about culture is that it is seemingly eating something.

What makes the saying especially catchy is that it decisively exploits the altogether analogous analog of eating, which is certainly a vital essence-of-life consideration. Presumably, those that don't eat are doomed to expire. You have to be eating. We all can relate to the notion that one thing is eating another, just as the eternal struggle of a predator seeking and eating its prey is always on our minds (somewhere in our deep recesses).

Most tracing of the "culture eating" aspects seem to credit the earliest known variant to the famous management guru Peter Drucker, though as will be explained in a moment, there is much haziness about this attribution.

Supposedly, this line was uttered about corporate strategy: *Culture eats strategy.*

To clarify it, I'll augment the line to say this: *Organizational culture beats organizational strategy.*

You see, there was a period of time when the corporate strategy was the hottest buzzword of the day. Top executives were supposed to get their act together and put together a vaunted corporate strategy. This entailed laying out where the firm was going and how it was proposing to get there. Without a roadmap about the strategy of the corporation, all else was likely to flounder and proceed without any substantive direction or purpose.

The corporate strategy seemed to be at the top pinnacle of things. If you had a corporate strategy, you were set. Nobody could try to refute such contention that you had to have a stated corporate strategy since the alternative of having no corporate strategy could be readily shot down as a grand omission and your organization would roam aimlessly and fruitlessly.

Along comes a presumed hidden factor that could knock the revered corporate strategy off its lofty perch.

Organizational culture.

Yes, it certainly makes sense that the culture of a firm can shape the fate of corporate strategy.

If the people within a company are not going to rally around its corporate strategy, the strategy will likely never see the light of day. It will be nothing more than a paper-based exercise. You need to be mindful as a leader and get the organizational culture to accept and promulgate the corporate strategy.

Of course, worse still, if the company culture is in opposition to the corporate strategy, for sure things are going to go awry. People inside the firm will readily find ways to subvert the corporate strategy, either doing so by outward intent or by the invisible hand of the company culture all told.

The beauty of the line that culture eats strategy is that it is entirely straightforward and doesn't necessarily need a bulky explanation to drive home the gist of the matter. For some leaders, this was a mundane point, yet they were nonetheless skirting past their company culture and trying to ramrod a new corporate strategy throughout the firm. Thus, despite the powerful nature of the line, many were not seeing the utility of the underlying assertion.

Other leaders saw this line as entirely inspirational and an eye-opening revelation. They were unsure of why their corporate strategies were flailing and not catching hold. It could be that they mindlessly walked right past their own company culture. This in turn led to a huge niche of consultants, books, courses, and the like that told leaders how to get their organizational culture to shift or be transformed as needed.

I'd like to think that Peter Drucker was the originating source, but nobody can seem to definitively pin down that Peter Drucker uttered this line as the deriving source. I knew Peter firsthand, primarily as an academic colleague, and can attest that it is the kind of catchphrase or clever witticism he was known for coming up with.

There is a cavalcade of references in the literature attributing the line to him as the initial source, but these are all secondhand and done without any specificity of when he said it and nor where or in what context. Adding some credence to the attribution, there are some documented indications that the CEO of Ford *attributed* the line to Peter (that was Mark Fields at the time), though again this is not fully cited and though perhaps adds to the potentiality of Peter being the keystone source, we are still left with a bit of a mystery.

Continuing, an additional twist to the line is the part about when the eating takes place.

Eating for humans seems to take place consisting of three general square meals a day, occurring at breakfast, lunch, and dinner. When you mention that something ate something else, you can embellish the phrasing by stating which meal of the day the act took place.

Therefore, we can state this: *Culture eats strategy for breakfast.*

Realize that without including the part about being "organizational" there is a bit of added generalization taking place. Anyone reading the line might assume that culture of any sort will always be eating a strategy of any kind, pushing us far beyond the boundaries of thinking about companies and how they operate. Whether this broader general case is applicable can be up for heated debate.

So, as more fully elaborated in this instance: *Organizational culture eats organizational strategy for breakfast.*

The nice thing about adding the time of day to the eating process is that you can then try to do a one-upmanship of the line. You can state that Y eats X for breakfast, while Z eats Y for lunch. Voila, Z is now the top line of the predatory scale.

To see how this works, assign "culture" to Y, assign "strategy" to X, and assign "power" to Z. Envision that we were to state that culture eats strategy for breakfast, and then we could try to do a grandiose topper by claiming that power eats culture for lunch. Boom, we just created a catchy phrase. Exciting!

But Z had better watch out since there is the chance that S eats Z for dinner (whatever you wish to assign to S, you are welcome to do so).

Do you see how that progression can be handy?

Though this might seem like somewhat cynical posturing about the mealtime aspects, please know that the mealtime does cleverly amplify the already meaningful expression. We relish those simplistic sayings that have a kernel of truth and can spoon-feed us with catchy wording.

Indeed, I have a new one for you: *Culture eats AI self-driving cars for lunch.*

Okay, I admit that this is once again a leveraging of the culture eating sage advice, but I assure you that it rings true and provides yet another hearty and memorable indicator of what we need to be watching out for. And in this case, I'm referring to societal culture rather than organizational culture, plus I've chosen the mealtime of lunch rather than breakfast or dinner (I'll explain why, shortly).

Before we can jump directly into the gist of this powerful message, it is important to ensure we are all on the same page about my reference to AI self-driving cars.

The future of cars consists of AI-based true self-driving cars. There isn't a human driver involved in a true self-driving car. Keep in mind that true self-driving cars are driven via an AI driving system. There isn't a need for a human driver at the wheel, and nor is there a provision for a human to drive the vehicle.

Here's an intriguing question that is worth pondering: *How will today's societal culture be a means of shaping the advent of AI-based true self-driving cars?*

Self-Driving Cars And Culture On Top

For Level 4 and Level 5 true self-driving vehicles, there won't be a human driver involved in the driving task.

All occupants will be passengers.

The AI is doing the driving.

One aspect to immediately discuss entails the fact that the AI involved in today's AI driving systems is not sentient. In other words, the AI is altogether a collective of computer-based programming and algorithms, and most assuredly not able to reason in the same manner that humans can.

Why this added emphasis about the AI not being sentient?

Because I want to underscore that when discussing the role of the AI driving system, I am not ascribing human qualities to the AI. Please be aware that there is an ongoing and dangerous tendency these days to anthropomorphize AI. In essence, people are assigning human-like sentience to today's AI, despite the undeniable and inarguable fact that no such AI exists as yet.

With that clarification, you can envision that the AI driving system won't natively somehow "know" about the facets of driving. Driving and all that it entails will need to be programmed as part of the hardware and software of the self-driving car.

Let's dive into the myriad of aspects that come to play on this topic.

The core premise that we want to examine is that culture purportedly eats AI self-driving cars for lunch.

First, what does that exactly mean?

Returning to the earlier discussion that provided some definitional fundamentals, when culture "eats" something there is an implied indication that culture is interceding in whatever that thing is. More so, culture will rule or win the day when it comes to whether that something will succeed or falter.

In this instance, the implied general assertion is that society and its cultural norms will bear heavily upon the advent of AI self-driving cars. The bearing will be so strong and persistent that the outcome of achieving self-driving cars might be determined by the pressures of culture.

This is somewhat surprising to some. If your attention is riveted solely on the technological elements of self-driving cars, you might fail to see that the cultural elements surrounding the fielding and use of self-driving cars are a huge determiner in whether self-driving cars are going to be accepted on our public roadways.

A classic technoid viewpoint of the world is that you can simply toss your technological creations into the midst of everyone and see how things perchance go. Fail fast, that's the touted mantra. The problem with this kind of witticism is that it utterly fails to gauge human reaction to technological innovations. Time and again, there are plenty of cases whereby technological wizardry was foisted upon the public and the reaction either dented the adoption or perilously undercut and nearly eviscerated any future potential for the presumed breakthrough.

Numerous possible paths are entailing how culture is potentially going to eat AI self-driving cars.

We begin with the proverbial 600-pound gorilla which is the nature of safety as it pertains to the use of self-driving cars. This serves in exploring the intertwining of cultural perceptions of safety pertaining to cars and correspondingly the perceptions about such safety as associated with the emergence of true self-driving cars.

In the United States alone, via today's conventional human-driven cars there are about 6.7 million car crashes annually (that is a count based on *reported* crashes, so there are likely a lot more crashes if you were to include unreported crashes too). Sadly, those abysmal crashes annually produce about 2.5 million injuries and approximately 40,000 fatalities. For more coverage on those kinds of driving-related statistics, see my discussion at **this link here**.

I bring up the existing litany of car crashes to try and ferret out the meaning of safety when it comes to driving a car.

One means to define safety is based on the existing "default standard" as accepted by society and our culture of today, per the numbers just highlighted. Presumably, if you can attain a lower number of car crashes, or a lower number of injuries, or a lower number of fatalities, you could contend that the driving circumstances are safer than they once were.

As an aside, this is a bit loosey-goosey because we would likely want to also include the number of miles driven. Rather than concentrating on the counts per se, we ought to even out the playing field by calculating ratios of the number of car crashes per the number of miles being driven. Likewise, we would want to compute the number of injuries per mile driven and the number of fatalities per mile driven. I say this because otherwise, you could potentially and easily trick the numbers by simply restricting how many miles can be driven, getting a hefty reduction in the foulness but cheating somewhat by that mathematical mischief.

Right now, how many car crashes and corresponding injuries and fatalities are we as a society willing to tolerate when it comes to true self-driving cars?

It would seem that we ought to be willing to accept some semblance of sizable counts, as long as those counts appeared to be lessening the counts (or ratios) associated with human-driven cars. In essence, we would rationally be willing to exchange human-driven cars for self-driving cars by the very logical thinking that we are stridently going to be reducing the number of injuries and fatalities related to cars of today, assuming that is indeed the case.

But that seems to be an unlikely sentiment as expressed by existing culture.

Some claim that any crashes by self-driving cars are not to be allowed, never ever. Meanwhile, some pundits and vendors are going around and recklessly touting that self-driving cars will be uncrashable.. All of this is fueling a perception that the number of car crashes that society will tolerate in the case of self-driving cars is zero.

That's unfortunate.

There is a zero chance of attaining zero car crashes involving self-driving cars.

We are going to have car crashes that encompass self-driving cars. As a quick example, consider that a self-driving car is coming down a street and a child suddenly darts into the middle of the street. The physics of the situation is going to come to the forefront. Even if the AI driving system immediately detects the child and slams on the brakes, the distances and timing are going to overtake any viable driving actions. I've covered these types of scenarios in many of my columns, so I won't continue herein to further expound on it.

The point overall is that our cultural predilections or societal perspective about what constitutes safety as it relates to driving are going to overtake the efforts of crafting and fielding true self-driving cars. If we only are willing to accept zero crashes as the safety metric for driverless cars, you might as well turn off the lights and send everyone home that is embarking upon devising them.

Thus, culture eats AI self-driving cars.

Conclusion

There are more twists and turns on this topic.

For example, one hope is that self-driving cars will bring forth an era of mobility-for-all.

The idea is that those in society that today are mobility disadvantaged will finally have an opportunity to make use of cars as a mode of travel. The presumption is that the cost of the use of self-driving cars will be a lot less than the comparable cost of utilizing human-driven cars (partially due to the excising of the labor component involved in driving). This will open widely the use of automotive transportation and we'll see a boon in vehicular travel as a result of self-driving car pervasiveness.

Suppose though that the pricing for the use of self-driving cars is somehow exorbitant.

Contemplate what society and our culture would do if it turned out that self-driving cars were only available to those with grand wealth. I'll let you ponder that one. I think it would be fair to assume that culture would end up eating self-driving cars in that somewhat glum scenario.

As a final word, for now, there is something else about these types of sage credos that is worth giving a modicum of attention to. You can usually reverse them and discover equally enlightening insights. Let's try that.

Going with the commonplace version of culture eats strategy, we can try reversing this saying and claim that strategy eats culture. How so? Well, if you prepare your corporate strategy wisely, it would presumably encompass how to shift the organizational culture to aid in attaining the corporate strategy being proffered. By anticipating the role of culture, you could overtake the overtaking that otherwise by a failure of omission potentially might occur.

The prey becomes the predator if you will. This makes indubitable sense. We can give it go with the topic of self-driving cars too. Perhaps true self-driving cars will eat culture. In essence, the advent of self-driving cars might shift our cultural norms and cause us to collectively rethink the nature of cars and our beliefs about automotive travel.

The initial thinking was this: *Culture eats AI self-driving cars for lunch*. But maybe we can also imagine this: *AI self-driving cars eat culture for dinner*. Well, all this talk about eating has made me hungry, so I'm off to get a bite to eat. While dining, I'll be giving more thought to this whole cultural thingamabob and the emergence of self-driving cars, and perhaps you might find it handy to do so during your next breakfast, lunch, or dinner.

Bon appétit.

CHAPTER 27
EXURBS
AND
SELF-DRIVING CARS

Are you ready for a fun driving trip?

Pretend that you are sitting in your car, doing so in the midst of a hectic downtown city. Please go ahead and start the engine of the vehicle.

Next, begin to drive out of the city.

Perhaps doing so brings a happy smile to your face.

You'll want to drive until you just get past the boundaries of the city proper. The odds are that you'll then enter into the vaunted suburbs. We all know what suburbs are. Usually, suburbs have homes that are larger than the ones typically found within the city. People enjoy a bit of a backyard and are likely to live near an expansive park or shimmering school grounds. Traffic isn't as congested in comparison to the hustle and bustle of the city vehicular snarl. And so on.

Continue driving on this indomitable outbound quest and seek to reach the boundaries of the suburb.

Where are you now?

Most people would tend to assume that beyond the suburbs are those somewhat barren or sparsely populated rural areas. Lots of farms. Very few homes. Not many people. Agriculture as far as the eye can see, or perhaps herds of grazing cattle. Acres and acres of open land. That's what you'd likely expect to see once you've stretched beyond the outer skirts of the suburbs.

But wait for a second, you are neglecting to include a zonal facet that sits between the end of the suburbs and the beginning of the rural areas.

I'd dare say many people have no idea that such a declarative zone exists. This seemingly unrecognized zone has a catchy name.

Exurbs.

Yes, the area that essentially resides in the buffer between the outer edge of the suburbs and the initial edge of a rural area is coined as the *exurbs*.

Think of this whole contrivance as a series of concentric circles. Assume that the innermost core is the city. Surrounding the city is the zone of the suburbs. Surrounding the suburbs is the zone of the exurbs. Surrounding the exurbs is the zone of the rural areas. To clarify, that's not a perfectly precise way to depict things, but it is evocative of the general gist. You'll have to discuss further the matter with specialists such as expert geographers to get further into the weeds, as it were.

The people that live in the exurbs are sometimes referred to as *exurbanites*.

That's an apparent tip of the hat to similarly sounding suburbanites living in suburban areas. Everyone gets a label, so it seems. I'm not sure that people are enamored of those labels and you'd be hard-pressed to find anyone exclaiming to the rooftops that they are a suburbanite and nor the same for those that are technically considered exurbanites.

Let's just stick with referring to this patch of land as the exurbs and merely acknowledge that people do live there.

If you've not heard or seen the word "exurbs" before, you probably assume it's one of those newfangled technoid catchphrases that somebody posted on the latest social media and now the darned thing is gaining a foothold. Actually, a book published in the 1950s is considered the origination point for the exurb moniker, written by Auguste Spectorsky and entitled *The Exurbanites* (well, I promised not to use that term again herein, but my excuse in this instance is that I'm merely providing the title of the book).

Generally, the notion of an exurb is that it is akin to adding an extra-urban layer to the multi-layer cake of land use that I've described as a series of concentric circles. You are certainly welcome to question whether such a layer is worthy of being explicitly called out. Some prefer to ignore the exurb and just emphasize that when you exit the suburbs you have then entered into rural lands.

Others stridently contend that acknowledging the existence of exurbs is assuredly valuable.

Exurbs are a bit of an odd beast. An exurb is similar to a suburb but characterized as even more sparse and less densely packed than a suburb would conventionally be. An exurb is also nearly akin to a rural area, but not quite as sparse and empty as the usual norms for a rural area. You can envision that residential life is the dominant foundation in an exurb. Business establishments and commerce are altogether secondary and scant.

Quantitative metrics such as population density can aid in being more definitive about the differences between an exurb and its neighboring suburbs and rural areas. An exurb tends to have a lower population density than a suburb, meaning that people are more scattered out. Meanwhile, an exurb tends to have a higher population density than a rural area. It is all a relative difference.

We can debate until the cows come home as to whether or not the exurbs are a real thing. For sake of discussion, assume that exurbs do exist.

There is a catch. An exurb doesn't always necessarily exist, such that a given locale might go directly from the suburbs and enter directly into rural lands (i.e., no exurb has sprung up in between those two boundaries). On the other hand, there might be a sliver of land that we could reasonably construe as being an exurb, or possibly a rather sizable area that almost unarguably constitutes an exurb.

As they say, your mileage may vary.

Why all this chatter about something that seems rather unfamiliar and perhaps esoteric?

Because people are moving to the exurbs.

Recent news reports about real estate and where communities are flourishing have exhorted that the exurbs are finally starting to see the light of day and becoming highly visible to those that previously had never heard of such outlying lands. Headlines tout the coming of the exurbs. Their time has arrived. But this is tempered at times by somewhat awkward or discourteous phrasing that makes exurbs seem somewhat oddball. Language such as referring to the exurbs as being on the fringe or having a far-flung positioning are apt to cloud what otherwise ought to be a simple and unsmeared piece of turf.

Despite any disquieting remarks, people that only once knew about suburbs are increasingly discovering the joys of moving into the exurbs. This has been sparked and then hastened as a result of the pandemic. City dwellers sought to get out of the cities. They often shifted into the suburbs. People living in the suburbs suddenly found themselves getting crowded, something they did not desire, and so they opted to shift into the exurbs.

This makes indubitable sense.

The other path was to go all the way into rural lands, but this was an outsized approach by many that led to a bit of shock when no longer immersed in the conventional comforts of living in modern cities or contemporary suburbs. You might last for a little while in a rural area, similar to when taking a short vacation and doing so temporarily. Eventually, the quietness and lack of conventional everyday activities were enough to convince those non-rural types to scoot back into an exurb or a suburb. We'll have to wait and see how many opt to go back into the cities, now that things are opening up again.

The recent revelation that remote work is a viable way of conducting business has stoked further the viability of living in the exurbs. As long as you can get high-speed Internet access, working from an exurb is no different than working from a suburb or anyplace else. They say that no one knows whether you are a dog while on the Internet (a famous and nearly outdated joke), and similarly no one knows or needs to know where you are located when you are getting work done remotely.

So-called knowledge workers are predicted to shift in droves from the cities or suburbs and relocate into the exurbs. The cost to buy a home there is a lot less and enables especially newbie career goers to afford a home of their own. The cost of living is less. All told the savings of your hard-earned dollars and cents add up to an alluring appeal.

There is one thing though that you'll need, which maybe you already have or maybe not.

A car.

When living in a fast-paced city, you can oftentimes get around via a subway system, a bus system, or some form of public transit. Many city dwellers of a younger bent seem to be eschewing the ownership and use of a car. They would rather walk, ride a bike, or use the transit systems.

Those that live already in a suburban locale, probably have a car since the other transportation options aren't particularly effective for their transit needs. Things are widely spread out. You can only ride your bike so far and will likely need to use a car at some juncture. The use of a car is somewhat sparingly undertaken. If an alternative transportation mode presents itself, the car will sit in the driveway and await just those journeys that are of necessity requiring an automobile.

You might be wondering what takes place in an exurb related to the use of a car.

Keep in mind that things are even further spread out in the exurbs. Furthermore, the availability of local mass transit tends to be even less than it was in the suburbs. In short, a car is pretty much a mandatory form of transportation.

And if you live as a family in the exurbs, the odds are that just one car won't do. You'll need to have two cars. This is seemingly an affordable purchase since the savings from the lowered cost of housing and the lowered cost of living can contribute towards having two cars. One of the cars might tend toward being a fancier car, while the other one might tend towards being a workhorse, such as an SUV or something that can handle the more remote roads and be used in the adjacent rural areas too.

Speaking of cars, the future of cars consists of AI-based true self-driving cars.

There isn't a human driver involved in a true self-driving car. Keep in mind that true self-driving cars are driven via an AI driving system. There isn't a need for a human driver at the wheel, and nor is there a provision for a human to drive the vehicle.

Here's an intriguing question that is worth pondering: *How might the advent of AI-based true self-driving cars impact the quest for being able to live in the proverbial exurbs?*

I've previously covered the trend toward people buying vacation homes in out-of-the-way places, which will be further fueled by the emergence of self-driving cars. There are many similarities to the somewhat analogous situation regarding the exurbs, though the exurbs are generally considered the place of your primary home and not particularly where your vacation home would reside.

I'd like to further clarify what is meant when I refer to true self-driving cars and then we can get into the details about the exurbs and the role of self-driving cars.

Self-Driving Cars And Exurbs

For Level 4 and Level 5 true self-driving vehicles, there won't be a human driver involved in the driving task.

All occupants will be passengers.

The AI is doing the driving.

One aspect to immediately discuss entails the fact that the AI involved in today's AI driving systems is not sentient. In other words, the AI is altogether a collective of computer-based programming and algorithms, and most assuredly not able to reason in the same manner that humans can.

Why this added emphasis about the AI not being sentient?

Because I want to underscore that when discussing the role of the AI driving system, I am not ascribing human qualities to the AI. Please be aware that there is an ongoing and dangerous tendency these days to anthropomorphize AI. In essence, people are assigning human-like sentience to today's AI, despite the undeniable and inarguable fact that no such AI exists as yet.

With that clarification, you can envision that the AI driving system won't natively somehow "know" about the facets of driving. Driving and all that it entails will need to be programmed as part of the hardware and software of the self-driving car.

Let's dive into the myriad of aspects that come to play on this topic.

The odds are that AI self-driving cars will help to encourage and potentially accelerate a shift toward living in the exurbs.

Here's why.

Those that live in the exurbs are at times going to want to visit the suburbs and nearby cities. This could be to make use of the more robust resources in the suburbs and the cities. Think of large shopping malls, ornate theatres, extensive museums, and other such attractions.

In addition, even if those that live in the exurbs are working remotely, they will certainly be asked to come and visit a local office or customers on occasion. Some employers are hopeful of having their employees make at least a daily visit to the office or perhaps a couple of times per week. The logic is that this aids in keeping the employees connected to the office and feel more so as being an integral part of the company. Direct face-to-face interactions over coffee or in an office setting can be crucial to ensuring seamless teamwork.

Someone driving a car from the exurbs to the city is going to endure a long haul that is decidedly unpleasant. In the exurbs, there is hardly any traffic congestion. People living in the exurbs get used to this delightfulness. Imagine the disgust they would experience the moment they found themselves driving amidst road rage traffic and having to contend with bumper-to-bumper nuttiness.

Also, the time to get to the city would be exorbitant. As a form of commute, this would be at the outer bounds of what any sane person could reasonably tolerate.

It might take an hour or two to get to the city, along with being miffed about the traffic. And then another hour or two to drive back out to your home in the exurbs. Doing this for work purposes provides some impetus. Doing this for recreation or enjoyment would turn out to be nonsensical since the angst of traveling would undercut any joy from having made the journey.

Those downsides are predicated on one key factor, a human having to drive a car.

Take the human driver out of the equation. Those living in the exurbs would make use of a self-driving car to drive them into the city or over to the nearby suburbs. The drive would be done without any hassle. The AI driving system has to cope with the crazy traffic.

Passengers inside the self-driving car would simply be whisked along and arrive at their desired destination. No need to think about what the best route might be. No need to deal with other human drivers that don't seem to know how to properly drive. That's entirely something the AI driving system will contend with.

Throughout the trek, passengers can idly look at the windows and enjoy the view. Or they can make use of a high-speed Internet connection available in-car and watch their favorite cat videos on their smartphones. There are also assuredly going to be LED displays inside self-driving cars, allowing passengers to watch movies on a bigger screen than available via their smartphones.

Sleeping inside a self-driving car is another possibility of how to use the time during a journey.

Passengers can catch a nap or enjoy an all-out snooze, depending upon the length of time for the ride. The interior of self-driving cars will be different than conventional cars since there is no longer a need to have a driver's seat. Various designs suggest that the seats will be swivel style to allow riders to look in any direction. You can bet too that the seats will recline to allow for resting and relaxing during a trek.

I trust you get the drift that those living in the exurbs would be able to readily take entertaining sojourns into the cities and suburbs by making use of self-driving cars.

You have your own private space during your travel and can do whatever best suits your time during the trip. No-fuss, no muss.

I've even emphasized that the use of self-driving cars will impact our perception of time and distance, in a manner akin to that which occurred during the transition from predominantly horsedrawn travel to automobiles.

Overall, self-driving cars will allow those that choose to live in the exurbs to feel as though they aren't living on some remote planet. They will be able to relish the less chaotic lifestyle of residing in an exurb, and yet still be able to tap into utilizing the cities and suburbs by the mere act of having a self-driving car perform the exasperating driving chore for them.

Conclusion

There are more twists and turns to be considered.

Those living in the exurbs might not need to own a car, or at least not own two cars.

They could use self-driving cars on ridesharing or ride-hailing basis for most of their traveling. Only when they have some specific reason to not use a self-driving car, perhaps going on a vacation trip and wanting to go off-road, they will otherwise nearly always use a self-driving car to get around.

The hope is that self-driving cars will be a lot less expensive to use than conventional cars. This makes sense since the labor required to drive a car is taken out of the cost aspects. In addition, self-driving cars will be available 24x7.

No need to have to try and find a human driver willing to provide lifts at late hours. The AI driving system and the self-driving car are always ready to roll (excluding when the autonomous vehicle is refueling, undergoing maintenance, and the like).

As with anything in the real world, there are some potential hiccups.

A big question yet to be figured out is whether self-driving cars will be made available in those out-of-the-way places. If a fleet operator of self-driving cars wants to maximize the usage of autonomous vehicles, they would presumably keep the fleet in a locale that has a lot of car traveling demand. This is assumed to be principally in cities.

Will there be sufficient need or demand for the use of self-driving cars to warrant having them located in the exurbs?

It is difficult to say.

Each circumstance will dictate what the ROI (return on investment) is going to look like. If a particular exurb is extensively using self-driving cars to get around town, plus using self-driving cars for those longer trips out-of-town, there is a substantive odds that having self-driving cars in that exurb would be highly profitable. On the other hand, if people in that exurb rarely used self-driving cars and insisted on using their own human-driven cars, there might not be sufficient revenue to be gained by having a fleet set up shop there.

The convenience and ease of using self-driving cars, along with the anticipated safety by not having any drunk driving or distracted driving by an AI driving system versus human drivers could be a huge appeal.

An exurb could be a tremendous money-maker for a savvy fleet operator and proffer a loyal base of riders.

You could say that self-driving cars will help grease the skids toward an exodus to the exurbs.

Time to start looking toward buying a comfortable home in a tranquil exurb of your choosing. And then keep an eye open for those handy dandy self-driving cars to provide you with your exurb driving needs.

CHAPTER 28
MANHOLE COVERS
AND
SELF-DRIVING CARS

Have you been asked about manhole covers in any of your recent high-tech company job interviews?

Probably you have.

Yes, oddly enough, manhole covers became a common topic for job interviews in the last several years, especially when seeking a job at a high-tech firm. You might assume that the jobs in question were somehow related to producing manhole covers or possibly working on street construction crews.

Nope.

The matter of manhole covers was suddenly being brought up in all kinds of job interviews for nearly any kind of job at a high-tech firm. Want to be a programmer at a high-tech firm? Better be ready for those manhole questions. Want to work in finance or marketing at a high-tech firm. Manhole covers are undoubtedly going to come up.

Here's the deal.

In one of those recruitment crazed trends, bringing up the offbeat topic of manhole covers became the hot new means to somehow screen candidates, supposedly separating the creative wheat from the dullard chaff. The interview questions about manhole covers were presumably aimed at eliciting how well someone thinks out-of-the-box or thinks on the spot, whichever of those two attributes the company is seeking to find in suitable applicants (or both qualities combined).

Let's start with one of the initial mind-bending questions that gained a lot of traction with interviewers.

Are you ready?

The interviewer looks at you with a seriously straight face and asks you to estimate how many manhole covers there are in New York City. You are given a moment or two to reflect on this deep-thinking question. The interviewer is watching you closely to see how you cope with this distressingly off-the-wall issue.

If you've not heard the question before, please go ahead and mull over the matter in your mind. Try not to show any outward indication of cold sweat or otherwise tip your hand that you are struggling with the keen query. It would be better for you to appear like a hipster calculating machine and that you are crafting the best possible answer for this altogether immensely fascinating question.

Of course, you might actually be thinking that it is an esoteric or eccentric question and doesn't have much to do with the job that you are applying for. Nonetheless, in the quirky nature of how job interviews go, you must not dare to challenge such a question and instead act like it is the best question since the making of sliced bread.

Since I don't want you to ever lose a potential juicy job at a high-tech firm simply because of the manhole question, I'll happily reveal the answer to you.

You are supposed to estimate the number of manhole covers by first mentally conjuring up a vision in your head that dreamily indicates the roadway layout of New York City. In essence, avenues run in one direction (typically north-south), and the streets go in a roughly perpendicular direction (usually east-west). This is a grid-style layout, akin to a matrix. Imagine a spreadsheet that has various rows and columns.

Next, you are seeing in your mind's eye that perhaps there is one manhole cover per each of the intersecting points of this matrix. Thus, if you multiply the number of avenues times the number of streets, which is the number of rows and columns of this imaginary matrix, you would then multiply that calculated amount by the estimate of one manhole cover and arrive at your total estimate.

You are welcome to get tricky and assume that there is less than one manhole cover per intersecting point, ergo multiple the rows by columns result with a fraction. Or you can go the other way and assume that there is more than one manhole cover per intersecting point. In that case, you would be multiplying the number of rows and columns result by a number greater than one.

Voila, you have the means to answer the question.

Kind of.

One big problem with this particular variant of a so-called "clever" question is that not everyone knows that New York City is arranged in a grid-style (those interviewers that do know this bit of arcane trivia are apt to assume everyone must know it). Without that piece of crucial knowledge, you are somewhat sunk on this oddball question. Even if you knew it was in a grid shape, you might not know how many avenues there are, or know how many streets there are.

You could also certainly argue that this is a huge generalization anyway since not all of New York City conforms to this shapely grid notion. But you'd be wise to not tilt at windmills, especially during a job interview.

The usual rationalization for this manhole cover query is that the interviewer is not expecting an arithmetically derived answer and instead indirectly trying to gauge how you think on your feet. If you were able to sketch out how you would solve this sneaky problem, this was considered a sufficiently evidential way of proving that you are a thinker and a problem solver.

The retort to that justification is that regrettably many interviewers are deplorable at doing interviews, and as such, they completely distorted the manhole cover conundrum. Some interviewers would eagerly wait for a number, and if you said anything other than providing a single number, you were marked as wrong. For those interviewees that did calculate a number, some interviewers would have the nervy gall to mark you as "wrong" if the number was not an exact match to the number of actual manhole covers in New York City.

Things got worse from there.

Some savvy interviewees that knew the question might be potentially asked (having been tipped by others that lamentedly got crushed by the question), shrewdly memorized the number of actual manhole covers (as reported by the New York City roadway infrastructure agency), and would simply proffer that number. This might allow you to skate through the question. On the other hand, some interviewers would then ask how you derived the number. If you could not tell the inspiring story of having deduced the matter via the grid method, you were sunk for not being creative in your thinking.

You would maybe have hoped that at least you would be granted a scored point for having done your homework before the interview.

Other manhole cover questions are used in interview settings.

Here's another one.

Are you ready this time?

I hope so, for your sake of getting this job. Well, actually, there isn't a job on the line in this case, but pretend that there was.

The question asks you to explain why manhole covers are round.

You see, your whole life you've probably seen just round manhole covers and never put much thought into why they are round. Perhaps there is some really good reason for this round shape. It could also simply be a tradition that few have ever sought to overturn.

Once again, this is a thinker or problem-solver type of question. You are expected to demonstrate that you can take a problem that you've not seen before, and turn it on its head, solving it in a few seconds and under the bright lights of a job interview.

Please note that many do not take much stock in these attempts to catch a job interviewer off-guard. Despite that, it is a commonplace tactic by interviewers. Indeed, it is sometimes the lazy way to undertake an interview. Merely scrape away at the interviewee with all kinds of problem-solving queries, and you've used up that allotted half-hour or hour of the interview. You can write up your notes and make it seem that you really grilled the interviewee, as though that was the purpose of the interview.

Once again, I'll share with you the answers to this rousing question. Note that you could straightforwardly assert that manhole covers are round because the manholes are round holes. Duh, what else would make sense to cover them with? Some interviewers won't like that answer and will severely ding you for being unduly smarmy.

Okay, here are the clever answers.

One reason to make manhole covers round is that the effort to put the cover back over the manhole is easily done and there is no struggle with the proper orientation. In contrast, if the holes were square and the manhole covers were squares, you would have a devil of a time trying to always make sure that the manhole cover was turned in the correct orientation to get it to nudge properly into the manhole.

Another suitable response is that after having lifted a manhole cover out of its hole covering spot, you can readily turn the round cover onto its edge and roll it to wherever you might want to temporarily store it. Try doing that with a square-shaped manhole cover. Additional responses include that the round shape is sturdier in many ways than other shapes, and making the cover round is generally easier than making other shapes.

While discussing manhole covers, you might find of overall interest that they are often made from cast iron and weigh around 250 pounds. There are plenty of variations, including manhole covers that weigh around 100 pounds and others that weigh more than 300 pounds. There are also manhole covers that are not round, though this is rare in the United States. The lip or width of a manhole cover is usually around an inch or so, sometimes being less and sometimes being thicker.

I suppose you probably do not give much thought daily to manhole covers.

You drive over them all the time, and yet they rarely register in your noggin as something to be noticed. Sure, there might be a construction crew that has removed a manhole cover, for which the roadway is usually blocked with cones and other obstructions to keep you from going over the now-open manhole.

In theory, you could likely straddle the open manhole with your vehicle and not suffer any damages to your car. Do not do this! A very bad idea. Plus, for all you know, there might be someone down below in the manhole. Think of the danger that a car passing over an open manhole presents to anyone that is within the manhole itself.

I would bet that nearly all of us would certainly avoid an open manhole, even if there weren't brightly colored cones blocking it off. The moment that you noticed up ahead that the roadway presented an open manhole, you would either come to a stop beforehand or at least maneuver into another lane to entirely avoid the gaping opening.

Suppose though that the manhole cover was only slightly ajar.

This presents a different situation in that you might or might not realize that the manhole cover is not fully seated in its proper spot. Also, consider the speed of your vehicle as a factor. If you are driving fast down a street and the manhole cover is ajar, perhaps you would fail to notice it out of place or spy it only at the last moment, allowing very little reaction time to cope with the unusual circumstance.

Most of us would likely say that luckily we've never had that kind of circumstance arise. Manhole covers are seemingly nearly always sitting in their proper placement over a manhole, or the manhole cover is fully off the manhole and sitting in the street by itself or been placed on the sidewalk. The odds of encountering a manhole cover that was neither completely implanted and nor completely removed would seem quite remote.

It happened recently, sadly so.

There is an unnerving video that was captured by a camera-wielding resident showcasing a recent tragic roadway incident involving a pick-up truck and a manhole cover. The video has been recently posted by the local police within the jurisdiction that the matter occurred. The dreadful incident occurred in Panorama City, California, which is in the city of Los Angeles.

Apparently, a young man in his 20s was for as yet unknown reasons down in a covered manhole and attempted to come up by propping out and over the manhole cover. Imagine trying to push up a manhole cover from underneath it. That's a lot of weight to try and displace.

Just as the manhole cover begins to shift up and slightly over, a pick-up truck comes into view of the video. The pick-up truck runs directly over the manhole cover, which is now askew and no longer fitted over the manhole per se. To give you a semblance of the forces involved, the tires of the pick-up truck thud upon the manhole cover, and the surprising result is that the manhole cover goes flying, akin to a frisbee disc. Or maybe think of a gigantic and highly dangerous tiddlywink that once you press strongly on the edge it will go flipping and flying. It is unimaginable that a hefty manhole cover could be so readily hurled into the air, but it does so with seeming ease.

Anyway, at the same time, it appears that the young man fell back down into the manhole as the pick-up truck proceeded overhead of the partially opened manhole. As you likely know, some manholes are relatively shallow and others can be dozens of feet in depth. In any case, according to the police, the young man died at the scene due to his injuries and was retrieved out of the manhole by the local fire department.

You might be wondering if the weather or roadway conditions or other factors were at play in this heartbreaking event. The video seems to indicate that the event happened on a Saturday morning around 10:30 a.m. and that there was daylight and the road was dry. This is worthwhile to consider since the matter would likely be given a different consideration if it was nighttime or perhaps the roadway was wet and it was raining out.

The driver of the pick-up truck kept driving and is now wanted by the police for questioning.

In California, there is a legal requirement that a driver must immediately (as soon as practical) come to a stop at an accident scene and remain there, regardless of whether the person believes they were not at fault and even if there isn't any apparent damages or injuries. Generally, those that do not stop and stay at the scene can be charged with a hit-and-run crime, ranging from being rated as a misdemeanor to a potential felony. In this case, there is also the grim matter of the fatality involved too.

The driver should have remained at the scene.

Shifting gears, besides the shocking nature of the incident, we can also consider what lessons might be learned.

The notion of a manhole cover being pushed up in the midst of an active roadway and without any other indicators or signage to forewarn the occurrence is a seemingly outlier or sometimes referred to as an edge or corner case. In the parlance of those that study occurrences of things, an edge or corner case is considered something that only has a remote chance of occurring. It can occur, but only with some semblance of rarity.

Perhaps this tragedy will spark us all to be cognizant of manhole covers, though on a day-to-day driving basis this would seem a somewhat extreme topic to keep at top of mind. When you are driving your car to work or simply to the local grocery store, you might occasionally take a second glance at those manhole covers. If you do so, please do not become unnecessarily distracted by the manhole covers since the attention ought to be predominantly on the overall roadway status.

Speaking of cars, the future of cars consists of AI-based true self-driving cars.

There isn't a human driver involved in a true self-driving car. Keep in mind that true self-driving cars are driven via an AI driving system. There isn't a need for a human driver at the wheel, and nor is there a provision for a human to drive the vehicle.

Here's an intriguing question that is worth pondering: *How might an AI-based true self-driving car contend with a manhole cover that is partially out of place?*

I'd like to first clarify what I mean when referring to AI-based true self-driving cars.

Self-Driving Cars And Manhole Covers

For Level 4 and Level 5 true self-driving vehicles, there won't be a human driver involved in the driving task.

All occupants will be passengers.

The AI is doing the driving.

One aspect to immediately discuss entails the fact that the AI involved in today's AI driving systems is not sentient. In other words, the AI is altogether a collective of computer-based programming and algorithms, and most assuredly not able to reason in the same manner that humans can.

Why this added emphasis about the AI not being sentient?

Because I want to underscore that when discussing the role of the AI driving system, I am not ascribing human qualities to the AI. Please be aware that there is an ongoing and dangerous tendency these days to anthropomorphize AI. In essence, people are assigning human-like sentience to today's AI, despite the undeniable and inarguable fact that no such AI exists as yet.

With that clarification, you can envision that the AI driving system won't natively somehow "know" about the facets of driving. Driving and all that it entails will need to be programmed as part of the hardware and software of the self-driving car.

Let's dive into the myriad of aspects that come to play on this topic.

First, it is important to realize that self-driving cars make use of various sensors to try and detect the driving scene. The types of sensors can include video cameras, radar, LIDAR, ultrasonic units, thermal imaging, and other such devices. All told, these are the eyes and ears of the AI driving system. Data is collected via the sensors and then various onboard computational analyses are made, oftentimes making use of Machine Learning (ML) and Deep Learning (DL). The driving scene is internally estimated based on the patterns found.

One of the most important aspects to be detected is something that might seem surprising to you, namely the detection of open space that is considered drivable. Humans are so used to eyeing the nature of drivable spaces that it is essentially second nature. You look at a street and can almost instantaneously gauge where the street is, along with where the curbs are and the medians are, and overall ascertain where you can suitably drive your car.

It seems that this is likely a learned facet. Think back to your childhood. An adult probably pointed out the street to you and told you to look both ways, explaining that cars go there and you have to be watchful of the monstrous beasts. After a while, you gradually became adept at figuring out streets, avenues, highways, etc. Your adult mind can nearly always look at an area around you and quickly identify where a car could be driven and where it could not be driven.

Using a computer to figure this out is not so easy. The video camera provides visual images that are examined computationally to try and identify the drivable spaces. Radar and LIDAR can be used for this purpose too. Inside the AI driving system, there is a kind of virtual database or computer model being maintained to try and keep track of where the self-driving car can go and where it ought to not go.

Why have I dragged you through that technological indication?

Because the key to this discussion is whether or not a self-driving car could detect a manhole and a partially ajar manhole cover.

Detecting the instance of a manhole that is covered entirely by its manhole cover is relatively straightforward. Likewise, detecting a manhole that is completely uncovered and lacking its manhole cover is somewhat uncomplicated, though this can be tricky in certain circumstances. Recall that earlier I had brought up the factor of various roadway conditions, such as whether it is raining out or nighttime. The roadway conditions could make detecting an open manhole a lot more difficult than it otherwise would normally be.

The really tough instance is when the manhole cover is only slightly ajar.

Suppose the visual images coming in from the video cameras are being obscured by the bright sunlight that might be coming directly into the camera lenses. Being able to get a crisp set of images of the street and the manhole could be confounded. The profile of the manhole cover is quite low to the ground and at only an inch thick is going to be hard to either directly see or have any radar or LIDAR returns providing a definitive indication of what is happening, especially as it happens in real-time.

Another concern is whether the AI developers conceived of the matter entailing a partially ajar manhole cover.

It could be that the programming of the AI driving system is only devised to determine whether the cover is in place or it is not in place. This might be a binary choice. Until the manhole itself is fully exposed, the internal program might be assigning a probability that the manhole cover is in place and won't mathematically make the switchover into the manhole cover being out of place until enough imagery or other sensory data seems to turn the tide in that determination.

You see, the developers and management might have decided that a partially ajar manhole cover is an edge or corner case that for now is not given much priority. The development team is doing all it can to just get their self-driving car to drive safely from point A to point B. Dealing with a partially open manhole is not something that they would likely consider a core part of the driving task.

The other added twist involves what to do even if the detection takes place with ideal accuracy.

Overall, the first crucial aspect entails identifying that such a situation exists, and the second and equally vital part of the matter involves the AI driving system computationally laying out what to do about this discovered anomaly in the roadway scene.

Should the AI driving system have the self-driving car come to a stop?

Maybe there isn't enough time available to stop before striking the manhole cover.

Should the AI driving system swerve into another lane?

But there might be other cars there or pedestrians nearby that could get hit by the veering self-driving car.

And so on.

Conclusion

There are many more entanglements to this problem.

Suppose the self-driving car does strike the manhole cover and takes a beating when the flying manhole cover smacks the underbody of the autonomous vehicle and perhaps rips up the tires.

Will the AI driving system be able to detect that this has happened?

As I've explained in my columns, the AI driving system only gets informed by whatever the sensors perchance detect and might not be able to readily detect when the vehicle itself has struck something or collided with objects.

Hitting and causing the manhole cover to go flying might or might not be detected by the sensors. If the sensors do detect it, the AI driving system has to be sufficiently programmed to interpret what the actions portend.

A human driver would certainly realize they hit something. They would likely realize it had to be the manhole cover, assuming they saw it at the last moment and felt the car shudder as it banged into the manhole cover. The odds are too that the human driver at the wheel in such a case would hear the sounds of the manhole cover as it clanged back down onto the roadway.

In short, it seems almost impossible to imagine that a human driver would not know they had struck the partially ajar manhole cover in this kind of situation.

On the other hand, it is conceivable that an AI driving system might not detect the matter.

Or that it detects the matter and has no provision for what to do and nor how to interpret the situation. That being said, all else being equal, most of the AI driving systems are programmed to try and safely come to the soonest practical stop if something untoward seems to have occurred. The AI driving system may ascertain that something unusual has happened and go into a type of failsafe mode that instructs the self-driving car to come to a stop.

A human driver would presumably know why they are stopping the car and would comprehend the fact that they hit a loose manhole cover. An AI driving system might simply come to a stop because something happened, which is unknown to the AI driving system and a catchall act entails coming to a prudent halt.

Now you know quite a bit on this narrow topic.

Various estimates suggest that there are approximately 20 million manholes in the United States. We can reasonably assume that means there are a corresponding 20 million manhole covers out on our streets too.

You readily pass over the ubiquitous and seeming unseen manhole covers each and every day. They largely go unnoted by human drivers.

When a manhole cover is missing, it seems nearly all human drivers would tend to notice the gaping hole. Most humans would hopefully and wisely try to divert away from the opening, and possibly warn other drivers about the matter.

Driving along and encountering a partially ajar manhole cover is something that few have likely ever witnessed, especially when the roadway wasn't flagged or coned to highlight the dangerous setting.

It seems likely you'll never be in the driver's seat of your car and see ahead of you a manhole cover as it is being pushed up and out of the way, but if you do, at least now you've thought about what to do and I trust you will do the right thing.

Keep your eyes open and your wits about you. In addition, as a spate of relief, perhaps, I'm sure that the AI driving systems will eventually incorporate the manhole ajar use case, and we can rest easy while riding inside a self-driving car that the autonomous vehicle will do the right thing too. That's an AI driving system that manages to cover all the bases.

CHAPTER 29
SUIING ROADWAYS AND SELF-DRIVING CARS

You are driving along on a highway and enjoying the open road.

Up ahead, a curve is coming. You are currently zipping along at the topmost allowed highway speed (well, plus a tad bit faster, though you would never admit that). The curve doesn't look overly onerous, at first glance.

So, you proceed apace.

Turns out that as you begin to take the curve, you suddenly and shockingly discover that you are moving way too fast for this curve. The wheels of the car begin to lose traction. You can feel the vehicle pulling fervently and you are fighting dearly with the steering wheel to stay on the roadway. It is pretty much too late to try and slow down since you are already deep into the curve.

Yikes!

Sweat pours down your forehead as you, the car, and the highway are doing battle. You glance over at the edge of the highway and realize that you might end up going into a ditch. Not what you want to do. Not what you had in mind. A tinge of fear and pure panic begins to overtake your mind as you scramble to save yourself and the vehicle from potential destruction.

Luckily, you somehow pull through the curve and pop out onto a straightaway. All is good. You faced the grim reaper and lived to tell the tale. The whole matter took only a handful of seconds to play out, and yet it seemed like a lifetime. This is a curve that you will never forget.

You gradually regain your composure. One thought that starts to go through your mind was whether or not there was any warning about the curve and the dangers of taking it too fast. Shouldn't there be a posted sign? Usually, roadway signs warn you about curves and provide a recommended reduced speed.

Sure, undoubtedly, you oftentimes ignore those signs, but at least you do glance at them. Your feeling is that you know how to drive your car and there is no need for some stupid sign to offer you advice. In this case, you mull over that perhaps those posted signs can be useful. It is conceivable that you might have instinctively slowed down by having seen a posted sign, even if you only noticed it fleetingly and didn't give it your complete concentration.

Later that day, you return home via that same path.

When you reach the point that the posted sign should have been present, you notice that it is laying on the ground. Nobody would see it unless they perchance were looking specifically for it and even then it was nearly impossible to see (laying partially obscured in a bunch of weeds and thick grass). The sign seemed to have gotten damaged and possibly knocked over, perhaps by some wayward prior driver. That's unfortunate.

Actually, that's a potentially life-threatening aspect, namely that this essential and downed sign ought to be put back into its proper place so that those approaching the curve will sufficiently be alerted and prudently on their toes.

You decide to call the government agency responsible for that stretch of road and inform them about the downed sign. Why so? Because you feel strongly that it is your duty as a responsible person and also wanting to aid in ensuring that no one else gets themselves into a terrible accident. It is your good deed for the day, perhaps for the week.

Two months later, you read in the news about a car that took that very same curve and flew uncontrollably into the ditch. The driver and two passengers were seriously injured. No one was killed, thankfully.

You are wondering whether that downed warning sign was ever put back into position. On your next occasional drive in that direction, you opt to go over to the curve and see if the sign is up.

Darn, the sign is still laying flat on the ground.

Without that posted sign, those innocent people in that wiped-out car did not seemingly get any heads-up about the curve and the kind of speeds to be safely going. They probably were cruising along at the prevailing highways speeds and simply took the curve without any special speed corrections. Perhaps, if the government agency had put that sign back up, those people would not have been injured and they would have taken the curve without any issues.

Somebody ought to sue.

What do you think?

Should the people in that car accident opt to go after the government agency that had responsibility for the posting of the warning sign? The act of suing that agency could potentially aid in recovering some of the costs of their totaled car and their hefty medical bills. In addition, the agency might get its act together and put that sign-up, along with being more diligent overall about such signage.

One question that might come up is whether the agency knew or should have known about the downed sign. In this instance, the phone call to them two months ago was seemingly sufficient notification. The two months elapsed time would ostensibly be plentiful for the agency to have put the sign-up or post a new sign.

All in all, it seems like the government agency dropped the ball and an unsuspecting driver and some passengers paid a harsh price accordingly.

The government might argue that the driver of the car is at fault.

Regardless of whether a posted sign was there or not, the driver was responsible for driving safely. The buck stops with the driver, as it were.

Furthermore, the government might question the capacity of the driver. Was the driver possibly drunk? Was the driver drowsy? Maybe the driver was watching cat videos and allowed themselves to be distracted from the roadway.

In contrast, the driver argues that their driving was completely lawful and fully abided by the speed limit on that highway. Without the posted sign being visible and apparent, nobody could have known that a reduction in prevailing speed was required. In short, the government cannot shirk its duty to ensure that proper signage exists for a public roadway that is known by the government to be inherently dangerous. Indeed, there was a sign already there, thus proving that the government knew this danger existed, and the agency failed to fulfill its duties properly by making sure that the sign was adequately posted.

Meanwhile, the government agency decides to claim that sovereign immunity applies. This is a legal way of saying that the agency is immune to civil lawsuits and cannot be sued accordingly. No litigation of this nature can be legally sought against the agency.

In reply, the attorney for the driver contends that there are various exceptions to the immunity provision and that this instance is indeed an exception. Per the attorney, the agency has flagrantly failed to properly maintain the roadways. And pursuant to the laws applicable in this case, the lack of suitable and timely roadway maintenance provides an opening to pierce through the usual immunity and bring the agency into court.

The plot somewhat thickens when it is discovered that a highway construction firm had been hired by the agency to do work in that area. They saw the downed sign. They did nothing about it. A decision is made by the driver to have the attorney go ahead and sue the construction company too.

It is all a bit of a sordid mess.

I certainly hope that none of you are ever embroiled in such a complicated circumstance.

Let's slightly shift gears.

The future of cars consists of AI-based true self-driving cars.

There isn't a human driver involved in a true self-driving car. Keep in mind that true self-driving cars are driven via an AI driving system. There isn't a need for a human driver at the wheel, and nor is there a provision for a human to drive the vehicle.

Here's an intriguing question that is worth pondering: *Is it conceivable that AI-based true self-driving cars might get enmeshed into lawsuits about the status of roadway conditions, and if so, what would that entail?*

I'd like to first further clarify what is meant when I refer to true self-driving cars.

Self-Driving Cars And Suing About Roadway Conditions

For Level 4 and Level 5 true self-driving vehicles, there won't be a human driver involved in the driving task.

All occupants will be passengers.

The AI is doing the driving.

One aspect to immediately discuss entails the fact that the AI involved in today's AI driving systems is not sentient. In other words, the AI is altogether a collective of computer-based programming and algorithms, and most assuredly not able to reason in the same manner that humans can.

Why is this added emphasis about the AI not being sentient?

Because I want to underscore that when discussing the role of the AI driving system, I am not ascribing human qualities to the AI. Please be aware that there is an ongoing and dangerous tendency these days to anthropomorphize AI. In essence, people are assigning human-like sentience to today's AI, despite the undeniable and inarguable fact that no such AI exists as yet.

With that clarification, you can envision that the AI driving system won't natively somehow "know" about the facets of driving. Driving and all that it entails will need to be programmed as part of the hardware and software of the self-driving car.

Let's dive into the myriad of aspects that come to play on this topic.

There are several ways AI self-driving cars can enter into the picture on this topic. We can consider each of the ways and delve into some of their particulars.

First, one aspect that is likely to arise in a case like this is whether there is any kind of evidence or indication about the roadway status at the time of the incident.

The driver might have to provide tangible indications that can demonstratively showcase the matter at hand. For example, are there any witnesses that the sign was not posted on the day and time of the incident? Can the driver provide any substantive proof that they were driving any the legal speed limit? Was the roadway dry or was it perchance wet from the rain?

All of this could be crucial to making the case against the government agency.

Here's where self-driving cars come in handy.

Self-driving cars are equipped with a slew of sensors. This includes video cameras, radar, LIDAR, ultrasonic units, and the like (not all self-driving cars have the same set of sensors). These sensors are used to detect the driving scene. Throughout a driving journey, the sensors are actively collecting data and feeding the data into the AI driving system. The AI driving system then interprets computationally the data to figure out where to drive and how to undertake the driving task.

Some of the time, the data is being stored in onboard computer memory. This can be handy for later on being uploaded into the cloud of the fleet operator via OTA (Over-the-Air) electronic communications. I've extensively emphasized that this will be a vast amount of data that can potentially be monetized by the fleet operator. In addition, on the downside of things, this can also portend for serious concerns about personal privacy issues.

I've labeled this capability as the roving eye.

So what, you might be wondering.

Once we have a prevalence of self-driving cars on our highways and byways, they will potentially be recording all sorts of aspects of our daily existence. If any self-driving cars were near to the incident of the human driver that crashed at the curve, there may be a lot of recorded data about the incident.

Potentially having been uploaded to the cloud of the fleet operator, both sides of the case might seek to get access to the data. The recorded video might well reveal that there wasn't a posted sign at the time of the incident. It might indicate the speed of the car that failed to make the curve. The roadway conditions might be apparent such as whether the roadway was dry or wet. Likewise, the radar, LIDAR, and other sensory data could be instrumental to the case.

There are several complexities to this.

You can expect that there will be numerous different automakers and self-driving tech firms that will be producing and fielding self-driving cars. Each of them will likely have their own clouds that store their autonomous vehicle procured data. They will undoubtedly also have their own proprietary formats for the data. They will probably have different retention policies about how long they keep their data intact.

This means that it might be difficult or costly to get this data. In addition, the data might need to be pieced together, taking some data from one brand of a self-driving car and trying to match it with the data from some other brand of a self-driving car. Kind of a technological nightmare.

Worse still, how would you even know which self-driving cars perchance came upon that specific driving scene within the realm of time pertinent to the incident?

You would seemingly not know which self-driving cars were there if any. As such, you might have to go to all of the fleet operators and ask all of them to produce whatever relevant data they might have. This again could be a huge undertaking for all parties involved.

The other question is whether the cloud owners are willing to give up that data. Maybe yes, maybe no. They might contend that the data reveals insider aspects about how their tech works. Numerous objections could be raised. This would seemingly play out in court with all kinds of legal wranglings taking place.

The odds are that this type of situation might become a court case in its own right. You can envision that a series of court cases about what the self-driving car firms have to provide or not provide in these matters could slowly wind its way through the judicial system.

Now that we've covered that angle on the topic, get ready for a different one.

Suppose a self-driving car is driving along and comes to that curve. The AI driving system is scanning for any nearby posted signs. None are detected, which in this case is because the posted sign is laying flat on the ground.

The AI driving system proceeds to take the curve.

Turns out that the algorithms used for the AI driving system were not expecting that the curve would be so dangerous. The AI driving system begins to lose control of the autonomous vehicle.

Oh no, the self-driving car goes into the ditch.

I realize that some smarmy insiders would say that this could never happen. They would argue that the AI driving system would have been established with extensive maps beforehand, clearly indicating that this dangerous curve existed. It would not matter whether the posted sign was there. The posted sign was essentially superfluous since the computer system already had lots of highly detailed maps.

Though it is the case that most of the AI driving systems are being devised to depend upon pre-mapping, this is not necessarily the case for all self-driving cars. Ergo, you cannot guarantee that all self-driving cars will have those kinds of pre-mapped indications at hand.

I'll also switch up the scenario to showcase that merely having maps does not solve all such roadway problems.

Assume that the curve was recently altered by the roadway construction crew that went out there to do maintenance (notice that I cleverly planted that seed in your mind, earlier). This change to the curve is not shown on any maps as yet. The maps of the roadway were undertaken a week ago, or whenever, and they are outdated about the status of the existing roadway.

This can and will happen, let no one contest that.

The AI driving system should always be scanning for any roadway signs. This is important in case a roadway sign has been put up to forewarn about some recent change to the roads. For example, pretend that a temporary warning sign was supposed to be put up in front of this particular curve, but it was not placed there.

Okay, so we have a self-driving car that based on the preloaded maps does not know that the curve is now dangerous, whereas before we'll say it was safe and easy to traverse. Furthermore, we are going to say that there is no signage to warn about the changes to the roadway.

Under these conditions, I would suggest it is possible that the AI driving system could computationally fail to ascertain how to take the curve, and might end up in a predicament that gets the self-driving car into a status that becomes uncontrollable.

Some of you might be pulling your hair out and yelling that this is rarely going to happen. Though I don't necessarily agree with that claim, let's assume I concede it. Nonetheless, there is now an existence proof, of sorts, that we both agree this could happen. Sure, it is perhaps a rarity, an edge or corner case, but it can in fact happen.

I'm going to then proceed with this discussion by standing tall on the aspect that it can happen.

If it did happen, the next consideration is a mind-bender.

Should the self-driving car company sue the government agency that is responsible for that stretch of roadway and/or the construction firm too?

Notice that I'm suggesting that the fleet operator or the maker of the self-driving car would do the suing. I mention this because it is not as though the AI is sentient and opts to sue the government. In the instance of a human driver, it would presumably be the human driver that did the suing. For a self-driving car, it is not the AI driving system that would do the suing.

That being said, you might be puzzled as to why any lawsuit would be warranted. If there wasn't a human driver, there would not seem to be any basis to bring a personal injury lawsuit. The AI isn't a person (which, as a side note, some believe that AI systems might eventually have some form of legal personhood, see my discussion at **this link here**).

Aha, there are at least two considerations to keep in mind.

There are the damages that the self-driving car incurred as a result of going into the ditch. Those damages to the autonomous vehicle can potentially be sought for recoupment.

More importantly, suppose there were passengers inside the self-driving car. Imagine that three people were inside the self-driving car. All three get injured when the self-driving car goes into the ditch.

Now you've got the potential for lawsuits galore.

The people are bound to sue the self-driving car company and the fleet operator. Those passengers might also sue the government and the construction contractor. The self-driving car company and fleet operator might sue the government and the construction contractor. Etc.

Courts are going to have their hands full with the advent of AI self-driving cars, I assure you.

We are going to have a lot of legal fireworks when it comes to the thorny socio-legal issues underlying the development and fielding of self-driving cars. In addition, you might take a look at this recent article about the legal issues entailing the future of autonomous vehicles, written by attorney Roger Royse of the Royse Law Firm and available online.

Conclusion

As eloquently proclaimed in the cherished movie *The Princess Bride*, I am only getting started on eliciting key facets on this engaging topic.

Here's one for you.

The government might try to argue that the AI driving system was insufficiently devised to properly take the curve.

Why would the government claim this?

For the same reason that the government might seek to suggest that a human driver was unsafe in their driving efforts. Pin the tail on the donkey, it's a worthwhile gambit. You can also expect that if the passengers opt to sue, they also will attack the veracity of the AI driving system and how it was devised, wanting to show that the AI driving system was not up to par.

Few of the self-driving car companies and automakers realize they are eventually going to get hauled into court and have to defend their AI driving systems. What decisions were made about how the AI driving system works? What provisions exist to handle situations like this?

On and on, the legal inquiry will go, trying to indicate that the AI driving system was poorly designed, poorly tested, poorly fielded and that the automaker or self-driving tech firms bear responsibility for what took place.

It could be that self-driving cars end up being a keystone for suing about dangerous roadway conditions. Similarly, it could be that self-driving cars are targeted as the source of why a roadway circumstance was not properly handled.

In your mind's eye, envision a courtroom filled with self-driving techies and engineers, trying to explain and justify the decisions they made when devising their AI driving systems.

I suppose some potential relief for them would be the day that the AI becomes sentient, in which case the AI could reside in the witness stand hot-seat and be pummeled by probing questions from the attorneys, saving those human technoids the trauma of having to do so.

CHAPTER 30
HIGHWAY HYPNOSIS AND SELF-DRIVING CARS

You are driving along on a lengthy stretch of an open highway.

Gloriously, you seem to have the roadway entirely to yourself. For miles on end, you haven't encountered any traffic. This is a relief in comparison to the daily commute that you undertake each day when going to work in a busy downtown city area.

Now, it is just you and the expansive highway.

The overall scenery on this highway is admittedly a bit drab. Nothing much to see. There aren't any flashy billboards or other eye-catching hallmarks. About the only manmade item is the laid-down asphalt of the highway and the painted roadway lines that seem to extend to the furthest horizon.

You begin to find yourself becoming somewhat preoccupied with the lines and lane markers of the highway. For driving purposes, you are merely having to keep your car within the lines of your lane. Your right foot is pressing down on the accelerator pedal with a constant amount of force and you are maintaining a consistent speed. Your hands are securely and fully on the steering wheel, occasionally making microscopic adjustments to ensure that the vehicle remains stridently going straight ahead on this everlasting straightaway.

Occasional bumps arise from having the tires go over a rough patch on the highway, providing an almost welcome respite from the otherwise tedium and boredom of this driving trek. When those gruff spots occur, it kind of sparks you to remember that you are driving a car. Indeed, you are driving a car at speeds exceeding 65 miles per hour and are hurdling along at a pace that doesn't seem fast to you, but if anyone was standing by the roadside you would zoom right past them.

The good news is that you are wide awake and had several cups of coffee before you got onto the highway.

You know that being sleepy while driving is a highly dangerous act. That is definitely not going to happen to you. You loathe people that try to drive while drowsy. Of course, it goes without saying that you have even worse opinions about those that try to drink and drive.

As the monotony of the driving journey starts to grab up your mind, you almost feel as though you are no longer occupying your body. It is as though your body, essentially your legs and arms, are working without you having to put any conscious thought into the matter. Your mind is floating away from the matters underway, meanwhile, your body and limbs are doing the right thing by staying glued to the driving controls.

The driving is so mesmerizing that you begin to lose a sense of time. How long have you been driving on this darned road? The lack of external stimuli such as pedestrians, other cars, bicycle riders, and the like has altered your perception of time and space. You are on a kind of highway treadmill that just seems to be endlessly running the same path over and over again.

If someone could see your face, they would probably notice a somewhat expressionless look. Your eyes have that glassy and faraway appearance. Your mind is operating on a sluggish basis and you almost have an emptiness of thought processes. There isn't anything worthy of devoting any mental contortions toward. The highway is a simple open path that requires no particular mental gymnastics to contend with.

What is happening to you during this long and uneventful drive?

Highway hypnosis.

Yes, you might remember learning in a driver training class about the dangers of highway hypnosis. It used to be that newbie teenage drivers were strictly forewarned about the evils of highway hypnosis. You were told repeatedly to be on the watch for your mind going into a kind of mental trance.

This trance could be induced via driving when there are little or no roadway changes or other alluring attractors that keep your head in the game. It is patently obvious that driving in a hectic city environment you are bombarded by stimuli and your mind has to be going at its peak performance (well, we hope so, for your sake and the other nearby drivers). In contrast, driving on a lengthy mountain road, or through an endless desert, or on any prolonged straightaway is oftentimes bereft of any notable visual stimuli.

The belief is that you can become somewhat hypnotized by the roadway.

Similar to the movies and TV shows that used to showcase a person being hypnotized by watching a spiraling line that keeps going and going, the same thing is said to affect you when it is a painted line on the highway that appears to go eternally. The quietness inside the car is coupled with the dullness of the external environment, and the next thing that you know this has combined to put your mind into a sort of dulled trance.

There is an ongoing heated debate about the nature of highway hypnosis.

Does it occur?

Is it a made-up excuse?

What causes it?

Some trace the origins of the discovery of highway hypnosis to the early days of driving and the initial formulations of automobiles. There are historical accounts that suggest the matter was originally coined as road hypnotism, which eventually was renamed highway hypnosis. The highway hypnosis moniker certainly is a catchier phrasing and seems to readily roll off the tongue.

Some experts do not like the catchphrase since it incorporates the notion of hypnotism into it. For various reasons, the mentioning of being hypnotized or being the subject of hypnotism is considered misleading and potentially outright misapplied. The preferred phrasing is something akin to saying that this is a phenomenon consisting of Driving Without Awareness (DWA).

Stating that this is *driving without awareness* is indubitably a more reasoned way to depict the situation, but the popularity and tangy beat of exhorting about the ominous soul-sapping of highway hypnosis is pretty hard to dislodge from the public vocabulary on this intriguing topic.

For sake of discussion, please allow me to continue to use the reference of *highway hypnosis*, and I do so with a proper head nod and apologies to those that vehemently prefer the DWA mantra. Regardless of the naming, the overall facet is that you mentally seem to fade away from the driving task at hand.

This can create a mental time gap, whereby you cannot immediately remember how long you have been at the wheel. You likely cannot recall what you've seen so far while being there in the driver's seat. It is as though your brain is no longer recording whatever you are seeing. In one ear, out the other, in a somewhat tongue-in-cheek homage to the sage piece of wisdom about how we sometimes skip the act of mental processing.

People that claim to have been entranced by highway hypnosis will often insist that this did not affect whatsoever on their driving. They reluctantly agree that they might have mentally been in a tropical paradise for a few moments, but assuredly they still were driving the car. They did not remove their hands from the wheel. They did not remove their foot from the pedals.

One distinction that some take toward the immersion into highway hypnosis is that it is not the same as the mental act of driving while distracted.

A distracted driver is fully cognizant of the driving task but has switched their mental attention to something other than the driving. For example, a driver might be watching a fascinating cat video via their in-car display, which is causing their mental attention to be split between the roadway and those cute kittens that are playing with a ball of string in that endearing video.

The person driving is still mentally alert. The bad news is that they are giving short shrift to the driving task. At one moment, they are looking and thinking about the highway. The next moment, they are glancing at the cat video or repositioning the mental energies toward the cat video. This kind of mental shifting is playing out like a vigorous ping pong match. The really bad news is that if something goes awry on the highway, their attention might at that instant be on the distracting aspect, such as the cat video, and therefore they are caught utterly unawares of the impending and possibly dire driving situation.

In contrast, the purist viewpoint about highway hypnosis is that you are not distracted by anything and that you are in fact devoted to the driving task. The problem is that you are mentally disengaged from the driving task. Some would argue that they are using their subconscious to do the driving, rather than their conscious mind per se (this is open to debate).

It is as though your mind has seemingly gone into a mindless state. The barebones fundamental operation of your body and about driving the car is still occurring. This is almost happening by so-called muscle memory. It is reflexive. Your mind is not necessarily thinking about other matters. One might liken this mental condition to being in the midst of some hefty meditation and you have zoned out of the driving chore.

The difficulty too is that your mind might not be telling you that you are immersed in this trance. If you were watching a cat video, your mind might be nagging you that you are not paying attention to the roadway. You override that nagging. Despite the overriding, at least the nagging is taking place. A claimed issue for highway hypnosis is that your mind lets itself go free and doesn't kick you in the mental butt about being more responsible to devote attention to the roadway.

Some try to argue that a lousy form of mental engagement is better than the lack of mental engagement regarding the driving task. In that sense, they would assert that driving while distracted is better than getting into the driving hypnotic state of mind. Others would counterargue that highway hypnosis is less threatening than the distracted driver.

We can add more fuel to the fire by including the drunk driver. Presumably, a drunk driver has a mental state that is totally messed up and unable to process properly the world around them. Almost everyone would likely tend to agree that a drunk driver poses a much greater threat than a distracted driver or a highway hypnotized driver. These comparisons though are problematic since there are varying degrees of each kind of mental overtaking.

Let's agree to something that we can all seemingly concur with, namely that driving ought to be a task that has the devoted and undivided attention of a fully cognizant and expressly unencumbered mind of the human driver at the wheel.

Period, full stop.

Arguing over which of the corrupted mental states is better or worse is akin to the famous saying that this is tantamount to trying to move around the chairs on the deck of the Titanic.

Now that I've dragged you through the morass about highway hypnosis, one aspect that might have come to your mind is that this driving without awareness is not worthy of discussion since the person is still at the wheel and presumably driving the car. In essence, there is the classic "so what" that needs to be addressed.

Why does this all matter?

Because a person that is embraced by highway hypnosis, if there is such a thing, can become dull in their driving and ergo have a delayed and potentially life-ending reaction to a sudden roadway mishap.

Take for example that while on that long stretch of highway there is a piece of tire piercing metal that perchance is laying on the roadway. It is not immediately obvious to the eye. The size, shape, and color allow it to blend into the overall appearance of the highway surface.

A driver that is engulfed in highway hypnosis might have a delayed and incorrect reaction to striking that tire ripping piece of debris. Whereas a driver that was mentally engaged might react with some surprise and concern, they would at least be likely aware that they must have struck something that was on the highway surface. Their mental processing would lead them in that mental calculation, very quickly. And, as such, they would react with a pre-canned mental template that tells them to gradually slow down the car and try to safely pull off the highway.

Someone that was zoned out via highway hypnosis would presumably be shocked back into awareness by the sounds and sudden response of the vehicle. This would get them back into the game. But their mind might be at wits end about what just happened. Did they hit something? Did the car itself fall apart or have some egregious problem?

They won't likely be able to recall where the car was before the incident. Did they miss something about the roadway? Their mind might begin to play tricks on them. Perhaps a deer entered into the highway and they were so zoned out mentally that they didn't even see it. The deer was somehow invisible to their mind.

At this juncture, the suddenly re-engaged mind might prod the driver to do something entirely inappropriate for the situation. This could be due to the mind not having a clue about what has just taken place. As a result, some semi-random choice of emergency driving action comes to the forefront of their thinking. This can make a bad situation turn into a deathly one.

Various claimed documented cases of drivers in car accidents that said they had highway hypnosis are at times seemingly reinforced by the forensic evidence at the scene of a crash. This might include the fact that no skid marks were indicated on the highway. Had the driver been aware and mentally engaged, the assumption is that they would have immediately hit their brakes and therefore there would be skid marks.

You have to be careful when trying to employ roadway evidence to support a contention that highway hypnosis was the culprit. There is usually a multitude of viable explanations. The tie between what the roadway evidence showcases and the true mental state of the driver are somewhat tenuous and altogether usually quite speculative.

There has been an off-and-on spate of scholarly research about highway hypnosis. One focus of the inquiry is that perhaps the biomechanics of the eyes is a contributor to the road hypnotic trance. It could be that the non-movement (or minimal movement) of the eyes are generating signals to the brain that somewhat lead to the brain going into this trance zone.

The research remains ongoing and continues to seek a better understanding of what makes *driving without awareness* (i.e., highway hypnosis) occur and how to resolve it.

Harking back to the days of learning about highway hypnosis while in driver training, you might recall that there were several pieces of handy advice about how to try and avert this seemingly temporary and possibly deadly mental condition. One proffered action entails moving your eyes back and forth to scan the roadway. This might seem to keep your eyes engaged and correspondingly your mind engaged.

More pieces of advice include creating your own engaging stimuli. Turn on the radio and listen to something that keeps your mind active. Chew gum. Open a window of the car to get wind whisking into the interior. These are all potential ways to keep highway hypnosis at bay. That being said, there is a fine line between seeking to remain mentally engaged and yet pushing you over into the distracted driving mode.

Let's slightly shift gears.

The future of cars consists of AI-based true self-driving cars.

There isn't a human driver involved in a true self-driving car. Keep in mind that true self-driving cars are driven via an AI driving system. There isn't a need for a human driver at the wheel, and nor is there a provision for a human to drive the vehicle.

Here's an intriguing question that is worth pondering: *Is it conceivable that AI-based true self-driving cars might somehow suffer from highway hypnosis, and if so, what can be done about this?*

I'd like to first further clarify what is meant when I refer to true self-driving cars.

Self-Driving Cars And Highway Hypnosis

For Level 4 and Level 5 true self-driving vehicles, there won't be a human driver involved in the driving task.

All occupants will be passengers.

The AI is doing the driving.

One aspect to immediately discuss entails the fact that the AI involved in today's AI driving systems is not sentient. In other words, the AI is altogether a collective of computer-based programming and algorithms, and most assuredly not able to reason in the same manner that humans can.

Why is this added emphasis about the AI not being sentient?

Because I want to underscore that when discussing the role of the AI driving system, I am not ascribing human qualities to the AI. Please be aware that there is an ongoing and dangerous tendency these days to anthropomorphize AI. In essence, people are assigning human-like sentience to today's AI, despite the undeniable and inarguable fact that no such AI exists as yet.

With that clarification, you can envision that the AI driving system won't natively somehow "know" about the facets of driving. Driving and all that it entails will need to be programmed as part of the hardware and software of the self-driving car.

Let's dive into the myriad of aspects that come to play on this topic.

First, consider what *could* happen if a self-driving encountered a human-driven car that was being driven by someone that had succumbed to a presumed dose of highway hypnosis.

The concern in this scenario is that the human driver might not adequately react to a roadway anomaly. Furthermore, the driver might inadvertently do something untoward during any ordinary driving task because they are mentally zoned out.

There's not particularly anything extraordinary that the self-driving car can do about such a circumstance.

Allow me to explain.

By and large, there are no outwardly evidentiary means to ferret out whether a human driver is driving with a full semblance of mental alertness versus whether they are in an alleged mental trance. About the only clues would be that the conventional human-driven car in question might seem to be driving without any apparent reaction to the roadway status.

For example, suppose the AI driving system detects via the self-driving car sensors that there is a large boulder in the roadway up ahead. The AI driving system might begin slowing down the self-driving car, anticipating the need to come to a stop before reaching the boulder. Meanwhile, imagine that the human-driven car nearby and traveling along at a tad ahead of the self-driving car seems to be making no overt indications of slowing or intending to stop.

This could be an indicator that the human driver of that car is incurring highway hypnosis.

Of course, it could be that the driver is distracted by watching enchanting online videos of a baby gurgling and fussing while eating some scrumptious baby food. Or the driver might be drunk and just barely able to keep the car moving forward and has not yet realized that the boulder is going to be a problem. And so on.

Since any of those are real possibilities, there are no immediate means to assume that the human driver is consumed necessarily by highway hypnosis. The AI driving system could either merely wait and see what happens to the conventional car or might take some proactive action to try and alert the human driver. For example, suppose the AI driving system opts to honk the horn of the self-driving car or perhaps turns the headlights on and off, attempting to gain the attention of the human driver.

This takes us to a brief but valuable side tangent.

Most people assume that AI driving systems are being programmed to focus exclusively on the well-being of the self-driving car. That could be the case. As such, the AI would not be exploring any concerns that are bereft of any specific bearing on the outcome of efforts entailing the self-driving car per se. If the crashing of the human-driven car into the boulder would not have any distinct impact upon the self-driving car, there would presumably be no cause for the AI driving system to do anything about the predicted catastrophe.

This is a somewhat vexing and ethically open question about whether we would expect or want self-driving cars to go further and try to assist other traffic, such as nearby human-driven cars. We would likely expect that other nearby human drivers would attempt to act in a good Samaritan fashion, and as such we might hope to have self-driving cars do likewise (as programmed by the AI developers to do so, not because the AI "divines" to do so).

In any case, there isn't much more to be fruitfully said about the use case of a human driver in the hypnotic highway haze and the overarching role of a nearby self-driving car. Generally, the AI driving system needs to be observing other nearby cars always and the AI programming needs to try and anticipate what those other cars are going to do, especially when those actions pertain to the driving of the self-driving car.

Moving on, we get the crux of this matter.

If you believe that there is such a thing as highway hypnosis and that it can overtake the mental acumen of human drivers, we can give some consideration to the curious possibility that AI driving systems might suffer the same potential fate.

I'd like to emphasize that one big problem with trying to make such a claim or connection is that it tends to imply that the AI driving system is sentient.

As mentioned earlier, none of today's AI driving systems are sentient. I would also easily win a wager that we won't have such AI in any near-term future and unlikely in any later-term future. I am not asserting that we will never have sentient AI, which some would argue is in fact never going to happen. I'll settle for now on the simpler notion that sentient AI is not in the cards for the foreseeable future.

Let's leave things at that for the moment.

Okay, if the AI isn't sentient, we would seem on the safe theoretical ground to proclaim that the AI driving system will decidedly <u>not</u> become a victim of highway hypnosis.

You see, we can be clear-cut about the undeniable aspect that the AI driving system does not have eyeballs (not now). It has video cameras and other sensors such as radar, LIDAR, and the like, but it doesn't have human eyes. Plus, AI does not have a brain. AI of today has various computer processors and other electronic circuitry, which is assuredly not a brain and should not be falsely compared to a human brain.

Here's why that is significant.

For those that are sticklers about the meaning of *highway hypnosis*, they would fervently say that to experience highway hypnosis you must have human eyes, a human brain, and your eyes and brain are the elements that would become ostensibly hypnotized by the highway driving. We've just stated that AI driving systems aren't composed in that manner and therefore strictly speaking could not be labeled as susceptible to highway hypnosis.

Case closed.

Wait for a second, let's be a bit more flexible about this. If you are willing to agree that highway hypnosis is more so about *driving without awareness*, and if we are willing to also define awareness in a more logically pliable fashion (even in the absence of sentience), we can constructively take a gander at seeing how this all applies to self-driving cars.

Shall we do so? Sure!

Imagine that a self-driving car is driving down a deserted highway. There aren't any other cars. There isn't anything to speak of, just lots of wide-open terrain that is relatively nondescript and unremarkable. The AI driving system is programmed to keep track of objects that are in the nearby driving scene. An internal list is being kept by the program. A software developer established the list such that it can contain up to a thousand detected objects at any point in time. Once an object is first detected, it is added to the list. When the object is no longer detectable, such as having passed a car that is now far behind the self-driving car and no longer within visual distance, the object is removed from the list.

Turns out, for every defined snippet of time, if there aren't any detected objects, the program places a marker of "nothing detected" into the list. The programmer never envisioned a scenario in which the self-driving car would be bereft of nearby objects for any substantive length of time. This seemed unimaginable, especially since the AI driving system was initially devised to handle inner-city driving.

Unfortunately, this is where things go awry on the monotonous long drive. After several hours of this mundane driving, the object list ends up with a thousand posted instances of "nothing detected" and the list now generates a buffer overflow error. But the rest of the AI system has no provision for dealing with the buffer overflow since it was not anticipated as a possibility.

The net result is that the AI driving system is still driving the self-driving car, but it no longer is actively tracking detected objects. Until a new object is detected, which will then cause a flush of the now exceeded list, the software is essentially in a "trance" and seemingly zoned out. In short, the program code has regrettably fallen into the likes of a type of highway hypnosis due to a bug or error that resides in the AI driving system.

Conclusion

Some smarmy AI developers might insist that this notion of such a bug or error being in the AI driving system code is utterly impossible and would never occur.

If you really think that, it is a bit unnerving. I'd strongly suggest that those of you having such a dogmatic faith in the purity of development for real-time systems as being altogether perfect and absent of any gotchas ought to see my analysis of the recent snafu in the code used for the NASA Mars helicopter known as Ingenuity. As an eye-opener for those that don't realize it, there are going to be bugs and errors in AI driving systems, despite whatever some pundits or vendors might say. Sorry to burst your bubble.

Though testing and simulation can do a lot to find them beforehand, there is nonetheless a bona fide and an altogether likely chance that some will still exist inside fielded self-driving cars. The key will be how good the error handling and contingency provisions are in the AI driving system to cope when those bugs rise up and do their roguish handiwork. Back to the matter of highway hypnosis.

I would not want anyone to go around and assert categorically that AI-based self-driving cars are going to have highway hypnosis. Doing so is a slippery slope toward anthropomorphizing AI. Let's just say that there are possibilities of AI driving systems to get into untoward states of processing, for which we could characterize this as somewhat akin to driving without the proper devoted and active attention to the driving task.

APPENDIX

APPENDIX A
TEACHING WITH THIS MATERIAL

The material in this book can be readily used either as a supplemental to other content for a class, or it can also be used as a core set of textbook material for a specialized class. Classes where this material is most likely used include any classes at the college or university level that want to augment the class by offering thought provoking and educational essays about AI and self-driving cars.

In particular, here are some aspects for class use:

- Computer Science. Studying AI, autonomous vehicles, etc.
- Business. Exploring technology and it adoption for business.
- Sociology. Sociological views on the adoption and advancement of technology.

Specialized classes at the undergraduate and graduate level can also make use of this material.

For each chapter, consider whether you think the chapter provides material relevant to your course topic. There is plenty of opportunity to get the students thinking about the topic and force them to decide whether they agree or disagree with the points offered and positions taken. I would also encourage you to have the students do additional research beyond the chapter material presented (I provide next some suggested assignments they can do).

RESEARCH ASSIGNMENTS ON THESE TOPICS

Your students can find background material on these topics, doing so in various business and technical publications. I list below the top ranked AI related journals. For business publications, I would suggest the usual culprits such as the Harvard Business Review, Forbes, Fortune, WSJ, and the like.

Here are some suggestions of homework or projects that you could assign to students:

a) Assignment for foundational AI research topic: Research and prepare a paper and a presentation on a specific aspect of Deep AI, Machine Learning, ANN, etc. The paper should cite at least 3 reputable sources. Compare and contrast to what has been stated in this book.

b) Assignment for the Self-Driving Car topic: Research and prepare a paper and Self-Driving Cars. Cite at least 3 reputable sources and analyze the characterizations. Compare and contrast to what has been stated in this book.

c) Assignment for a Business topic: Research and prepare a paper and a presentation on businesses and advanced technology. What is hot, and what is not? Cite at least 3 reputable sources. Compare and contrast to the depictions in this book.

d) Assignment to do a Startup: Have the students prepare a paper about how they might startup a business in this realm. They must submit a sound Business Plan for the startup. They could also be asked to present their Business Plan and so should also have a presentation deck to coincide with it.

You can certainly adjust the aforementioned assignments to fit to your particular needs and the class structure. You'll notice that I ask for 3 reputable cited sources for the paper writing based assignments. I usually steer students toward "reputable" publications, since otherwise they will cite some oddball source that has no credentials other than that they happened to write something and post it onto the Internet. You can define "reputable" in whatever way you prefer, for example some faculty think Wikipedia is not reputable while others believe it is reputable and allow students to cite it.

The reason that I usually ask for at least 3 citations is that if the student only does one or two citations they usually settle on whatever they happened to find the fastest. By requiring three citations, it usually seems to force them to look around, explore, and end-up probably finding five or more, and then whittling it down to 3 that they will actually use.

I have not specified the length of their papers, and leave that to you to tell the students what you prefer. For each of those assignments, you could end-up with a short one to two pager, or you could do a dissertation length paper. Base the length on whatever best fits for your class, and the credit amount of the assignment within the context of the other grading metrics you'll be using for the class.

I mention in the assignments that they are to do a paper and prepare a presentation. I usually try to get students to present their work. This is a good practice for what they will do in the business world. Most of the time, they will be required to prepare an analysis and present it. If you don't have the class time or inclination to have the students present, then you can of course cut out the aspect of them putting together a presentation.

If you want to point students toward highly ranked journals in AI, here's a list of the top journals as reported by *various citation counts sources* (this list changes year to year):

- Communications of the ACM
- Artificial Intelligence
- Cognitive Science
- IEEE Transactions on Pattern Analysis and Machine Intelligence
- Foundations and Trends in Machine Learning
- Journal of Memory and Language
- Cognitive Psychology
- Neural Networks
- IEEE Transactions on Neural Networks and Learning Systems
- IEEE Intelligent Systems
- Knowledge-based Systems

GUIDE TO USING THE CHAPTERS

For each of the chapters, I provide next some various ways to use the chapter material. You can assign the tasks as individual homework assignments, or the tasks can be used with team projects for the class. You can easily layout a series of assignments, such as indicating that the students are to do item "a" below for say Chapter 1, then "b" for the next chapter of the book, and so on.

a) What is the main point of the chapter and describe in your own words the significance of the topic,

b) Identify at least two aspects in the chapter that you agree with, and support your concurrence by providing at least one other outside researched item as support; make sure to explain your basis for disagreeing with the aspects,

c) Identify at least two aspects in the chapter that you disagree with, and support your disagreement by providing at least one other outside researched item as support; make sure to explain your basis for disagreeing with the aspects,

d) Find an aspect that was not covered in the chapter, doing so by conducting outside research, and then explain how that aspect ties into the chapter and what significance it brings to the topic,

e) Interview a specialist in industry about the topic of the chapter, collect from them their thoughts and opinions, and readdress the chapter by citing your source and how they compared and contrasted to the material,

f) Interview a relevant academic professor or researcher in a college or university about the topic of the chapter, collect from them their thoughts and opinions, and readdress the chapter by citing your source and how they compared and contrasted to the material,

g) Try to update a chapter by finding out the latest on the topic, and ascertain whether the issue or topic has now been solved or whether it is still being addressed, explain what you come up with.

The above are all ways in which you can get the students of your class involved in considering the material of a given chapter. You could mix things up by having one of those above assignments per each week, covering the chapters over the course of the semester or quarter.

As a reminder, here are the chapters of the book and you can select whichever chapters you find most valued for your particular class:

Companion Book By This Author

Advances in AI and Autonomous Vehicles: Cybernetic Self-Driving Cars

Practical Advances in Artificial Intelligence (AI) and Machine Learning

by

Dr. Lance B. Eliot, MBA, PhD

Chapter Title

1 Genetic Algorithms for Self-Driving Cars
2 Blockchain for Self-Driving Cars
3 Machine Learning and Data for Self-Driving Cars
4 Edge Problems at Core of True Self-Driving Cars
5 Solving the Roundabout Traversal Problem for SD Cars
6 Parallel Parking Mindless Task for SD Cars: Step It Up
7 Caveats of Open Source for Self-Driving Cars
8 Catastrophic Cyber Hacking of Self-Driving Cars
9 Conspicuity for Self-Driving Cars
10 Accident Scene Traversal for Self-Driving Cars
11 Emergency Vehicle Awareness for Self-Driving Cars
12 Are Left Turns Right for Self-Driving Cars
13 Going Blind: When Sensors Fail on Self-Driving Cars
14 Roadway Debris Cognition for Self-Driving Cars
15 Avoiding Pedestrian Roadkill by Self-Driving Cars
16 When Accidents Happen to Self-Driving Cars
17 Illegal Driving for Self-Driving Cars
18 Making AI Sense of Road Signs
19 Parking Your Car the AI Way
20 Not Fast Enough: Human Factors in Self-Driving Cars
21 State of Government Reporting on Self-Driving Cars
22 The Head Nod Problem for Self-Driving Cars
23 CES Reveals Self-Driving Car Differences

This title is available via Amazon and other book sellers

Companion Book By This Author

Self-Driving Cars:
"The Mother of All AI Projects"

by Dr. Lance B. Eliot, MBA, PhD

Chapter Title

This title is available via Amazon and other book seller

Companion Book By This Author

Innovation and Thought Leadership on Self-Driving Driverless Cars

by Dr. Lance B. Eliot, MBA, PhD

Chapter Title

This title is available via Amazon and other book sellers

Companion Book By This Author

New Advances in AI Autonomous Driverless Cars Self-Driving Cars

by Dr. Lance B. Eliot, MBA, PhD

Chapter Title

This title is available via Amazon and other book sellers

Companion Book By This Author

Introduction to Driverless Self-Driving Cars

by Dr. Lance B. Eliot, MBA, PhD

Chapter Title

This title is available via Amazon and other book sellers

Companion Book By This Author

Autonomous Vehicle Driverless Self-Driving Cars and Artificial Intelligence

by Dr. Lance B. Eliot, MBA, PhD

Chapter Title

This title is available via Amazon and other book sellers

Companion Book By This Author

Transformative Artificial Intelligence Driverless Self-Driving Cars

by Dr. Lance B. Eliot, MBA, PhD

Chapter Title

This title is available via Amazon and other book sellers

Companion Book By This Author

Disruptive Artificial Intelligence and Driverless Self-Driving Cars

by Dr. Lance B. Eliot, MBA, PhD

Chapter Title

This title is available via Amazon and other book sellers

Companion Book By This Author

State-of-the-Art
AI Driverless Self-Driving Cars

by Dr. Lance B. Eliot, MBA, PhD

Chapter Title

This title is available via Amazon and other book sellers

Companion Book By This Author

Top Trends in AI Self-Driving Cars

by Dr. Lance B. Eliot, MBA, PhD

Chapter Title

1 Eliot Framework for AI Self-Driving Cars

2 Responsibility and Self-Driving Cars

3 Changing Lanes and Self-Driving Cars

4 Procrastination and Self-Driving Cars

5 NTSB Report and Tesla Car Crash

6 Start Over AI and Self-Driving Cars

7 Freezing Robot Problem and Self-Driving Cars

8 Canarying and Self-Driving Cars

9 Nighttime Driving and Self-Driving Cars

10 Zombie-Cars Taxes and Self-Driving Cars

11 Traffic Lights and Self-Driving Cars

12 Reverse Engineering and Self-Driving Cars

13 Singularity AI and Self-Driving Cars

This title is available via Amazon and other book sellers

Companion Book By This Author

AI Innovations and Self-Driving Cars

by Dr. Lance B. Eliot, MBA, PhD

Chapter Title

This title is available via Amazon and other book sellers

Companion Book By This Author

Crucial Advances for AI Self-Driving Cars

by Dr. Lance B. Eliot, MBA, PhD

Chapter Title

This title is available via Amazon and other book sellers

Companion Book By This Author

Sociotechnical Insights and AI Driverless Cars

by Dr. Lance B. Eliot, MBA, PhD

Chapter Title

This title is available via Amazon and other book sellers

Companion Book By This Author

Pioneering Advances for AI Driverless Cars

by Dr. Lance B. Eliot, MBA, PhD

Chapter Title

This title is available via Amazon and other book sellers

Companion Book By This Author

Leading Edge Trends for AI Driverless Cars

by Dr. Lance B. Eliot, MBA, PhD

Chapter Title

This title is available via Amazon and other book sellers

Companion Book By This Author

The Cutting Edge of AI Autonomous Cars

by Dr. Lance B. Eliot, MBA, PhD

Chapter Title

1 Eliot Framework for AI Self-Driving Cars

2 Driving Controls and AI Self-Driving Cars

3 Bug Bounty and AI Self-Driving Cars

4 Lane Splitting and AI Self-Driving Cars

5 Drunk Drivers versus AI Self-Driving Cars

6 Internal Naysayers and AI Self-Driving Cars

7 Debugging and AI Self-Driving Cars

8 Ethics Review Boards and AI Self-Driving Cars

9 Road Diets and AI Self-Driving Cars

10 Wrong Way Driving and AI Self-Driving Cars

11 World Safety Summit and AI Self-Driving Cars

This title is available via Amazon and other book sellers

Companion Book By This Author

The Next Wave of AI Self-Driving Cars

by Dr. Lance B. Eliot, MBA, PhD

Chapter Title

This title is available via Amazon and other book sellers

Companion Book By This Author

Revolutionary Innovations of AI Self-Driving Cars

by Dr. Lance B. Eliot, MBA, PhD

Chapter Title

This title is available via Amazon and other book sellers

Companion Book By This Author

AI Self-Driving Cars
Breakthroughs

by Dr. Lance B. Eliot, MBA, PhD

Chapter Title

Companion Book By This Author

Trailblazing Trends for
AI Self-Driving Cars

by Dr. Lance B. Eliot, MBA, PhD

Chapter Title

This title is available via Amazon and other book sellers

Companion Book By This Author

Ingenious Strides for
AI Driverless Cars

by Dr. Lance B. Eliot, MBA, PhD

Chapter Title

This title is available via Amazon and other book sellers

Companion Book By This Author

AI Self-Driving Cars
Inventiveness

by Dr. Lance B. Eliot, MBA, PhD

Chapter Title

This title is available via Amazon and other book sellers

Companion Book By This Author

Visionary Secrets of AI Driverless Cars

by Dr. Lance B. Eliot, MBA, PhD

Chapter Title

This title is available via Amazon and other book sellers

Companion Book By This Author

Spearheading
AI Self-Driving Cars

by Dr. Lance B. Eliot, MBA, PhD

Chapter Title

1 Eliot Framework for AI Self-Driving Cars

2 Artificial Pain and AI Self-Driving Cars

3 Stop-and-Frisks and AI Self-Driving Cars

4 Cars Careening and AI Self-Driving Cars

5 Sounding Out Car Noises and AI Self-Driving Cars

6 No Speed Limit Autobahn and AI Self-Driving Car

7 Noble Cause Corruption and AI Self-Driving Cars

8 AI Rockstars and AI Self-Driving Cars

This title is available via Amazon and other book sellers

Companion Book By This Author

Spurring
AI Self-Driving Cars

by Dr. Lance B. Eliot, MBA, PhD

Chapter Title

This title is available via Amazon and other book sellers

Companion Book By This Author

Avant-Garde
AI Driverless Cars

by Dr. Lance B. Eliot, MBA, PhD

Chapter Title

Companion Book By This Author

AI Self-Driving Cars
Evolvement

by Dr. Lance B. Eliot, MBA, PhD

Chapter Title

Companion Book By This Author

AI Driverless Cars Chrysalis

by Dr. Lance B. Eliot, MBA, PhD

Chapter Title

1 Eliot Framework for AI Self-Driving Cars

2 Object Poses and AI Self-Driving Cars

3 Human In-The-Loop and AI Self-Driving Cars

4 Genius Shortage and AI Self-Driving Cars

5 Salvage Yards and AI Self-Driving Cars

6 Precision Scheduling and AI Self-Driving Car

7 Human Driving Extinction and AI Self-Driving Cars

This title is available via Amazon and other book sellers

Companion Book By This Author

Boosting
AI Autonomous Cars

by Dr. Lance B. Eliot, MBA, PhD

Chapter Title

This title is available via Amazon and other book sellers

Companion Book By This Author

AI Self-Driving Cars Trendsetting

by Dr. Lance B. Eliot, MBA, PhD

Chapter Title

This title is available via Amazon and other book sellers

Companion Book By This Author

AI Autonomous Cars Forefront

by Dr. Lance B. Eliot, MBA, PhD

Chapter Title

This title is available via Amazon and other book sellers

Companion Book By This Author

AI Autonomous Cars Emergence

by Dr. Lance B. Eliot, MBA, PhD

Chapter Title

This title is available via Amazon and other book sellers

Companion Book By This Author

AI Autonomous Cars Progress

by Dr. Lance B. Eliot, MBA, PhD

Chapter Title

This title is available via Amazon and other book sellers

Companion Book By This Author

AI Self-Driving Cars Prognosis

by Dr. Lance B. Eliot, MBA, PhD

Chapter Title

This title is available via Amazon and other book sellers

Companion Book By This Author

AI Self-Driving Cars
Momentum

by Dr. Lance B. Eliot, MBA, PhD

Chapter Title

This title is available via Amazon and other book sellers

Companion Book By This Author

AI Self-Driving Cars
Headway

by Dr. Lance B. Eliot, MBA, PhD

Chapter Title

Companion Book By This Author

AI Self-Driving Cars
Vicissitude

by Dr. Lance B. Eliot, MBA, PhD

Chapter Title

1 Eliot Framework for AI Self-Driving Cars

2 Leaving A Tip and AI Self-Driving Cars

3 Digital Nudging and AI Self-Driving Cars

4 Carpool Lanes and AI Self-Driving Cars

5 Sleep Solving and AI Self-Driving Cars

6 Nostradamus and AI Self-Driving Cars

7 Advanced Driving and AI Self-Driving Cars

8 Cybertruck Windows Shattered Mystery

9 Artificial Stupidity and AI Self-Driving Cars

10 Revenue Estimates Of AI Self-Driving Cars

11 Survivalists and AI Self-Driving Cars

This title is available via Amazon and other book sellers

Companion Book By This Author

AI Self-Driving Cars Autonomy

by Dr. Lance B. Eliot, MBA, PhD

Chapter Title

This title is available via Amazon and other book sellers

Companion Book By This Author

AI Driverless Cars Transmutation

by Dr. Lance B. Eliot, MBA, PhD

Chapter Title

This title is available via Amazon and other book sellers

Companion Book By This Author

AI Driverless Cars Potentiality

by Dr. Lance B. Eliot, MBA, PhD

Chapter Title

This title is available via Amazon and other book sellers

Companion Book By This Author

AI Driverless Cars Realities

by Dr. Lance B. Eliot, MBA, PhD

Chapter Title

This title is available via Amazon and other book sellers

Companion Book By This Author

AI Self-Driving Cars Materiality

by Dr. Lance B. Eliot, MBA, PhD

Chapter Title

This title is available via Amazon and other book sellers

Companion Book By This Author

AI Self-Driving Cars Accordance

by Dr. Lance B. Eliot, MBA, PhD

Chapter Title

This title is available via Amazon and other book sellers

Companion Book By This Author

AI Self-Driving Cars
Equanimity

by Dr. Lance B. Eliot, MBA, PhD

Chapter Title

This title is available via Amazon and other book sellers

Companion Book By This Author

AI Self-Driving Cars Divulgement

by Dr. Lance B. Eliot, MBA, PhD

Chapter Title

This title is available via Amazon and other book sellers

Companion Book By This Author

AI Self-Driving Cars Consonance

by Dr. Lance B. Eliot, MBA, PhD

Chapter Title

1 Eliot Framework for AI Self-Driving Cars

2 Baby Yoda on Hoods Life and AI Self-Driving Cars

3 Ugliest Cars Looks and AI Self-Driving Cars

4 MacGyver Shrewdness and AI Self-Driving Cars

5 Strong vs Weak AI and AI Self-Driving Cars

6 Trolley Problem and AI Self-Driving Cars

7 Evasive Maneuvering and AI Self-Driving Cars

8 Movie Miscasting AI and AI Self-Driving Cars

9 Snakes In A Car and AI Self-Driving Cars

10 Cognitive Tests and AI Self-Driving Cars

11 Lightning Strikes and AI Self-Driving Cars

12 Neanderthal DNA and AI Self-Driving Cars

13 Plane Lands on Highway and AI Self-Driving Cars

14 Turing Test and AI Self-Driving Cars

This title is available via Amazon and other book sellers

Companion Book By This Author

Revelatory AI Self-Driving Cars

by Dr. Lance B. Eliot, MBA, PhD

Chapter Title

This title is available via Amazon and other book sellers

Companion Book By This Author

Edifying AI Self-Driving Cars

by Dr. Lance B. Eliot, MBA, PhD

Chapter Title

This title is available via Amazon and other book sellers

Companion Book By This Author

Apprising AI Driverless Cars

by Dr. Lance B. Eliot, MBA, PhD

Chapter Title

This title is available via Amazon and other book sellers

Companion Book By This Author

Improving AI Self-Driving Cars

by Dr. Lance B. Eliot, MBA, PhD

Chapter Title

This title is available via Amazon and other book sellers

Companion Book By This Author

Progressing AI Driverless Cars

by Dr. Lance B. Eliot, MBA, PhD

Chapter Title

This title is available via Amazon and other book sellers

ABOUT THE AUTHOR

Dr. Lance B. Eliot, Ph.D., MBA is a Stanford Fellow and a globally recognized AI expert and thought leader, an experienced executive and leader, a successful serial entrepreneur, and a noted scholar on AI, including that his Forbes and AI Trends columns have amassed over 4.5+ million views, his books on AI are frequently ranked in the Top 10 of all-time AI books, his articles are widely cited, and he has developed dozens of advanced AI systems.

He currently serves as the CEO of Techbruim, Inc. and has over twenty years of industry experience including serving as a corporate officer in billion-dollar sized firms and was a partner in a major consulting firm. He is also a successful entrepreneur having founded, ran, and sold several high-tech firms.

Dr. Eliot previously hosted the popular radio show *Technotrends* that was also available on American Airlines flights via their in-flight audio program, he has made appearances on CNN, has been a frequent speaker at industry conferences, and his podcasts have been downloaded over 100,000 times.

A former professor at the University of Southern California (USC), he founded and led an innovative research lab on Artificial Intelligence. He also previously served on the faculty of the University of California Los Angeles (UCLA) and was a visiting professor at other major universities. He was elected to the International Board of the Society for Information Management (SIM), a prestigious association of over 3,000 high-tech executives worldwide.

He has performed extensive community service, including serving as Senior Science Adviser to the Congressional Vice-Chair of the Congressional Committee on Science & Technology. He has served on the Board of the OC Science & Engineering Fair (OCSEF), where he is also has been a Grand Sweepstakes judge, and likewise served as a judge for the Intel International SEF (ISEF). He served as the Vice-Chair of the Association for Computing Machinery (ACM) Chapter, a prestigious association of computer scientists. Dr. Eliot has been a shark tank judge for the USC Mark Stevens Center for Innovation on start-up pitch competitions and served as a mentor for several incubators and accelerators in Silicon Valley and in Silicon Beach.

Dr. Eliot holds a Ph.D. from USC, MBA, and Bachelor's in Computer Science, and earned the CDP, CCP, CSP, CDE, and CISA certifications.

ADDENDUM

Progressing AI Driverless Cars

Practical Advances in Artificial Intelligence (AI) and Machine Learning

By

Dr. Lance B. Eliot, MBA, PhD

For supplemental materials of this book, visit:

www.ai-selfdriving-cars.guru

For special orders of this book, contact:

LBE Press Publishing

Email: LBE.Press.Publishing@gmail.com

Made in the USA
Monee, IL
05 November 2026

67886754R00252